The Story of a Street Cat Named Bob

Also by James Bowen

Bob: No Ordinary Cat
Where in the World is Bob?
For the Love of Bob
A Gift from Bob

The Story of a Street Cat Named Bob

A Special Two-Book Omnibus

James Bowen

HODDER &
STOUGHTON

First published in Great Britain in 2012 & 2013 by Hodder & Stoughton
An Hachette UK company

1

Copyright © James Bowen 2012 & 2013

The right of James Bowen and Garry Jenkins to be
identified as the Authors of the Work have been asserted
by them in accordance with the Copyright, Designs and Patents Act 1988.

A CIP catalogue record for this title is available
from the British Library

ISBN 978 1 473 66876 8

Printed and bound by CPI Group (UK) Ltd, Croydon, CR0 4YY

Hodder & Stoughton policy is to use papers that are natural,
renewable and recyclable products and made from wood grown
in sustainable forests. The logging and manufacturing processes
are expected to conform to the environmental regulations
of the country of origin.

Hodder & Stoughton Ltd
Carmelite House
50 Victoria Embankment
London EC4Y 0DZ

www.hodder.co.uk

Contents

A Street Cat Named Bob

JAMES BOWEN

To Bryn Fox . . . and anyone who has lost a friend

Contents

Chapter 1

Fellow Travellers

There's a famous quote I read somewhere. It says we are all given second chances every day of our lives. They are there for the taking, it's just that we don't usually take them.

I spent a big chunk of my life proving that quote. I was given a lot of opportunities, sometimes on a daily basis. For a long time I failed to take any of them, but then, in the early spring of 2007, that finally began to change. It was then that I befriended Bob. Looking back on it, something tells me it might have been his second chance too.

I first encountered him on a gloomy, Thursday evening in March. London hadn't quite shaken off the winter and it was still bitingly cold on the streets, especially when the winds blew in off the Thames. There had even been a hint of frost in the air that night, which was why I'd arrived back at my new, sheltered accommodation in Tottenham, north London, a little earlier than usual after a day busking around Covent Garden.

As normal, I had my black guitar case and rucksack slung over my shoulders but this evening I also had my closest friend, Belle, with me. We'd gone out together years ago but were just mates now. We were going to eat a cheap takeaway curry and watch a movie on the small black and white television set I'd managed to find in a charity shop round the corner.

As usual, the lift in the apartment block wasn't working so we headed for the first flight of stairs, resigned to making the long trudge up to the fifth floor.

The strip lighting in the hallway was broken and part of the ground floor was swathed in darkness, but as we made our way to the stairwell I couldn't help noticing a pair of glowing eyes in the gloom. When I heard a gentle, slightly plaintive meowing I realised what it was.

Edging closer, in the half-light I could see a ginger cat curled up on a doormat outside one of the ground-floor flats in the corridor that led off the hallway.

I'd grown up with cats and had always had a bit of a soft spot for them. As I moved in and got a good look I could tell he was a tom, a male.

I hadn't seen him around the flats before, but even in the darkness I could tell there was something about him, I could already tell that he had something of a personality. He wasn't in the slightest bit nervous, in fact, completely the opposite. There was a quiet, unflappable confidence about him. He looked like he was very much at home here in the shadows and to judge by the way he was fixing me with a steady, curious, intelligent stare, I was the one who was straying into his territory. It was as if he was saying: 'So who are you and what brings you here?'

I couldn't resist kneeling down and introducing myself.

'Hello, mate. I've not seen you before, do you live here?' I said.

He just looked at me with the same studious, slightly aloof expression, as if he was still weighing me up.

I decided to stroke his neck, partly to make friends but partly to see if he was wearing a collar or any form of identification. It was hard to tell in the dark, but I realised there was nothing, which immediately suggested to me that he was a stray. London had more than its fair share of those.

He seemed to be enjoying the affection, and began brushing himself lightly against me. As I petted him a little more, I could feel that his coat was in poor condition, with uneven bald patches here and there. He was clearly in need of a good meal. From the way he was rubbing against me, he was also in need of a bit of TLC.

'Poor chap, I think he's a stray. He's not got a collar and he's really thin,' I said, looking up at Belle, who was waiting patiently by the foot of the stairs.

She knew I had a weakness for cats.

'No, James, you can't have him,' she said, nodding towards the door of the flat that the cat was sitting outside. 'He can't have just wandered in here and settled on this spot, he must belong to whoever lives there. Probably waiting for them to come home and let him in.'

Reluctantly, I agreed with her. I couldn't just pick up a cat and take him home with me, even if all the signs pointed to the fact it was homeless. I'd barely moved into this place myself and was still trying to sort out my flat. What if it did belong to the person living in that flat? They weren't going to take too kindly to someone carrying off their pet, were they?

Besides, the last thing I needed right now was the extra responsibility of a cat. I was a failed musician and recovering drug addict living a hand-to-mouth existence in sheltered accommodation. Taking responsibility for myself was hard enough.

The following morning, Friday, I headed downstairs to find the ginger tom still sitting there. It was as if he hadn't shifted from the same spot in the past twelve hours or so.

Once again I dropped down on one knee and stroked him. Once again it was obvious that he loved it. He was purring away, appreciating the attention he was getting. He hadn't learned to trust me 100 per cent yet. But I could tell he thought I was OK.

In the daylight I could see that he was a gorgeous creature. He had a really striking face with amazingly piercing green eyes, although, looking closer, I could tell that he must have been in a fight or an accident because there were scratches on his face and legs. As I'd guessed the previous evening, his coat was in very poor condition. It was very thin and wiry in places with at least half a dozen bald patches where you could see the skin. I was now feeling genuinely concerned about him, but again I told myself that I had more than enough to worry about getting myself straightened out. So, more than a little reluctantly, I headed off to catch the bus from Tottenham to central London and Covent Garden where I was going to once more try and earn a few quid busking.

By the time I got back that night it was pretty late, almost ten o'clock. I immediately headed for the corridor where I'd seen the ginger tom but there was no sign of him. Part of me was disappointed. I'd taken a bit of a shine to him. But mostly I felt relieved. I assumed he must have been let in by his owner when they'd got back from wherever it was they had been.

My heart sank a bit when I went down again the next day and saw him back in the same position again. By now he was slightly more vulnerable and dishevelled than before. He looked cold and hungry and he was shaking a little.

'Still here then,' I said, stroking him. 'Not looking so good today.'

I decided that this had gone on for long enough.

So I knocked on the door of the flat. I felt I had to say something. If this was their pet, it was no way to treat him. He needed something to eat and drink – and maybe even some medical attention.

A guy appeared at the door. He was unshaven, wearing a T-shirt and a pair of tracksuit bottoms and looked like he'd been sleeping even though it was the middle of the afternoon.

'Sorry to bother you, mate. Is this your cat?' I asked him.

For a second he looked at me as if I was slightly mad.

'What cat?' he said, before looking down and seeing the ginger tom curled up in a ball on the doormat.

'Oh. No,' he said, with a disinterested shrug. 'Nothing to do with me, mate.'

'He's been there for days,' I said, again drawing a blank look.

'Has he? Must have smelled cooking or something. Well, as I say, nothing to do with me.'

He then slammed the door shut.

I made my mind up immediately.

'OK, mate, you are coming with me,' I said, digging into my rucksack for the box of biscuits I carried specifically to give treats to the cats and dogs that regularly approached me when I was busking.

I rattled it at him and he was immediately up on all fours, following me.

I could see he was a bit uneasy on his feet and was carrying one of his back legs in an awkward manner, so we took our time climbing the five flights of stairs. A few minutes later we were safely ensconced in my flat.

My flat was threadbare, it's fair to say. Apart from the telly, all I had in there was a second-hand sofa bed, a mattress in the corner of the small bedroom, and in the kitchen area a half-working refrigerator, a microwave, a kettle and a toaster. There was no cooker. The only other things in the flat were my books, videos and knick-knacks.

I'm a bit of a magpie; I collect all sorts of stuff from the street. At that time I had a broken parking meter in one corner, and a broken mannequin with a cowboy hat on its head in another. A friend once called my place 'the old curiosity shop', but as he sussed out his new environment the only thing the tom was curious about was the kitchen.

I fished out some milk from the fridge, poured it into a saucer and mixed it with a bit of water. I know that – contrary to popular opinion – milk can be bad for cats because, in fact, they are actually lactose intolerant. He lapped it up in seconds.

I had a bit of tuna in the fridge so I mixed it up with some mashed up biscuits and gave that to him as well. Again, he wolfed it down. *Poor thing, he must be absolutely starving*, I thought to myself.

After the cold and dark of the corridor, the flat was five-star luxury as far as the tom was concerned. He seemed very pleased to be there and after being fed in the kitchen he headed for the living room where he curled up on the floor, near the radiator.

As I sat and watched him more carefully, there was no doubt in my mind that there was something wrong with his leg. Sure enough, when I sat on the floor next to him and started examining him I found that he had a big abscess on the back of his rear right leg. The wound was the size of a large, canine-like tooth, which gave me a good idea how he'd got it. He'd probably been attacked by a dog, or possibly a fox, that had stuck its teeth into his leg and clung on to him as he'd tried to escape. He also had a lot of scratches, one on his face not far from his eye, and others on his coat and legs.

I sterilised the wound as best as I could by putting him in the bathtub then putting some non-alcoholic moisturiser around the wound and some Vaseline on the wound itself. A lot of cats would have created havoc if I'd tried to treat them like that but he was as good as gold.

He spent most of the rest of the day curled up on what was already his favourite spot, near the radiator.

But he also roamed around the flat a bit every now and again, jumping up and scratching at whatever he could find. Having ignored it earlier on, he now began to find the mannequin in the corner a bit of a magnet. I didn't mind. He could do whatever he liked to it.

I knew ginger toms could be very lively and could tell he had a lot of pent-up energy. When I went to stroke him, he jumped up and started pawing at me. At one point he got quite animated, scratching furiously and almost cutting my hand

'OK, mate, calm down,' I said, lifting him off me and putting him down on the floor. I knew that young males who hadn't been neutered could become extremely lively. My guess was that he was still 'complete' and was well into puberty. I couldn't be sure, of course, but it again underlined the nagging feeling that he must have come off the streets rather than from a home.

I spent the evening watching television, the tom curled up by the radiator, seemingly content to be there. He only moved when I went to bed, picking himself up and following me into the bedroom where he wrapped himself up into a ball by my feet at the edge of the bed.

As I listened to his gentle purring in the dark, it felt good to have him there. He was company, I guess. I'd not had a lot of that lately.

On Sunday morning I got up reasonably early and decided to hit the streets to see if I could find his owner. I figured that someone might have stuck up a 'Lost Cat' poster. There was almost always a photocopied appeal for the return of a missing pet plastered on local lamp-posts, noticeboards and even bus stops. There seemed to be so many missing moggies that there were times when I wondered whether there was a cat-napping gang at work in the area.

Just in case I found the owner quickly, I took the cat with me, attaching him to a leash I'd made out of a shoelace to keep him safe. He was happy to walk by my side as we took the stairs to the ground floor.

Outside the block of flats the cat began pulling on the string lead as if he wanted to head off. I guessed that he wanted to do his business. Sure enough he headed off into a patch of greenery and bushes adjoining a neighbouring building and disappeared for a minute or two to heed nature's call. He then returned to me and happily slipped back into the lead.

He must really trust me, I thought to myself. I immediately felt that I had to repay that trust and try and help him out.

My first port of call was the lady who lived across the street. She was known locally for looking after cats. She fed the neighbourhood strays and got them neutered, if necessary. When she opened the door I saw at least five cats living inside. Goodness knows how many more she had out the back. It seemed that every cat for miles headed to her backyard knowing it was the best place to get some food. I didn't know how she could afford to feed them all.

She saw the tom and took a shine to him straight away, offering him a little treat.

She was a lovely lady but didn't know anything about where he'd come from. She'd not seen him around the area.

'I bet he's come from somewhere else in London. Wouldn't surprise me if he's been dumped,' she said. She said she'd keep her eyes and ears open in case she heard anything.

I had a feeling she was right about him being from somewhere far from Tottenham.

Out of interest, I took the cat off his lead to see if he knew what direction to go in. But as we walked the streets, it was obvious he didn't know where he was. He seemed completely lost. He looked at me as if to say: 'I don't know where I am; I want to stay with you.'

We were out for a few hours. At one point he scurried off into a bush to do his business again, leaving me to ask any passing locals whether they recognised him. All I got was blank looks and shrugs.

It was obvious that he didn't want to leave me. As we wandered around, I couldn't help wondering about his story: where he'd come from and what sort of life he'd led before he'd come and sat on the mat downstairs.

Part of me was convinced that the 'cat lady' across the street was right and he was a family pet. He was a fine-looking cat and had probably been bought for Christmas or someone's birthday. Gingers can be a bit mental and worse if not neutered, as I'd already seen. They can get very dominant, much more so than other cats. My hunch was that when he'd become boisterous and frisky he had also become a little too much to handle.

I imagined the parents saying 'enough is enough' and – rather than taking him to a refuge or the RSPCA – sticking him in the back of the family car, taking him for a drive and throwing him out into the street or on to the roadside.

Cats have a great sense of direction, but he'd obviously been let loose far from home and hadn't gone back. Or maybe he'd known that it wasn't really home at all and decided to find a new one.

My other theory was that he'd belonged to an old person who had passed away.

Of course, it was possible that wasn't the case at all. The fact that he wasn't house-trained was the main argument against him having been domesticated. But the more I got to know him the more convinced I was that he had definitely been used to being around one person. He seemed to latch on to people whom he thought would look after him. That's what he'd done with me.

The biggest clue about his background was his injury, which looked nasty. He'd definitely picked that up in a fight. From the way it was leaking pus, the wound must have been a few days old, maybe even a week. That suggested another possibility to me.

London has always had a large population of street cats, strays who wander the streets living off scraps and the comfort of strangers. Five or six hundred years ago, places like Gresham Street in the City, Clerkenwell Green and Drury Lane used to be known as 'cat streets' and were overrun with them. These strays are the flotsam and jetsam of the city, running around fighting for survival on a daily basis. A lot of them were like this ginger tom: slightly battered, broken creatures.

Maybe he'd spotted a kindred spirit in me.

Chapter 2
Road To Recovery

I'd been around cats since I was a child and I felt like I had a pretty good understanding of them. While I was growing up my family had several Siamese and I remember that at one stage we also had a beautiful tortoiseshell cat. My memories of all of them were generally fond ones, but inevitably I suppose the one that stuck most vividly in my mind was the darkest.

I'd grown up in England and Australia and for a while we'd lived in a place called Craigie in Western Australia. While we were there we had a lovely, white fluffy kitten. I can't remember where we got it from but I have a feeling it might have been from a local farmer. Wherever it had come from, it was a terrible home. For whatever reason it hadn't been checked out medically before being handed over to us. It turned out the poor little thing was flea-ridden.

It hadn't been immediately apparent. The problem was that because the kitten had such thick white fur the fleas were festering in there and nobody knew. Fleas are parasites, of course. They draw the life out of other creatures to sustain their own. They basically drained this poor kitten of all its blood. By the time we spotted it, it was too late. My mother took it to the vet's but she was told that it had passed the point of no return. It had all sorts of infections and other problems. It died within a couple of weeks of us getting it. I was five or six at the time and was devastated – as was my mother.

I'd thought about the kitten often over the years, usually whenever I saw a white cat. But he had been on my mind a lot this weekend as I'd spent time with the tom. I could tell his coat was in a bad state. It really was threadbare in places. I had an awful feeling that it would suffer the same fate as the white kitten.

Sitting in the flat with him that Sunday evening, I made a decision: I wasn't going to let that happen. I wasn't going to assume that the care I had given him was going to make him better. I wasn't going to take anything for granted.

I had to take him to a vet. I knew my makeshift medication wasn't going to be good enough to heal the wound. But I had no idea what other underlying health issues he might have. I wasn't going to take the risk of waiting, so I decided to get up early the next morning and take him to the nearest RSPCA centre, down the other end of Seven Sisters Road towards Finsbury Park.

I set my alarm early and got up to give the cat a bowl of mashed biscuits and tuna. It was another grey morning, but I knew I couldn't use that as an excuse.

Given the state of his leg, I knew he wasn't going to be up to the ninety-minute walk, so I decided to carry him and placed him in a green recycling box. It wasn't ideal but I couldn't find anything else. No sooner had we set off than it was clear that he didn't like it. He kept moving, sticking his paw over the top of the box and attempting to climb out. So eventually I gave up.

'Come on, I'll carry you,' I said, picking him up with my spare arm while carrying the recycling box in the other. He was soon scrambling up on to my shoulders where he settled. I let him sit there while I carried the empty box with me all the way to the RSPCA centre.

Inside the centre, it was like stepping into a scene from hell. It was packed, mostly with dogs and their owners, most of whom seemed to be young teenage blokes with skinhead haircuts and aggressive tattoos. Seventy per cent of the dogs were Staffordshire Bull Terriers that had almost certainly been injured in fights with other dogs, probably for people's amusement.

People always talk about Britain as a 'nation of animal lovers'. There wasn't much love on display here, that was for sure. The way some people treat their pets really disgusts me.

The cat sat on my lap or on my shoulder. I could tell he was nervous, and I couldn't blame him. He was getting snarled at by most of the dogs in the waiting room. One or two were being held tightly on their leashes as they strained to get closer to him.

One by one, the dogs were ushered into the treatment room. Each time the nurse appeared, however, we were disappointed. In the end it took us four and a half hours to be seen.

Eventually, she said, 'Mr Bowen, the vet will see you now.'

He was a middle-aged vet. He had that kind of world-weary, seen-it-all expression you see on some people's faces. Maybe it was all the aggression I'd been surrounded by outside, but I felt on edge with him immediately.

'So what seems to be the problem?' he asked me.

I knew the guy was only doing his job, but I felt like saying, 'Well, if I knew that I wouldn't be here' but resisted the temptation.

I told him how I'd found the cat in the hallway of my building and pointed out the abscess on the back of his leg.

'OK, let's have a quick look at him,' he said.

He could tell the cat was in pain and gave him a small dose of diazepam to help relieve it. He then explained that he was going to issue a prescription for a two-week course of cat-strength amoxicillin.

'Come back and see me again if things haven't improved in a fortnight,' he said.

I thought I'd take the opportunity and ask about fleas. He had a quick look around his coat but said he could find nothing.

'But it's probably worth you giving him some tablets for that. It can be a problem in young cats,' he said.

Again, I resisted the temptation to tell him that I knew that. I watched as he wrote a prescription out for that as well.

To his credit, he also checked to see if the tom was microchipped. He wasn't, which again suggested to me he was a street cat.

'You should get that done when you have a chance,' he said. 'I think he should also be neutered quite soon as well,' he added, handing me a brochure and a form advertising a free neutering scheme for strays. Given the way he tore around the house and was so boister-ous with me I nodded in agreement with his diagnosis. 'I think that's a good idea,' I smiled, expecting him to at least ask a follow-up 'why?'

But the vet didn't seem interested. He was only concerned with tapping his notes into a computer screen and printing off the prescription. We were obvi-ously on a production line that needed to be processed and pushed out the door ready for the next patient to come in. It wasn't his fault – it was the system.

Within a few minutes we were finished. Leaving the vet's surgery, I went up to the counter at the dispensary and handed over the prescription.

The white-coated lady there was a bit friendlier.

'He's a lovely-looking fellow,' she said. 'My mum had a ginger tom once. Best companion she ever had. Amazing temperament. Used to sit there at her feet watching the world go by. A bomb could have gone off and he wouldn't have left her.'

She punched in the details to the till and produced a bill.

'That will be twenty-two pounds please, love,' she said.

My heart sank.

'Twenty-two pounds! Really,' I said. I had just over thirty pounds in the whole world at that point.

'Afraid so, love,' the nurse said, looking sympathetic but implacable at the same time.

I handed over the thirty pounds in cash and took the change.

It was a lot of money for me. A day's wages. But I knew I had no option: I couldn't let my new friend down.

'Looks like we're stuck with each other for the next fortnight,' I said to the tom as we headed out of the door and began the long walk back to the flat.

It was the truth. There was no way I was going to get rid of the cat for at least a fortnight, not until he completed his course of medicine. No one else was going to make sure he took his tablets and I couldn't let him out on the streets in case he picked up an infection.

I don't know why, but the responsibility of having him to look after galvanised me a little bit. I felt like I had an extra purpose in my life, something positive to do for someone – or something – other than myself.

That afternoon I headed to a local pet store and got him a couple of weeks' worth of food. I'd been given a sample of scientific formula food at the RSPCA and tried it on him the previous night. He'd liked it so I bought a bag of that. I also got him a supply of cat food. It cost me around nine pounds, which really was the last money I had.

That night I had to leave him on his own and head to Covent Garden with my guitar. I now had two mouths to feed.

Over the course of the next few days, as I nursed him back to health, I got to know him a little better. By now I'd given him a name: Bob. I got the idea while watching a DVD of one of my old favourite TV series, *Twin Peaks*. There was a character in that called Killer Bob. He was actually schizophrenic, a kind of Jekyll and Hyde character. Part of the time he would be a normal, sane guy, the next he would be kind of crazy and out of control. The tom was a bit like that. When he was happy and content you couldn't have wished to see a calmer, kinder cat. But when the mood took him he could be an absolute maniac, charging around the flat. I was talking to my friend Belle one night when it dawned on me.

'He's a bit like Killer Bob in *Twin Peaks*,' I said, drawing a blank look from her.

But it didn't matter. Bob it was.

It was pretty clear to me now that Bob must have lived outdoors. When it came to toilet time, he absolutely refused to go in the litter tray that I'd bought for him. Instead I had to take him downstairs and let him do his business in the gardens that surrounded the flats. He'd dash off into a bit of overgrowth and do whatever was needed then scratch up the ground to cover up the evidence.

Watching him going through his ritual one morning, I wondered whether he'd belonged to travellers. There were quite a few of them around the Tottenham area. In fact, there was a camp of them on some land near my block of flats. Maybe he'd been part of a travelling family and had somehow got left behind when they moved on. He was definitely not a house cat, that much I knew now.

There was no doubt that he was forming an affection for me. As, indeed, I was for him. At first he had been affectionate, but still a bit wary of me. But as the days passed he became more and more confident – and friendly. He could still be very boisterous and even aggressive at times. But by now I knew that was down to the fact that he needed to be neutered.

Our life settled into a bit of a routine. I'd leave Bob in the flat in the morning and head to Covent Garden where I'd play until I got enough cash. When I got home he'd be waiting for me at the front door. He would then follow me to the sofa in the front room and watch telly with me.

By now I was beginning to realise what a smart cat he was. I could see that he understood everything I was saying to him.

When I patted the sofa and invited him to come and sit next to me he did. He also knew what I meant when I told him it was time for him to have his meds. Each time he would look at me as if to say 'Do I have to?' But he wouldn't struggle while I put tablets in his mouth and rubbed his throat gently until he swallowed it. Most cats would go mad if you try to open their mouths. But he already trusted me.

It was around that point I began to realise there was something rather special about him. I'd certainly never encountered a cat quite like Bob.

He wasn't perfect, by any means. He knew where the food lived and would regularly crash around the kitchen, knocking over pots and pans as he searched for food. The cupboards and fridge door already bore scratch marks from where he'd been frantically trying to get access to something tasty to eat.

To be fair to him, he listened if I said no.

All I had to do was say, 'No, get away from there, Bob,' and he'd slink off. Again it showed how intelligent he was. And again it raised all sorts of questions about his background. Would a feral or a street cat pay attention to what a human told them in that way? I doubted it.

I really enjoyed Bob's company but I knew I had to be careful. I couldn't form too strong a friendship because sooner or later he would want to return to the streets. He wasn't the sort of cat that was going to enjoy being cooped up permanently. He wasn't a house cat.

For the short term, however, I was his guardian and I was determined to try and fulfil that role to the best of my ability. I knew I needed to do all I could to prepare him for his return to the streets, so one morning I filled in the form the RSPCA vet had given me for the free neutering service. I stuck it in the post and, to my mild amazement, got a reply within a couple of days. The letter contained a certificate entitling us to a free neutering.

The next morning I took Bob down to do his business outside again. The litter trays I'd bought him remained unsoiled and unused. He just didn't like them.

He headed for the same spot in the bushes adjoining the neighbouring houses. It seemed to be a favourite area for some reason. I suspected it was something to do with him marking his territory, something I'd read about in a science article somewhere.

As usual, he was in there for a minute or two then spent some time afterwards clearing up after him. The cleanliness and tidiness of cats never ceases to amaze me. Why was it so important to them?

He had satisfied himself that everything was right and was making his way out when he suddenly froze and tensed up, as if he'd seen something. I was about to go over to see what was bothering him when it became quite obvious what it was.

All of a sudden, Bob lunged forward at lightning speed. It really did all happen in a blur. Before I knew it, Bob had grabbed at something in the grass near the hedge. I moved in to take a closer look and saw that it was a little grey mouse, no more than three inches long.

The little fellow had clearly been trying to scurry past him but hadn't stood a chance. Bob had pounced with lightning speed and precision and now had the creature clamped between his teeth. It wasn't the prettiest of sights. The mouse's legs were thrashing around and Bob was carefully repositioning its body in his teeth so that he could finish off the mouse. It wasn't long before the inevitable happened and the little creature gave up the fight. It was at that point that Bob released it from his mouth and laid it on the ground.

I knew what was likely to happen next but I didn't want Bob to eat it. Mice were notorious breeding grounds for disease. So I knelt down and attempted to pick up his prey. He wasn't too happy about it and made a little noise that was part growl and part hiss. He then picked the mouse up again.

'Give it to me Bob,' I said, refusing to back down. 'Give it to me.'

He really wasn't too keen and this time gave me a look as if to say: 'Why should I?'

I fished around in my coat and found a nibble, offering him a trade. 'Take this instead, Bob, it will be much better for you.'

He still wasn't convinced but after a few more moments the stand-off came to a halt and he gave in. As soon as he stepped away from the mouse, I picked it up by its tail and disposed of it.

It was another reminder of what, to me anyway, is one of the many fascinating things about cats: they are lethal predators by nature. A lot of people don't like to think of their cute little kitty as a mass murderer, but that's what cats are, given half a chance. In some parts of the world, including Australia, they have strict rules on cats being let out at night because of the carnage they cause in the local bird and rodent population.

Bob had proven the point. His coolness, his speed and his skill as a killer was amazing to behold. He knew exactly what to do and how to do it.

It set me thinking again about the life he must have led before he had arrived in the hallway of the block of flats. What sort of existence had it been? Where had he lived and how had he survived? Had he relied on finding and eating prey like this every day? Had he been raised in a domestic environment or had he always lived off the land like this? How had he become the cat he

26

was today? I would love to have known. I was sure my street cat friend had a tale or two to tell.

In many ways, this was something else that Bob and I had in common.

Ever since I'd ended up living rough on the streets, people had wondered about my past life. How had I landed myself in this position, they'd ask me? Some did it professionally, of course. I'd spoken to dozens of social workers, psychologists and even police officers who'd quizzed me about how I'd ended up living on the streets. But a lot of ordinary people would ask me about it too.

I don't know why, but people seem to be fascinated to learn how some members of society fall through the cracks. I think it's partly that feeling that 'there for the grace of God go I', that it could happen to anyone. But I think it also makes people feel better about their own lives. It makes them think, 'Well, I may think my life is bad, but it could be worse, I could be that poor sod.'

The answer to how people like me end up on the streets is always different, of course. But there are usually some similarities. Often drugs and alcohol play a big part in the story. But in an awful lot of instances, the road that led them to living on the streets stretches all the way back to their childhoods and their relation-ship with their family. That was certainly the way it was for me.

I lived quite a rootless childhood, mainly because I spent it travelling between the UK and Australia. I was born in Surrey but when I was three my family moved to Melbourne. My mother and father had separated by this time. While my father stayed in Surrey, my mother had got away from all the aggravation by landing a job selling for Rank Xerox, the photocopying company, in Melbourne. She was really good at it too, she was one of the company's top saleswomen.

My mother had itchy feet, however, and within about two years we had moved from Melbourne to Western Australia. We stayed there for about three or four years until I was nine or so. Life in Australia was pretty good. We lived in a succession of large bungalows, each of which had vast garden areas at the back. I had all the space a boy could want to play in and explore the world and I loved the Australian landscape. The trouble was that I didn't have any friends.

I found it very hard to fit in at school, mainly, I think, because we'd moved a lot. The chances of me settling into life in Australia disappeared when I was nine and we moved back to the UK and to Sussex, near Horsham. I enjoyed being back in England and have some happy memories of that period. I was just getting back into life in the northern hemisphere when we had to move yet again – back to Western Australia, when I was around twelve.

This time we ended up in a place called Quinn's Rock. It was there that I think a lot of my problems really began. Because of all this travelling around, we never lived in one house for more than a couple of years. My mother was always buying and selling, moving all the time. I never had a family home and never grew up in one place. We were definitely living some kind of gypsy-like existence.

I'm no psychologist, although I've met my fair share of them over the years. There is no doubt in my mind that we moved home way too much, and it was not good for a growing child. It made it very hard for me to become socially adept. At school it was very hard to make friends. I was always trying too hard. I was too eager to impress, which isn't good when you are a kid. It had the opposite result: I ended up being bullied at every school I went to. It was particularly bad in Quinn's Rock.

I probably stuck out with a British accent and my eager-to-please attitude. I was a sitting target, really. One day they decided to stone me. Literally. Quinn's Rock was called Quinn's Rock for a reason and these kids took advantage of all the nice lumps of limestone that were lying around wherever you looked. I got concussion after being bombarded on the way home from school.

Things weren't helped by the fact that I didn't get on at all with my stepfather at the time, a guy called Nick. In my teenage opinion, he was a prick – and that was what I called him. Nick the Prick. My mother had met him when she joined the police back in Horsham and he had come with her out to Australia.

We continued living this same nomadic existence throughout my early teens. It was usually connected to my mother's many business ventures. She was a very successful woman. At one point she started doing tele-marketing training videos. That did quite well for a while. Then she set up a woman's magazine called *City Woman*, which didn't do so well. Sometimes we'd have plenty of money and other times we'd be strapped for cash. But that never lasted for long; she was a proper entrepreneur.

By the time I was in my mid-teens I'd pretty much quit school. I left because I was just sick to death of the bullying I encountered there. I didn't get along with Nick either. And I was very independent-minded.

I became a tearaway, a wild kid who was always out late, always defying my mother and generally thumb-ing his nose at authority, no matter what form it took. It wasn't surprising that I had soon developed a knack for getting myself into trouble, something I have never quite shaken off.

Predictably, I got into drugs, at first sniffing glue, probably to escape from reality. I didn't get addicted to it. I only did it a couple of times after seeing another kid doing it. But it was the start of the process. After that I started smoking dope and sniffing toluene, an indus-trial solvent you find in nail varnish and glue. It was all connected, it was all part of a cycle of behaviour, one thing led back to another, which led back to another and so on. I was angry. I felt like I hadn't had the best breaks.

Show me the child of seven and I'll show you the man, they say. I'm not so sure that you'd have spotted my future when I was seven, but you could certainly have guessed what lay ahead when I was seventeen. I was set on the road to self-destruction.

My mother tried her hardest to get me off drugs. She could see the damage I was doing – and the even worse problems I was going to cause myself if I didn't kick the habits I was forming. She did all the things mothers do. She went through my pockets trying to find drugs and even locked me in my bedroom a few times. But the locks in our house were those ones with buttons in the middle. I learned to pick them really easily with a Bobby pin. They just popped out and I was free. I wasn't going to be hemmed in by her – or anyone else for that matter. We argued even more then, of course, and inevitably things went from bad to worse. Mum got me to go to a psychiatrist at one point. They diagnosed me with everything from schizophrenia, to manic depression to ADHD, or Attention Deficit Hyperactivity Disorder. Of course, I thought it was all bullshit. I was a messed-up teenager who thought he knew better than everyone. With the benefit of hindsight I can see that my mother must have been worried sick. She must have felt powerless and terrified of what was going to happen to me. But I was oblivious to other people's feelings. I didn't care and I didn't listen to anyone.

The situation got so bad between us that for a while I lived in Christian charity accommodation. I just passed my time away there, taking drugs and playing guitar. Not necessarily in that order.

Around my eighteenth birthday, I announced that I was going to move back to London to live with my half-sister from my father's previous marriage. It marked the beginning of the downward spiral.

At the time, it had seemed like I was setting out into the world like any normal teenager. My mother had taken me to the airport and dropped me off in the car. We'd come to a stop at a red light and I'd jumped out giving her a peck on the cheek and a wave goodbye. We were both thinking that I'd be gone for six months or so. That was the plan. I would stay for six months, hang out with my half-sister and pursue my grand dreams of making it as a musician. But things wouldn't exactly go to plan.

At first, I went to stay with my half-sister in south London. My brother-in-law hadn't taken too kindly to my arrival. As I say, I was a rebellious teenager who dressed like a Goth and was – probably – a complete pain in the arse, especially as I wasn't contributing to the household bills.

In Australia I'd worked in IT and sold mobile phones but back in the UK I couldn't land a decent job. The first I'd been able to get had been working as a bartender. But my face hadn't fitted and they'd sacked me after using me to cover for other people's holidays during Christmas 1997. As if that wasn't bad enough, they wrote the dole office a letter saying I'd quit the job, which meant I couldn't collect the benefits I was eligible for by virtue of having been born in England.

After that I'd been even less welcome in my brother-in-law's house. Eventually, my half-sister and he had kicked me out. I had made contact with my dad and been to see him a couple of times, but it was clear we weren't going to be able to get on. We barely knew each other, so living there was out of the question. I started sleeping on friends' floors and sofas. Soon I was leading a nomadic existence, carrying my sleeping bag with me to various flats and squats around London. Then when I ran out of floors I moved to the streets.

Things headed downwards fast from there.

Living on the streets of London strips away your dignity, your identity – your everything, really. Worst of all, it strips away people's opinion of you. They see you are living on the streets and treat you as a non-person. They don't want anything to do with you. Soon you haven't got a real friend in the world. While I was sleeping rough I managed to get a job working as a kitchen porter. But they sacked me when they found out I was homeless, even though I'd done nothing wrong at work. When you are homeless you really stand very little chance.

The one thing that might have saved me was going back to Australia. I had a return ticket but lost my passport two weeks before the flight. I had no paper-work and besides I didn't have the money to get a new one. Any hope I had of getting back to my family in Australia disappeared. And so, in a way, did I.

The next phase of my life was a fog of drugs, drink, petty crime – and, well, hopelessness. It wasn't helped by the fact that I developed a heroin habit.

I took it at first simply to help me get to sleep at night on the streets. It anaesthetised me from the cold and the loneliness. It took me to another place. Unfortunately, it had also taken a hold of my soul as well. By 1998 I was totally dependent on it. I probably came close to death a few times, although, to be honest, I was so out of it at times that I had no idea.

During that period it didn't occur to me to contact anyone in my family. I had disappeared off the face of the earth – and I didn't really care. I was too wrapped up in surviving. Looking back at the time now, I can only imagine that they must have been going through hell. They must have been worried sick.

I got an inkling of the grief I was causing about a year after I had arrived in London and about nine months or so after I'd taken to the streets.

I had made contact with my father when I'd arrived in London but hadn't spoken to him in months. It was around Christmas time that I decided to give him a call. His wife – my stepmother – had answered the phone. He refused to come to the phone and kept me waiting for a few minutes, he was so angry with me.

'Where the f*** have you been? We've all been worried sick about you,' he said, when he had collected himself enough to talk to me.

I made some pathetic excuses but he just shouted at me.

He told me that my mother had been in contact with him desperately trying to find out where I was. That was a measure of how worried she'd become. The two of them never spoke. He shouted and screamed at me for fully five minutes. I realise now it was a mixture of release and anger. He had probably thought I was dead, which, in a way, I had been.

That period of my life lasted a year or so. I'd eventually been picked up off the streets by a homeless charity. I'd stayed in various shelters. Connections, just off St Martin's Lane, was one of them. I'd been sleeping rough in the market next door around that time.

I ended up on what's known as the 'vulnerable housing' list, which qualified me as a priority for sheltered accommodation. The problem was that for the best part of the next decade I ended up living in horrendous hostels, B&Bs and houses, sharing my space with heroin and crack addicts who would steal anything that wasn't nailed down. Everything I had was stolen at some point. I had to sleep with my most important possessions tucked inside my clothes. Survival was all I could think about.

Inevitably, my drug dependency got worse. By the time I was in my late twenties, my habit had got so bad I ended up in rehab. I spent a couple of months getting straightened out and was then put on a drug rehabilitation programme. For a while, the daily trip to the chemist and the fortnightly bus ride to my drug dependency unit in Camden became the focus of my life. They became an almost reflex. I'd get out of bed and go and do one or the other on auto-pilot, as if in a daze, which, if I'm honest, I often was.

I did some counselling there as well. I talked endlessly about my habit, how it had started – and how I was going to bring it to an end.

It's easy to come up with excuses for drug addiction, but I'm certain I know the reason for mine. It was pure and simple loneliness. Heroin allowed me to anaesthetise myself to my isolation, to the fact that I didn't have family or a huge circle of friends. I was on my own and, strange and unfathomable as it will seem to most people, heroin was my friend.

Deep down, however, I knew it was killing me – literally. So over a period of a few years I'd moved off heroin on to methadone, the synthetic opioid that is used as a substitute to wean morphine and heroin addicts off their habits. By the spring of 2007, the plan was that I would eventually start weaning myself off that and get completely straight.

The move to the flat in Tottenham was a key part of that process. It was an ordinary apartment block full of ordinary families. I knew I had a chance to put my life back on track there.

To help pay the rent I'd started busking in Covent Garden. It wasn't much but it helped put food on the table and pay the gas and electricity. It also helped to keep me on an even keel. I knew it was my chance to turn the corner. And I knew I had to take it this time. If I'd been a cat, I'd have been on my ninth life.

Chapter 3
The Snip

As we approached the end of Bob's second week of medication, he was looking a lot brighter. The wound at the back of his leg was healing nicely and the bald and thin patches on his coat had begun to disappear and were being replaced with new, thicker fur. He also seemed happier in his face, his eyes had a more lustrous gleam to them. There was a beautiful, green and yellow glow to them that hadn't been there before.

He was definitely on the road to recovery, and his boisterousness around the flat was the ultimate proof of it. He had been a whirling dervish, flying around the place since day one, but in the past week or so he'd become even more of a ball of energy. I hadn't thought it possible. There were times when he would jump and run around the place like some kind of maniac. He would claw furiously at everything and anything he could find, including me.

There were scratches on every wooden surface in the flat. I even had scratches on the back of my hand and arm. I didn't mind, I knew it wasn't malicious and that he was only playing.

He had become such a menace in the kitchen, where he would claw at the cupboards and fridge door in an attempt to break into my food supplies, that I'd had to buy a couple of cheap plastic child-locks.

I also had to be careful about leaving anything lying around that might become a plaything for him. A pair of shoes or item of clothing could be scratched to bits within minutes.

All Bob's actions showed that there was something that needed to be done. I'd been around enough cats in my life to recognise the tell-tale signs. He was a young male with way too much testosterone flying around his body. There was no doubt in my mind that he needed neutering. So a couple of days before his course of medicine finished I decided to call the local vets, the Abbey Clinic on Dalston Lane.

I knew the pros and cons of keeping him 'entire', and they were mostly cons. If I didn't castrate him there would be times when Bob's hormones would completely take over and he just wouldn't be able to stop himself from roaming the streets in search of willing females. It could mean that he would go missing for days – even weeks – at a time. He'd also be far more likely to get run over and to get into fights with other cats. As far as I knew, that might have been the cause of the fight that had caused his injury. Male toms are very protective of their territory and produce a distinctive odour to signal their 'patch'. Bob might have wandered into someone else's territory and paid the price. I knew it was probably paranoia on my part, but there was also a risk, albeit a very small one, of him contracting diseases like FeLV and FIV, the feline equivalent of HIV, if he wasn't neutered. Last, but far from least, if he stayed with me, he would also be a much calmer, more even-tempered pet. He wouldn't be so prone to running around like a maniac all the time.

By contrast the pros in favour of doing nothing amounted to a very short list. It would avoid him having to undergo a small bit of surgery. That was about it.

It was a no-brainer.

I rang the vets' surgery and spoke to a female nurse.

I explained my situation and asked whether he was eligible for a free operation. She said yes provided I had a certificate from a vet, which I did after my first visits to sort out his leg and get his flea and worm medications.

The only thing that worried me was the medication he was still taking. I explained that he was coming to the end of a course of antibiotics but she said that shouldn't be a problem. She recommended that I book him in for an operation in two days' time.

'Just bring him in and leave him with us in the morning. If everything goes to plan, you'll be able to pick him up at the end of the day,' she said.

I got up nice and early on the day of the operation, knowing that I had to get him into the surgery by 10a.m. It was the first time that we'd travelled any distance from the flat together since our visit to the RSPCA.

I hadn't let him out of the flat, apart from to do his business downstairs, because he was still on his antibiotics. So I stuck him in the same green, plastic recycling box I'd used a fortnight earlier to take him to the RSPCA. The weather was miserable so I took the lid and let it rest loosely on the box once we were out and about. He wasn't much more comfortable in it that day than he was the first time I put him in it. He kept sticking his head out and watching the world go by.

The Abbey Clinic is a small place, sandwiched between a newsagent and a medical centre on a parade of shops on Dalston Lane. We got there in plenty of time for his appointment and found the place packed. It was the usual, chaotic scene, with dogs tugging on their owners' leashes and growling at the cats inside their smart carriers. Bob stood out like a sore thumb in his improvised carrier so was immediately a target for their aggression. Once again, there were several Staffies there with their Neanderthal-looking owners.

Some cats would have bolted, I'm sure. But Bob wasn't fazed at all. He seemed to have placed his trust in me.

When my name was called out a young nurse in her twenties came out to meet us. She had some paperwork and led me into a room where she asked me what were obviously standard questions.

'Once it's been carried out, the operation can't be reversed. So are you certain you don't want to breed from Bob at some future date?' she said.

I just smiled and nodded.

'Yeah, I'm quite certain,' I said, rubbing Bob on the head.

Her next question stumped me, however.

'And how old is Bob?' she smiled.

'Ah. I really don't know,' I said, before briefly explaining his story.

'Hmm, let's take a look.' She explained that the fact that he hadn't been neutered was a good clue about his age.

'Male and female cats tend to become sexually mature at around six months of age. If they are left "entire" after that they go through some distinct physical changes. For instance, toms get fuller in the face, particularly around the cheeks. They also develop thicker skins and generally become quite big, certainly bigger than those cats that have been neutered,' she told me. 'He's not that big, so I'd guess that he's maybe nine to ten months old,' she said.

As she passed me the release forms, she explained that there was a minor risk of complications but that it was a really tiny chance. 'We will give him a thorough examination and maybe run a blood test before we go ahead with it,' she said. 'If there's a problem we will contact you.'

'OK,' I said, looking slightly sheepish. I didn't have a working mobile so they would have trouble contacting me.

She then took me through the procedure itself. 'The operation happens under general anaesthetic and is usually pretty straightforward. The testicles are removed through two small incisions made into the scrotal sacs.'

'Ouch, Bob,' I said giving him a playful ruffle.

'If everything goes OK, you can come and collect Bob in six hours,' she said, looking down at her watch. 'So at around four thirty. Is that OK?'

'Yeah, great,' I nodded. 'See you then.'

After giving Bob a final cuddle, I headed back out into the overcast streets. There was rain brewing once more.

I didn't have time to head all the way into central London. By the time I'd set up and sung a few songs, it would be time to turn around again. So I decided to take my chances around the nearest railway station, Dalston Kingsland. It wasn't the greatest pitch in the world, but it provided me with a few quid and a place to while away the hours as I waited for Bob. There was also a very friendly cobbler's shop next to the station where I knew I would get shelter from the inevitable rain when it came.

I tried to block Bob out of my thoughts as I played. I didn't want to think about him in the operating theatre. He had probably lived his life on the street and could well have had all sorts of other things wrong. I'd heard stories of cats and dogs going into vets' surgeries for the most minor procedures and never coming out again. I struggled to keep my darkest thoughts at bay. It didn't help that there were big black clouds glowering over me.

Time passed very, very slowly. Eventually, however, the clock reached 4.15p.m. and I began packing up. I almost ran the last few hundred yards to the clinic.

The nurse I'd seen earlier was at the reception desk talking to a colleague and greeted me with a warm smile.

'How is he? Did it all go all right?' I asked, still breathing heavily.

'He's fine, absolutely fine. Don't worry,' she said. 'Get your breath back and I'll take you through.'

It was weird, I hadn't felt this concerned about someone – or something – for years.

I went into the surgical area and saw Bob lying in a nice warm cage.

'Hello, Bob mate, how you doing?' I said.

He was still very dopey and drowsy so didn't recognise me for a while, but when he did he sat upright and started clawing at the doors of the cage as if to say: 'Let me outta here.'

The nurse got me to sign a discharge notice and then gave Bob a good once over to make sure he was fit to leave.

She was really lovely and very helpful, which made a pleasant change after the previous experience I'd had at the vets'. She showed me where the incisions had been made. 'It will stay swollen and sore around there for a couple of days, but that's normal,' she said. 'Just check every now and again to make sure there's no discharge or anything like that. If you notice that then give us a ring or bring him back in so we can check him out. I'm sure he'll be fine.'

'How long will he be groggy?' I asked her.

'Could be a couple of days before he's back to his normal bright-eyed and bushy-tailed self,' she said. 'It varies a lot, some cats bounce back immediately. With others it kind of knocks the stuffing out of them for a couple of days. But they are normally as right as rain within forty-eight hours.

'He probably won't want to eat much the day after but his appetite will return fairly soon. But if he stays very sleepy and lethargic give us a ring or bring him in for a check-up. It's very rare but cats sometimes get infections from the operation,' she said.

I'd brought the recycling box along with me again, and was just about to pick Bob up when she told me to wait.

'Hang on,' she said. 'I think we can do better than that.'

She went away for a couple of minutes and then produced a lovely, sky-blue carrying case.

'Oh, that's not mine,' I said.

'Oh, don't worry, it's OK. We've got loads of spares, you can have this one. Just drop it back in when you're next passing.'

'Really?'

I had no idea how it had got there. Maybe someone had left it behind. Or maybe someone had brought their cat in and returned to discover that it would not be needed any more. I didn't want to dwell on it too much.

It was obvious that the op had taken a lot out of Bob. In the carrier on the way home, he just lay there half asleep. The moment we got into the flat he slowly padded over to his favourite spot by the radiator and lay down. He slept there all night.

I took the day off work the next day to make sure he was OK. The advice from the vet was that he should be supervised for twenty-four to forty-eight hours after the operation to make sure there weren't any side effects. I was to particularly look out for continuing drowsiness, which wasn't a good sign. It was approaching the end of the week so I knew I'd need some money. But I could never have forgiven myself if something had gone wrong, so I stayed in the flat on twenty-four-hour Bob watch.

Fortunately, he was absolutely fine. The following morning, he was a bit perkier and ate a little bit of breakfast. As the nurse had predicted, he didn't have his normal appetite but he ate half a bowl of his favourite food, which was encouraging. He also wandered around the flat a little bit, although, again, he wasn't his normal ebullient self.

Over the next couple of days he began becoming more like the old Bob. Within three days of the op, he was wolfing down his food just like before. I could tell he was still in the occasional bit of pain. He would wince or come to a sudden stop every now and again, but it wasn't a major problem.

I knew that he'd still have the odd mad half-hour, but I was glad I'd acted.

Chapter 4
Ticket To Ride

As the fortnight drew to a close, I realised that I had to think about getting Bob out of the flat and back on to the streets. That's where he had come from – and I assumed that's where he would want to return.

He'd continued to make really good progress and looked much healthier than he had done when I first met him. He'd fattened up a lot more too.

So a day or two after I'd completed the course of medicine and he'd recovered fully from his op, I took Bob downstairs and out through the hallway. I led him down the path and out towards the gate then pointed him in the direction of the street.

He just stood there, fixed to the spot, looking at me confused, as if to say: 'What do you want me to do?'

'Go, go, go on,' I said, making sweeping movements with my hands.

It had no effect whatsoever.

For a moment I just stood there, engaged in a miniature staring competition with him. But then he just turned on his heels and padded off, not in the direction of the street but towards the patch of ground where he liked to do his business. He then dug a hole, covered it all up, and strolled back towards me.

This time his expression said: 'OK, I did what you wanted. What now?'

It was then that, for the first time, a thought began to crystallise in my head.

'I think you want to hang around,' I said quietly to him.

Part of me was pleased. I enjoyed his company and he was certainly a character. But, being sensible about it, I knew I shouldn't let it happen. I was still struggling to look after myself. I was still on a drug dependency programme, and would be for the foreseeable future. How on earth was I going to look after a cat, even one as intelligent and self-sufficient as Bob? It wasn't fair – on either of us.

So, with a heavy heart, I decided that I'd have to slowly start easing him out of the flat during the day. When I went to work in the morning, I would no longer leave him in the flat. I'd take him out with me, then leave him outside in the gardens.

'Tough love,' I told myself.

He didn't like it one bit.

The first time I did it, he shot me a look that said 'traitor'. As I headed off with my guitar over my shoulder, he followed, quietly stalking me, zigzagging across the pavement like some spy, trying to remain unseen. Except it was easy to spot his distinctive ginger fur, bobbing and weaving around.

Each time I saw him, I'd stop and wave my arms, flamboyantly waving him back. He'd limp away, reluctantly, throwing me a few betrayed looks as he went. Eventually he'd get the message and disappear.

When I got back six or so hours later, he would be waiting for me at the entrance to the flats. Part of me wanted to prevent him from coming in. But that part was overwhelmed by the one that wanted to invite him up to the flat once more to curl up at my feet.

Over the course of the next few days the pair of us settled into a bit of a routine.

Each day I'd leave him outside and each night when I got back from busking, I'd find him waiting for me, either outside in an alleyway or – if someone had let him in during the day – sitting on the mat outside my flat. He wasn't going away, that was obvious.

I decided I had to take the ultimate step and leave him out overnight. The first night I did it I saw him lurking in the area where the bins were kept. I tried to sneak in without him seeing me. It was a stupid move. He was a cat, he had more senses in one of his whiskers than I had in my entire body. No sooner had I opened the door to the building than he was there squeezing his way in. I left him outside in the hallway that night, but he was on my doormat when I emerged again in the morning. For the next few days we went through the same performance.

Each day I stepped outside he'd either be hanging around the hallway or would be waiting outside. Each night he'd find a way of getting into the building.

Eventually he decided that he'd won that particular battle. So I was soon dealing with another problem. He began following me down the main road.

The first time he came as far as the main road, but returned to the block when I shooed him away. The next time he tailed me for a hundred yards or so down the road, towards Tottenham High Road where I got the bus to Covent Garden.

A part of me admired his tenacity and sheer perseverance. But another part of me was cursing him. I simply couldn't shake him off.

Each day after that he got further and further – becoming bolder and bolder. Part of me wondered whether one day, after I left him, he'd actually keep going and find somewhere else to go. But each night I got home, there he was – waiting. I knew that something had to give eventually though. And it did.

One day I headed out for work as usual. I had packed my large black acoustic guitar with its red trim on the edge of the body, slung it over my shoulder along with my rucksack and headed downstairs.

I saw Bob was sitting in an alleyway and said hello. When he started to follow me, I shooed him away, as usual.

'Stay there, you can't come where I'm going,' I said.

This time he seemed to get the message and slunk off. As I headed down the road, I looked back occasionally to see if he was there, but there was no sign of him. *Perhaps he's finally getting the message*, I said to myself.

To get to the bus stop that would take me to Covent Garden, I had to cross Tottenham High Road, one of the busiest and most dangerous roads in north London. This morning, as usual, cars, lorries and motorbikes were carving their way along the road, trying to pick their way through the clogged traffic.

As I stood on the pavement, trying to spot a gap so that I could run for the bus that was looming into view a hundred yards or so down the traffic-packed street, I felt someone – or something – rub against my leg. Instinctively, I looked down. I saw a familiar figure standing alongside me. To my horror, I could see that Bob was going through the same process as me, looking for his opportunity to cross.

'What the hell are you doing here?' I said to him.

He just looked at me dismissively, as if I'd just asked a really stupid question. Then he focused once more on the road, nudging himself nearer the edge of the kerb as if getting ready to make a dash for it.

I couldn't let him risk it. It would almost certainly be suicide. So I swept him up and put him on my shoulder, where I knew he liked to sit. He sat there, snuggled up against the side of my head, as I sidestepped and weaved my way through the traffic and crossed the road.

'All right, Bob, that's far enough,' I said to him as I put him down on the pavement and shooed him away again.

He sidled off down the street into the throng. *Maybe now I've seen the last of him*, I thought to myself. He really was a long way from home now.

A few moments later the bus pulled up. It was an old-fashioned red double-decker bus that you could jump on at the back. I went to sit on the bench at the back of the bus and was placing my guitar case in the storage space near where the conductor was standing when, behind me, I saw a sudden flash of ginger fur. Before I knew it, Bob had jumped up and plonked himself on the seat next to where I was sitting.

I was gobsmacked. I realised – finally – that I wasn't ever going to shake this cat off. But then I realised something else.

I invited Bob to jump on my lap, which he did in the blink of an eye. A moment or two later, the conductor appeared. She was a cheerful West Indian lady and smiled at Bob, then me.

'Is he yours?' she said, stroking him.

'I guess he must be,' I said.

Chapter 5

Centre of Attention

For the next forty-five minutes or so, Bob sat quietly next to me, his face pressed against the glass of the bus window, watching the world go by. He seemed to be fascinated by all the cars, cyclists, vans and pedestrians whizzing past us; he wasn't fazed at all.

The only time he pulled away from the window and looked to me for a little reassurance was when the blare of a police siren, a fire engine or an ambulance got a bit too close for comfort. This surprised me a bit and once more set me thinking about where he had spent his early life. If he had grown up on the streets he would have got used to this noise a long, long time ago.

'Nothing to worry about,' I told him, each time giving him a friendly stroke on the back of the neck. 'This is what the middle of London sounds like, Bob, better get used to it.'

It was odd, even though I knew he was a street cat and could run away at any time, I had this deep-seated feeling that he was here in my life to stay. Somehow I sensed this wouldn't be the last time we'd make this trip together.

I was going to get off at my usual bus stop near Tottenham Court Road tube station. As it loomed into view, I picked up my guitar, scooped up Bob and headed for the exit. On the pavement, I fished around in my coat pocket and found the makeshift shoelace lead that I'd left in there after taking Bob out to do his business the evening before.

I put it around his neck then placed him down. I didn't want him wandering off. The junction of Tottenham Court Road and New Oxford Street was bustling with shoppers, tourists and ordinary Londoners getting on with their day. He'd have been lost in a second – or, even worse, crushed by one of the buses or black cabs whistling towards and from Oxford Street.

Understandably, it was all a bit intimidating for Bob. It was unfamiliar territory for him – well, I assumed it was. I couldn't be sure, of course. As we picked our way along I could tell from his slightly uptight body language and the way he kept looking up at me that he was uneasy. So I decided to take one of my normal short cuts through the back streets to get to Covent Garden.

'Come on, Bob, let's get you out of the crowds,' I said.

Even then he wasn't 100 per cent happy. Weaving our way through the throng, he kept shooting me looks as if to say he wasn't quite sure about this. After only a few yards I could tell that he wanted me to pick him up.

'All right, but don't make a habit of it,' I said, gathering him up and placing him on my shoulders just as I'd done crossing Tottenham High Road. He'd soon settled into a comfortable spot, at a slight angle across my right shoulder blade, with his front paws placed on the top of my arm, looking out like the occupant of the bird's nest on some pirate ship. I couldn't help smiling inwardly. I must look a bit like Long John Silver, except I had a puss rather than a parrot sailing along with me.

He certainly seemed to be very comfortable there. I could feel him purring lightly as we walked through the throng, across New Oxford Street and into the smaller streets leading down towards Covent Garden.

The crowds had thinned out by now and after a while I began to forget Bob was there. Instead I started to immerse myself in the usual thoughts that went through my mind on the way to work. Was the weather going to be good enough for me to get a solid five hours' busking? Answer: Probably. It was overcast, but the clouds were white and high in the sky. There wasn't much chance of rain. What sort of crowd would there be in Covent Garden? Well, it was getting close to Easter so there were a lot of tourists. How long would it take me to make the twenty or thirty pounds I needed to get me – and now Bob – through the next few days? Well, it had taken me the best part of five hours the previous day. Maybe it would be better today, maybe it wouldn't. That was the thing with busking; you just never knew.

I was mulling all these things over still when I was suddenly aware of something.

Ordinarily, no one would engage or even exchange a look with me. I was a busker and this was London. I didn't exist. I was a person to be avoided, shunned even. But as I walked down Neal Street that afternoon almost every person we passed was looking at me. Well, more to the point, they were looking at Bob.

One or two had quizzical, slightly confused looks on their faces, which was understandable, I guess. It must have looked slightly incongruous, a tall, long-haired bloke walking along with a large, ginger tom on his shoulders. Not something you see every day – even on the streets of London.

Most people, however, were reacting more warmly. The moment they saw Bob their faces would break into broad smiles. It wasn't long before people were stopping us.

'Ah, look at you two,' said one well-dressed, middle-aged lady laden down with shopping bags. 'He's gorgeous. Can I stroke him?'

'Of course,' I said, thinking it would be a one-off event.

She plonked down her bags and placed her face right up to his.

'What a lovely fellow you are, aren't you?' she said. 'He is a boy, isn't he?'

'He is,' I said.

'Isn't he good to sit there on your shoulders like that? Don't see that very often. He must really trust you.'

I'd barely said goodbye to the lady when we were approached by two young girls. They'd seen the lady making a fuss of Bob so I guess they thought they could do the same. They turned out to be Swedish teenagers on holiday.

'What is his name? Can we take his picture?' they said, snapping away with their cameras the instant I nodded.

'His name's Bob,' I said.

'Ah, Bob. Cool.'

We chatted for a minute or two. One of them had a cat herself and produced a picture of it for me. I had to politely excuse myself after a couple of minutes, other-wise they would have spent hours drooling over him.

We carried on towards the bottom of Neal Street in the direction of Long Acre. But the going was slow. No sooner had the latest admirer gone away than the same thing was happening again – and again. I'd barely go three feet without being stopped by someone who wanted to stroke or talk to Bob.

The novelty soon wore off. At this rate I wasn't going to get anywhere, I began to realise. It normally took me not much more than ten minutes to get from my normal bus stop to my pitch at Covent Garden. But it had already taken me twice that because everyone had seemed to want to stop and talk to Bob. It was a bit ridiculous.

By the time we got to Covent Garden it was almost an hour after I normally got set up.

Thanks a lot, Bob, you've probably cost me a few quid in lost earnings, I heard myself saying in my head, half-jokingly.

It was a serious issue though. If he was going to slow me down this much every day, I really couldn't let him follow me on to the bus again, I thought. It wasn't long before I was thinking a bit differently.

By this point, I'd been busking around Covent Garden for about a year and a half. I generally started at about two or three in the afternoon and carried on until around eight in the evening. It was the best time to capture tourists and people finishing off their shopping or on the way home from work. At the weekends I would go earlier and do lunchtimes. On Thursday, Friday and Saturday I'd carry on until quite late, trying to take advantage of the extra numbers of Londoners that hung around at the end of the working week.

I'd learned to be flexible in finding an audience. My main pitch was on a patch of pavement directly outside Covent Garden tube station on James Street. I'd work that until about 6.30p.m., when the main evening rush hour was at its peak. Then for the last couple of hours I'd walk around all the pubs in Covent Garden where people were standing outside smoking and drinking. In the summer months this could be quite productive as office workers unwound after their day's work with a pint and a fag in the evening sunshine.

It could be a bit risky at times. Some people took exception to me approaching them and could be rude and even abusive at times. 'Piss off you scrounger'; 'Get yourself a proper job you lazy f******.' That kind of stuff. But that came with the territory. I was used to it. There were plenty of people who were happy to hear me play a song then slip me a quid.

Busking at James Street was a bit of a gamble as well. Technically speaking, I wasn't supposed to be there.

The Covent Garden area is divided up very specifically into areas when it comes to street people. It's regulated by officials from the local council, an officious bunch that we referred to as Covent Guardians.

My pitch should have been on the eastern side of Covent Garden, near the Royal Opera House and Bow Street. That's where the musicians were supposed to operate, according to the Covent Guardians. The other side of the piazza, the western side, was where the street performers were supposed to ply their trade. The jugglers and entertainers generally pitched themselves under the balcony of the Punch and Judy pub where they usually found a rowdy audience willing to watch them.

James Street, where I had begun playing, was meant to be the domain of the human statues. There were a few of them around, one guy dressed as Charlie Chaplin used to do quite well but only worked now and again. But it was normally clear so I had taken advantage and made it my own little patch. I knew there was always the risk of getting moved along by the Covent Guardians but I took my chances and it usually paid off. The volume of people coming out of the tube station there was huge. If only one in a thousand of them made a 'drop' then I could do OK.

It was just after 3p.m. when I got to my pitch – finally. Just as we turned into James Street we were stopped for the umpteenth time, on this occasion by an obviously gay guy on his way home from the gym, judging by the sweaty kit he was wearing.

He made a complete fuss of Bob and even asked me – I think jokingly – whether he could buy him off me.

'No, mate, he's not for sale,' I said politely, just in case he was serious. Walking away from the guy I just looked at Bob and shook my head. 'Only in London, mate, only in London.'

Arriving at the pitch, I firstly checked to make sure the coast was clear. There was no sign of the Covent Guardians. There were also a couple of people who worked at the tube station who sometimes gave me some hassle because they knew I wasn't supposed to be there. But they didn't seem to be around either. So I put Bob down on the pavement near the wall, unzipped my guitar case, took off my jacket and got ready to tune up.

Ordinarily it would take me a good ten minutes to get tuned, start playing and get people to pay me some attention.

Today though a couple of people slowed down in front of me and lobbed small denomination coins into my guitar case even before I'd played a note. *Generous of them*, I thought.

It was as I fiddled around, tuning my guitar, that the penny eventually dropped!

My back was turned to the crowd when I again heard the distinctive clinking of one coin hitting another. Behind me I heard a male voice. 'Nice cat, mate,' he said.

I turned and saw an ordinary-looking guy in his mid-twenties giving me a thumbs up sign and walking off with a smile on his face.

I was taken aback. Bob had curled himself up in a comfortable ball in the middle of the empty guitar case. I knew he was a charmer. But this was something else.

I'd taught myself to play the guitar when I was a teenager living back in Australia. People would show me things and then I'd work my way through them on my own. I got my first guitar when I was fifteen or sixteen. It was quite late to start playing, I suppose. I bought an old electric guitar from a Cash Converters in Melbourne. I'd always played on my friends' acoustic guitars, but I fancied an electric one. I loved Jimi Hendrix, I thought he was fantastic and wanted to play like him.

The set I'd put together for my busking featured some of the things that I'd enjoyed playing for years. Kurt Cobain had always been a bit of a hero of mine, so there was some Nirvana in there. But I also played some Bob Dylan and a fair bit by Johnny Cash. One of the most popular things I played was 'Hurt', originally by Nine Inch Nails but then covered by Johnny Cash. It was easier to play that version because it was an acoustic piece. I also played 'The Man In Black' by Johnny Cash. That was a good busking song – and it was kind of appropriate too. I generally wore black. The most popular song in my set was 'Wonderwall' by Oasis. That always worked best, especially outside the pubs when I wandered around later in the evenings.

I played pretty much the same stuff over and over every day. It was what people liked. That's what the tourists wanted to hear. I would usually start with a song like 'About A Girl' by Nirvana just to get the fingers going. That's what I did today, as Bob sat in front of me, watching the crowds walk out of the tube station.

🐾

I'd barely been playing for more than a few minutes when a group of kids stopped. They were obviously from Brazil and were all wearing Brazilian football shirts and speaking what I recognised as Portuguese. One of them, a young girl, bent down and began stroking Bob.

'Ah, *gato bonito*,' she said.

'She is saying you have a beautiful cat,' one of the boys said, helpfully translating her Portuguese.

They were just kids on a trip to London, but they were fascinated. Almost immediately other people were stopping to see what the fuss was about. About half a dozen of the Brazilian kids and other passers-by began fishing around in their pockets and started raining coins into the bag.

'Looks like you may not be such a bad companion after all, Bob. I'll invite you out for the day more often,' I smiled at him.

I'd not planned on bringing him along with me so I didn't have much to give him. There was a half-empty packet of his favourite cat treats in my rucksack so I gave him one of them every now and again. Like me, he'd have to wait until later to get a decent meal.

As the late afternoon turned into the early evening and the crowds thickened with people heading home from work or out into the West End for the evening, more and more people were slowing down and looking at Bob. There was clearly something about him that fascinated people.

As darkness was beginning to descend, one middle-aged lady stopped for a chat.

'How long have you had him?' she asked, bending down to stroke Bob.

'Oh, only a few weeks,' I said. 'We sort of found each other.'

'Found each other? Sounds interesting.'

At first I was a bit suspicious. I wondered whether she was some kind of animal welfare person and might tell me that I had no right to keep him or something. But she turned out simply to be a real cat lover.

She smiled as I explained the story of how we'd met and how I'd spent a fortnight nursing him back to health.

'I had a ginger tom very much like this one a few years ago,' she said, looking a bit emotional. For a moment I thought she was going to burst into tears. 'You are lucky to have found him. They are just the best companions, they are so quiet and docile. You've found yourself a real friend there,' she said.

'I think you are right,' I smiled.

She placed a fiver into the guitar case before leaving.

He was definitely a lady puller, I realised. I estimated that something like 70 per cent of the people who had stopped so far had been females.

After just over an hour, I had as much as what I'd normally make in a good day, just over twenty pounds.

This is brilliant, I thought to myself.

But something inside me was saying that I shouldn't call it quits, that I should carry on for tonight.

The truth was I was still torn about Bob. Despite the gut feeling I had that this cat and I were somehow destined to be together, a large part of me still figured that he'd eventually go off and make his own way. It was only logical. He'd wandered into my life and he was going to wander back out again at some point. This couldn't carry on. So as the passers-by continued to slow down and make a fuss of him, I figured I might as well make the most of it. Make hay while the sun shines and all that.

'If he wants to come out and have fun with me, that's great,' I said to myself. 'And I'm making a bit of cash as well, then that's great too.'

Except that it was more than just a bit of cash by now.

I had been used to making around twenty pounds a day, which was enough to get me through a few days and to cover all the expenses of running my flat. But that night, by the time I finished up at around 8p.m., it was clear that I'd made a lot more than that.

After packing up my guitar, it took me all of five minutes to count out all the coins that had piled up. There were what looked like hundreds of coins of all denominations as well as a few notes scattered amongst them.

When I finally totted it all up, I shook my head quietly. I had made the princely sum of £63.77. To most of the people walking around Covent Garden that might not have seemed like a lot of money. But it was to me.

I transferred all the coins into my rucksack and hauled it on to my shoulders. It was rattling like a giant piggy bank. It also weighed a ton! But I was ecstatic. That was the most I'd ever made in a day's work on the streets, three times what I'd make on a normal day.

I picked up Bob, giving him a stroke on the back of the neck.

'Well done, mate,' I said. 'That was what I call a good evening's work.'

I decided that I didn't need to wander around the pubs. Besides, I knew Bob was hungry – as was I. We needed to head home.

I walked back towards Tottenham Court Road and the bus stop with Bob once more positioned on my shoulder. I wasn't rude to anyone, but I decided not to engage with absolutely everyone who stopped and smiled at us. I couldn't. There were too many of them. I wanted to get home this side of midnight.

'We'll have something nice to eat tonight, Bob,' I said as we settled on to the bus for the trip back up to Tottenham. Again, he pinned his nose up against the window watching the bright lights and the traffic.

I got off the bus near a really nice Indian restaurant on

Tottenham High Road. I'd walked past it many times, savouring the lengthy menu, but never had enough spare money to be able to afford anything. I'd always had to make do with something from a cheaper place nearer to the block of flats.

I went in and ordered a chicken tikka masala with lemon rice, a peshwari naan and a sag paneer. The waiters threw me a few, funny looks when they saw Bob on a lead beside me. So I said I'd pop back in twenty minutes and headed off with Bob to a supermarket across the road.

With the money we'd made I treated Bob to a nice pouch of posh cat food, a couple of packs of his favourite nibbles and some 'cat milk'. I also treated myself to a couple of nice tins of lager.

'Let's push the boat out, Bob,' I said to him. 'It's been a day to remember.'

After picking up our dinner, I almost ran home, I was so overwhelmed by the tempting smells coming out from the brown paper carrier bag from the upmarket curry house. When we got inside Bob and I both wolfed down our food as if there was no tomorrow. I hadn't eaten so well in months – well, maybe years. I'm pretty sure he hadn't either.

We then curled up for a couple of hours, me watching television and him snuggled up in his favourite spot under the radiator. We both slept like logs that night.

Chapter 6

One Man and His Cat

The next morning I was woken by a sudden, loud, crashing sound. It took me a moment to get my bearings, but when I did so I immediately guessed what it was. The metallic, clanging noise had come from the kitchen. That probably meant that once again Bob was trying to open the cupboards where I kept his food and had knocked something over.

I squinted at the clock. It was mid-morning. After the excitement of the previous night I had given myself a lie in, but Bob had obviously decided he couldn't wait any longer. This was his way of saying: 'Get up, I want my breakfast.'

I hauled myself out of bed and stumbled into the kitchen. The small, tin saucepan I used to boil milk was lying on the floor.

As soon as he saw me Bob slid his way purposefully towards his bowl.

'OK, mate, I get the picture,' I said, unlocking the cupboards and reaching for a sachet of his favourite chicken dish. I spooned a couple of portions into the bowl and watched him devour it in seconds. He then gulped down the water in his bowl, licked his face and paws clean and trotted off into the living room, where, looking very satisfied with himself, he took his favourite position under the radiator.

If only all our lives were that simple, I thought to myself.

I'd considered not going to work, but then thought better of it. We may have had a lucky break last night, but that money wouldn't keep us going for long. The electricity and gas bills were due soon. Given the cold weather we'd had in recent months, they weren't going to make for pleasant reading. It had also begun to dawn on me that I had a new responsibility in my life. I had an extra mouth to feed – a rather hungry and manipulative one.

So after wolfing down some breakfast of my own, I started getting my stuff together.

I wasn't sure whether Bob would want to come out busking with me again today. Yesterday might have been a one-off; he might simply have been satisfying his curiosity about where I went when I left home most days. But I put some snacks in the bag for him just in case he did decide to follow me again.

It was early afternoon as I headed off. It was obvious what I was doing; I had my rucksack and guitar lashed across my back. If he didn't want to go out of the flat with me, which was rare, he generally let me know by slinking off behind the sofa. For a moment I thought that was what he was going to do today. When I took the chain off the front door, he headed in that direction. But then as I was about to shut the door behind me he bolted towards me and followed me out into the corridor and towards the staircase.

When we got to the ground floor and out into the open air he scurried off into the bushes to do his business. Afterwards, rather than heading to me, he trotted off towards the area where the bins were kept.

The bins were becoming more and more of a fascination for him. Goodness knows what he was finding – and eating – in there. I thought that this might be the only reason he'd wanted to come down with me. I wasn't too happy about him rooting around in the rubbish so went to check what was there. You never knew when the local bin men would come. Fortunately, there must have been a collection earlier that morning because there was no stray rubbish around. There were slim pickings, Bob wasn't going to have much joy. Reassured, I decided to head off without him. I knew he'd get back inside the building somehow, especially now that a lot of the neighbours knew him. One or two had started making a real fuss of him whenever they saw him. One lady who lived on the floor below me always gave him a treat.

He would probably be waiting on the landing for me when I got home that evening.

Fair enough, I thought as I set off for Tottenham High Road. Bob had done me a huge favour the previous day. I wasn't going to exploit our relationship by demanding he come along with me every day. He was my companion, not my employee!

The skies were grey and there was a hint of rain in the air. If it was like this in central London it was going to be a waste of time. Busking on a rainy day was never a good idea. Instead of feeling sympathy for you, people simply rushed by that bit quicker. If it was bucketing down in the centre of town, I told myself, I'd simply turn around and head back home. I would rather spend the day hanging out with Bob. I wanted to use the money we'd made the previous night to get him a decent lead and collar.

I was about two hundred yards or so down the road when I sensed something behind me. I turned round and saw a familiar figure, padding along the pavement.

'Ah, changed our mind have we,' I said, as he approached me.

Bob tilted his head ever so slightly to one side and gave me one of those pitying looks, as if to say: 'well, why else would I be standing here?'

I still had the shoestring lead in my pocket. I put it on and we started walking down the road together.

The streets of Tottenham are very different to those of Covent Garden, but just like the day before people immediately began staring at us. And just like the day before, one or two looked at me disapprovingly. They clearly thought I was off my rocker, leading a ginger tom around on a piece of string.

'If this is going to become a regular thing I really am going to have to get you a proper lead,' I said quietly to Bob, suddenly feeling a bit self-conscious.

But for every person that gave me a dirty look another half dozen smiled and nodded at me. One West Indian lady, weighed down with bags of shopping, gave us a big, sunny grin.

'Don't you two make a pretty picture,' she said.

No one had engaged me in conversation on the streets around my flat in all the months I'd lived here. It was odd, but also amazing. It was as if my Harry Potter invisibility cloak had slipped off my shoulders.

When we got to the crossing point at Tottenham High Road, Bob gave me a look as if to say: 'Come on, you know what to do now' and I plonked him on my shoulders.

Soon we were on the bus, with Bob taking his favourite position with his head pressed against the glass. We were on the road again.

I'd been right about the weather. Soon the rain was hammering down, forming intricate patterns on the window where Bob had once more pressed his face tight against the glass. Outside you could just make out a sea of umbrellas. There were people running, splashing through the streets to avoid the downpour.

Thankfully, the rain had eased off by the time we reached the centre of town. Despite the weather there were even bigger crowds in the centre of town than there had been the previous day.

'We'll give it a go for a couple of hours,' I said to Bob as I plonked him on my shoulders and headed off towards Covent Garden. 'But if it starts to rain again we'll head back, I promise.'

Walking down Neal Street, once again people were stopping us all the time. I was happy to let them fuss over Bob, within reason. In the space of ten minutes, half a dozen people had stopped us and at least half of them had asked to take a picture.

I quickly learned that the key was to keep moving, otherwise you'd be surrounded before you knew it.

It was as we were reaching the end of Neal Street near where I turned towards James Street that something interesting happened.

I suddenly felt Bob's paws readjusting themselves on my shoulder. Before I knew it he was sliding off my shoulder and clambering down my arm. When I let him hop on to the pavement he began walking ahead of me. I extended the lead to its full length and let him go. It was obvious that he recognised where we were and was going to take it from here. He was leading the way.

He marched ahead of me all the way to the pitch where we'd been the previous night. He then stood there, waiting for me to take out my guitar and lay the guitar case down for him.

'There you go, Bob,' I said. He instantly sat down on the soft case as if it was where he belonged. He positioned himself so that he could watch the world walk by – which, this being Covent Garden, it was.

There had been a time when I'd had ambitions of making it as a real musician. I'd harboured dreams of becoming the next Kurt Cobain. As naive and completely stupid as it sounds now, it had been part of my grand plan when I'd come back to England from Australia.

That's what I'd told my mother and everyone else when I'd set off.

I'd had my moments and, for a brief time, I felt like I might actually get somewhere.

It was hard for a while, but things changed around 2002, when I'd got off the streets and into some sheltered accommodation in Dalston. One thing had led to another and I'd formed a band with some guys I'd met. We were a four-piece guitar band called Hyper Fury, which told you a lot about my and my band mates' state of mind at the time. The name certainly summed me up. I was an angry young man. I really was hyper-furious – about life in general and about feeling that I'd not had a fair break in particular. My music was an outlet for my anger and angst.

For that reason we weren't very mainstream. Our songs were edgy and dark and our lyrics even more so, which was hardly surprising, I suppose, given that our influences were bands like Nine Inch Nails and Nirvana.

We actually managed to put out two albums, though EPs might be a more accurate description. The first came out in September 2003 with another band, Corrision. It was called *Corrision v Hyper Fury* and featured two pretty heavy tracks, called 'Onslaught' and 'Retaliator'. Again, the titles offer a fairly strong indication to our musical philosophy. We followed that up six months later in March 2004 with a second album called *Profound Destruction Unit*, which featured three songs, 'Sorry', 'Profound' and another version of 'Retaliator'. It sold a few copies but it didn't really set the world on fire. Put it this way: we didn't get booked for Glastonbury.

We did have some fans, though, and managed to get some gigs, mainly in north London and places like Camden, in particular. There was a big Gothy kind of scene going on there and we fitted in well with it. We looked and certainly sounded the part. We did gigs in pubs, we played at squat parties, basically we played wherever we were invited. There was a moment when we might have started to make progress. The biggest gig we did was at The Dublin Castle, a famous music pub in north London, where we played a couple of times. In particular, we played in the Gothic Summer festival there, which was quite a big deal at the time.

Things were going so well for us at one point that I teamed up with a guy called Pete from Corrision and started our own independent label, Corrupt Drive Records.

But it didn't really work or, to be more accurate, I didn't really work.

At the time my best friend Belle and I were in what would be a brief relationship together. We got on great as friends. She is a really caring person and looked after me, but as a relationship it was kind of doomed from the beginning. The problem was that she was on drugs as well and she was co-dependent. It really didn't help me – or her – as we struggled to kick our habits. When one of us was trying to get clean the other one was using and vice versa. That's co-dependency all over.

So it made it really difficult for me to break the cycle.

I was trying to break the cycle, but, looking back on it, if I'm honest I wouldn't say I was trying hard. I think part of it was that I didn't really feel like it was ever going to become a reality. Mentally, at least, the band was something I put on the back-burner. It was too easy to slip back into old habits – quite literally.

By 2005 I'd accepted that the band was a hobby, not a way of making a living. Pete carried on with the record label and still runs it now, I believe. But I was struggling so badly with my habit that I fell by the wayside – again. It became another one of those second chances that I let slip through my fingers. I guess I'll never know what might have been.

I'd never given up on music, however. Even when the band broke up and it was clear that I wasn't going to get anywhere professionally, I would spend hours most days playing on the guitar, improvising songs. It was a great outlet for me. God knows where I'd have been without it. And busking had certainly made a difference to my life in recent years. Without it – and the money it generated – I dread to think what I would have ended up doing to earn cash. That really didn't bear thinking about.

That evening, as I settled down into the session, the tourists were once more out in force.

It was a repeat of the previous day. The moment I sat down – or, more precisely, the moment Bob sat down – people who would normally have rushed by began to slow down and interact with him.

Again, it was women rather than men who showed the most interest.

Not long after I'd started playing, a rather stony-faced traffic warden walked past. I saw her look down at Bob and watched as her face melted into a warm smile.

'Aah, look at you,' she said, stopping and kneeling down to stroke Bob.

She barely gave me a second glance and didn't drop anything into the guitar case. But that was fine. I was beginning to love the way that Bob seemed to be able to brighten up people's days.

He was a beautiful creature, there was no doubt about that. But it wasn't just that. There was something else about Bob. It was his personality that was attracting the attention. People could sense something about him.

I could sense it myself. There was something special about him. He had an unusual rapport with people, well, people he knew had his best interests at heart, at least.

Every now and again I'd see him bridle a bit when he saw someone he didn't like. As we settled down, a very smart, rich-looking Middle-Eastern guy walked past, arm-in-arm with a really attractive blonde. She could easily have been a model.

'Oh, look. What a gorgeous cat,' she said, suddenly stopping in her tracks and pulling on the guy's arm to slow him down. The guy looked distinctly unimpressed and flicked his hand dismissively, as if to say, 'So what?'

The instant he did so Bob's body language changed. He arched his back ever so slightly and shifted his body position so that he was a few inches closer to me. It was subtle – but to me it was really telling.

I wonder whether this guy reminds Bob of someone from his past? I thought to myself as the couple walked on. *I wonder whether he had seen that look before?*

I'd have given anything to know his story, discover what had led him to the hallway of my block of flats that evening. But that was something I never was going to know. It would always be guesswork.

As I settled into my set I was much more relaxed than twenty-four hours earlier. I think having Bob there the previous day had thrown me a bit, psychologically. I'd been used to having to engage and draw in the crowds myself. It had been hard work. Eking out every penny was tough. With Bob it was different. The way he'd sucked in the audience for me had been a bit odd at first. I'd also felt very responsible for him with so many people around. Covent Garden – like the rest of London – has its share of weirdoes. I was terrified that someone would just grab him and run off with him.

But that day felt different, however. That day I felt like we were safe, like we kind of belonged here.

As I began singing and the coins started tinkling into the case at the same rate as the previous day, I thought to myself: *I'm enjoying this.*

It had been a long time since I'd said that.

By the time we headed home three hours later my rucksack was once more jangling with the weight of coins. We'd collected well over sixty pounds again.

This time I wasn't going to spend it on an expensive curry. I had more practical uses for the money. The following day the weather was even worse, with the forecast of really heavy rain that night.

So I decided to spend some time on Bob rather than busking. If he was going to hang out with me on a regular basis then I needed to have better equipment for him. I couldn't walk around with him attached to a leash made out of a shoelace. Apart from anything else, it was uncomfortable – not to mention dangerous.

Bob and I hopped on a bus and headed off in the direction of Archway. I knew the north London branch of the Cats Protection charity was there.

Bob seemed to sense immediately that this wasn't the same route we'd taken the previous couple of days. Every now and again he would turn and look at me as if to say: 'So, where are you taking me today?' He wasn't anxious, just curious.

The Cats Protection shop was a smart, modern place with all sorts of equipment, toys and books about cats. There were loads of free pamphlets and brochures on every aspect of caring for a cat – from microchipping to toxoplasmosis, diet tips to neutering advice. I picked up a few for future reading.

There were only a couple of people working there and the place was quiet. So they couldn't resist coming over for a chat as I took a look around with Bob sitting on my shoulder.

'He's a good-looking boy isn't he?' one lady said, stroking Bob. He could tell he was in safe hands because he was leaning his body into her as she smoothed his coat and cooed over him.

We then fell into a conversation about how Bob and I had met. I then explained what had happened the previous two days. Both women smiled and nodded.

'A lot of cats like to go out for a walk with their owners,' one told me. 'They like to go for a walk in the park or for a short stroll down the street. But I have to say Bob's a bit unusual isn't he?'

'He is,' her friend said. 'I think you've got yourself a bit of a jewel there. He's obviously decided to attach himself to you.'

It was nice to hear them confirming what, deep down, I knew already. Every now and again, I had a little pang of doubt about whether I should try harder to put him back on the streets, whether I was doing the right thing in keeping him in the flat with me. Their words were a real boost for me.

What I didn't know, however, was how best to manage Bob if he was going to be my constant companion on the streets of London. It wasn't the safest of environments, to put it mildly. Apart from the obvious traffic, there were all sorts of potential threats and dangers out there.

'The best thing you can do is to get a harness like this,' one of the ladies said, unhooking a nice-looking blue, woven nylon harness, collar and matching lead.

She explained the pros and cons of it.

'It's not a great idea just to fix a leash to a cat collar. The worst collars can harm your cat's neck and even choke the cat. And the problem with the better quality collars is that they are made from elastic or are what they call "breakaway" collars so that the cat can escape if the collar gets caught on something. There's a good chance that at some point you'll have an empty leash dangling in your hand,' the lady explained. 'I think you would be much better off with a cat harness and a leash, especially given you are out all the time,' she said.

'Isn't it going to feel funny for him?' I asked. 'It's not going to feel natural.'

'You'll need to ease him into it,' she agreed. 'It might take you a week or so. Start him off wearing it for a few minutes a day before you are ready to go outside together. Then build it up from there.' She could see me mulling it over. 'Why not try it on him?'

'Why not?' I said.

Bob was sitting comfortably and didn't offer too much resistance, although I could tell that he was uncertain about what was happening.

'Just leave it on him and let him get used to the sensation of having it on his body,' the lady said.

The harness, lead and collar cost about thirteen pounds. It was one of the most expensive they had, but I figured he was worth it.

If I'd been a businessman, chief executive of James & Bob Inc, I'd have been thinking you've got to look after your employees, you've got to invest in your human resources – except in this case it was my feline resources.

It only took me a couple of days to introduce Bob to the harness. I began just by letting him wear it around the house, sometimes with the lead attached. At first he was a bit confused at having this extra-long, leather tail trailing behind him. But he soon got used to it. Every time he wore it I made sure to praise him for doing so. I knew the worst thing I could do was to shout at him, not that I ever did that anyway.

After a couple of days we progressed to going on short walks with it on. When we were out busking, I stuck to the old collar most of the time, but then every now and again I'd slip the harness on for a short section of the walk to work. Slowly but surely it became second nature to him to have the harness on.

Bob was still coming with me every day.

We didn't stay out too long. I didn't want to inflict that on him. Even though I already had a feeling he would follow me to the ends of the earth, and even though he was always sitting on my shoulders and didn't have to walk, I wasn't going to do that to him.

It was during the third week of us busking together that he first decided he didn't want to join me. Ordinarily, the minute he saw me putting on my coat and packing my rucksack, he'd be up and moving towards me, ready for me to put his lead on. But then, one day, as I went through the normal routine, he just shuffled off behind the sofa for a bit then went and laid down underneath the radiator. It was as if to say 'I'm having a day off.'

I could tell he was tired.

'Don't fancy it today, Bob?' I said, stroking him.

He looked at me in that knowing way of his.

'No problem,' I said, heading to the kitchen to put some snacks in a bowl to keep him going for the rest of the day until I got home that evening.

I'd read a report once that said leaving the TV on made pets feel less lonely when their owners are out. I didn't know whether that was true, but I switched the TV set on in any case. He immediately shuffled towards his favourite spot and started staring at it.

Going out that day really brought home to me the difference Bob had made to my life. With him on my shoulder or walking on the lead in front of me, I turned heads everywhere. On my own I was invisible again. By now we were well known enough to the locals for a few people to express concern.

'Where's the cat today?' one local stall-owner said as he passed me by that evening.

'He's having a day off,' I said.

'Oh, good. I was worried something had happened to the little fella,' he smiled, giving me the thumbs-up.

A couple of other people stopped and asked the same question. As soon as I'd told them Bob was fine they moved on. No one was quite as interested in stopping for a talk as they did when Bob was around. I may not have liked it, but I accepted it. That's the way it was.

On the pavement at James Street, the sound of coins landing in the bag had become music to my ears; I couldn't deny that. But without Bob I couldn't help noticing that the music slowed down significantly. As I played I was conscious that I wasn't making anywhere near as much money. It took me a few more hours to earn about half the cash I had made on a good day with Bob. It was back to the old days before Bob, but that was OK.

It was as I walked back that evening that something began to sink in. It wasn't all about making money. I wasn't going to starve. And my life was much richer for having Bob in it.

It was such a pleasure to have such great company, such a great companion. But somehow it felt like I'd been given a chance to get back on track.

It's not easy when you are working on the streets. People don't want to give you a chance. Before I had Bob, if I would try to approach people in the pubs with my guitar strap on, people would go 'no, sorry' before I'd even had a chance to say hello.

I could have been asking someone for the time. But they'd say to me: 'no change, sorry' before I opened my mouth. That happened all the time. They wouldn't even give me the opportunity.

People don't want to listen. All they see is someone they think is trying to get a free ride. They don't understand I'm working, I'm not begging. I was actually trying to make a living. Just because I wasn't wearing a suit and a tie and carrying a briefcase or a computer, just because I didn't have a payslip and a P45, it didn't mean that I was freeloading.

Having Bob there gave me a chance to interact with people.

They would ask about Bob and I would get a chance to explain my situation at the same time. They would ask where he came from and I'd then be able to explain how we got together and how we were making money to pay our rent, food, electricity and gas bills. People would give me more of a fair hearing.

Psychologically, people also began to see me in a different light.

Cats are notoriously picky about who they like. And if a cat doesn't like its owner it will go and find another one. Cats do that all the time. They go and live with somebody else. Seeing me with my cat softened me in their eyes. It humanised me. Especially after I'd been so dehumanised. In some ways it was giving me back my identity. I had been a non-person; I was becoming a person again.

Chapter 7

The Two Musketeers

Bob wasn't just changing people's attitude to me: he was changing my attitude to others as well.

I'd never really had any responsibilities towards others in my life. I'd had the odd job here and there when I was younger in Australia and I'd also been in a band, which required a bit of teamwork. But the truth was that, since I left home as a teenager, my main responsibility had always been to myself. I'd always had to look after number one, simply because there wasn't anyone else to do it. As a result, my life had become a very selfish one. It was all about my day-to-day survival.

Bob's arrival in my life had dramatically changed all that. I'd suddenly taken on an extra responsibility. Another being's health and happiness was down to me.

It had come as a bit of a shock, but I had begun to adapt to it. In fact, I enjoyed it. I knew it may sound silly to a lot of people, but for the first time I had an idea what it must be like looking after a child. Bob was my baby and making sure he was warm, well fed and safe was really rewarding. It was scary too.

I worried about him constantly, in particular, when I was out on the streets. In Covent Garden and elsewhere I was always in protective mode, my instincts were always telling me that I had to watch out for him at every turn. With good cause.

I hadn't been lulled into a false sense of security by the way people treated me with Bob. The streets of London weren't all filled with kind-hearted tourists and cat lovers. Not everyone was going to react the same way when they saw a long-haired busker and his cat singing for their suppers on street corners. It happened less now that I had Bob, but I still got a volley of abuse every now and again, usually from drunken young blokes who felt the fact they were picking up a pay packet at the end of the week made them somehow superior to me.

'Get off your arse and do a proper day's work you long-haired layabout,' they would say, albeit almost always in more colourful language than that.

I let their insults wash over me. I was used to them. It was a different matter when people turned their aggression on Bob. That's when my protective instincts really took over.

Some people saw me and Bob as easy targets. Almost every day, we'd be approached by idiots of some kind. They would shout stupid comments or stand there laughing at us. Occasionally, they would threaten to turn violent.

One Friday evening, quite soon after Bob and I had first come to Covent Garden together, I was playing at James Street when a bunch of young, very rowdy, black lads came past. They had real attitude, and were obviously on the lookout for trouble. A couple of them spotted Bob sitting on the pavement next to me and started making 'woof' and 'meow' noises, much to the amusement of their mates.

I could have coped with that. It was just stupid, puerile stuff. But then, for no reason whatsoever, one of them kicked the guitar case with Bob sitting in it. It wasn't a playful tap with his toes, it had real venom in it, and sent the case – and Bob – sliding a foot or so along the pavement.

Bob was really distressed. He made a loud noise, almost like a scream, and jumped out of the case. Thankfully his lead was attached to the case otherwise he would almost certainly have run off into the crowds. I might never have seen him again. Instead, restrained by the lead, he had no option but to hide behind my rucksack, which was standing nearby.

I got up immediately and confronted the guy.

'What the f*** did you do that for?' I said, standing toe-to-toe with him. I'm quite tall and towered over him, but it didn't seem to faze him.

'I just wanted to see if the cat was real,' he said, laughing as if he'd cracked a brilliant joke.

I didn't see the funny side of it.

'That's really clever, you f******idiot,' I said.

That was the signal for it all to kick off. They all began circling me and one of them began shoving into me with his chest and shoulders, but I stood my ground and shoved him back. For a split second or two there was a stand-off, but then I pointed to a CCTV camera that I knew was positioned on the corner near us.

'Go on then, do what you want. But just remember: you're on camera; see how far you get afterwards.'

The look on their faces was a picture I'd love to have captured – on CCTV or anywhere. They were obviously street smart enough to know you couldn't get away with violence on camera. One of them gave me a look as if to say: 'I will get you for that.'

Of course, they couldn't back down without raining down another wave of insults. But they were soon moving on, waving their arms and making every offensive gesture known to man. Sticks and stones and all that. I wasn't worried. In fact, I felt good about seeing them off. But I didn't hang around much longer that evening. I knew their type. They didn't take kindly to being 'dissed'.

The incident proved a couple of things to me. First, it was always a good idea to be near a CCTV camera. It had been another busker who had first given me the advice to always try and pitch yourself near one. 'You'll be safer there,' he said. Of course, I was too much of a know-all back then. Wasn't it going to give the authorities evidence if I was busking illegally? I'd ignored the advice for a while. Slowly but surely, however, I'd seen the wisdom of his words and incidents like this underlined them.

That was the positive. The negative was that I'd been reminded of something I'd also known. I really was on my own when trouble flared like this. There wasn't a policeman in sight. There wasn't a whiff of a Covent Guardian or even any assistance from the staff in the tube station. Despite the fact that quite a lot of people were milling around when the gang confronted me, none of the passers-by offered to intervene. In fact, people did their best to melt into the background and shuffle off. Nobody was going to come to my aid. In that respect, nothing had changed. Except, of course, I now had Bob.

As we headed back up to Tottenham that evening he cozied up to me on the bus. 'It's you and me against the world,' I said to him. 'We're the two Musketeers.'

He nuzzled up to me and purred lightly, as if in agreement.

The hard reality was that London was full of people who we had to treat with caution. Ever since I'd started bringing Bob with me I'd been wary of dogs, for instance. There were a lot of them, obviously, and it was no surprise that many of them took an instant interest in Bob. To be fair, in the vast majority of cases, people would notice if their dog was getting too close and give them a gentle tug on the lead. But others came too close for my comfort.

Fortunately Bob didn't seem to be bothered about them at all. He just ignored them. If they came up to him he would just stare them out. Again, it underlined my suspicion that he'd begun his life on the streets, he'd learned to handle himself there. Just how well he could handle himself I found out a week or so after the incident with the gang.

We were sitting in Neal Street in the late afternoon when a guy with a Staffordshire Bull Terrier loomed into view. Arseholes always have Staffs, it's a fact of London life, and this guy really looked like an arse- hole. He was shaven-headed, swigging extra-strength lager and wearing a tatty tracksuit. From the way he was slaloming around the street, he was off his head already, even though it was barely 4p.m.

They slowed down when they got to us purely because the Staff was straining at the leash as it tried to move in the direction of me and Bob.

As it happened, the dog wasn't threatening, he was just checking Bob out. Well, not even that, he was checking out the biscuits Bob had in front of him. He wasn't eating them at the time so the Staffie started inching his way towards the bowl, sniffing excitedly at the prospect of a free titbit or two.

I couldn't believe what happened next.

I'd seen Bob around dogs a fair bit by now. His

normal policy was not to give them the time of day. On this occasion, however, he must have felt some action was necessary.

He'd been snoozing peacefully at my side. But as the Staffie leaned in towards the biscuits, he calmly looked up, picked himself up and then just bopped the dog on the nose with his paw. It was so lightning fast it was a punch to do Muhammad Ali proud.

The dog couldn't believe it. He just jumped back in shock and then carried on backtracking.

I was almost as shocked as the dog, I think. I just laughed out loud.

The owner looked at me and then looked down at his dog. I think he was so drunk he couldn't fully comprehend what had just happened, especially as it had occurred in the blink of an eye. He gave the dog a whack around the head then tugged on its lead to move on. I think he was embarrassed that his fearsome-looking beast had been made to look stupid by a cat.

Bob watched quietly as the dog, his head hung in shame, walked away. Within a few seconds he'd reverted back to his previous position, snoozing at my feet. It was as if it was a minor annoyance for him, like swatting a pesky fly. But for me it was a really revealing moment. It told me so much more about my companion and the life he had led before our fateful meeting at the bottom of the stairs. He wasn't afraid to defend himself. In fact, he knew how to look after himself rather well. He must have learned to do that somewhere, maybe in an environment where there were lots of dogs – and aggressive ones at that.

Once more I found myself fascinated by the same old questions. Where had he grown up? What adventures had he had before he had joined up with me and become the second Musketeer?

Living with Bob was fun. As our little run-in with the Staffie proved, there was never a dull moment. He was a real personality, of that there was no doubt. He had all sorts of quirks to his character, and I was discovering more and more of them every day.

By now there was little doubt in my mind that he must have grown up on the streets. It wasn't just his street-fighter skills, he wasn't really domesticated in any way, he was a bit rough around the edges. Even now, after he'd been living with me for the best part of a month, he still didn't like using the litter trays I'd bought for him. He really hated those things and would scamper away whenever I put one down anywhere near him. Instead he would hold on until he saw me going out of the door, and then do his business downstairs in the gardens of the flats.

I didn't want it to carry on like this. For a start, it wasn't much fun walking down – and up – five flights of stairs to take the cat out whenever he wanted to go to the toilet. So I decided to try and give Bob no option but to use the litter trays. One day during that third week I said to myself that I would go twenty-four hours without letting him out, so that he would have no alternative but to use the litter tray. But he won that contest hands down. He bottled everything up and waited – and waited and waited until I had to go out. Then he squeezed past me as I went out the door and bolted down the stairwell to get outside. Game, set and match to Bob. I realised it was a fight I was unlikely to win.

He also had a wild side to his personality. He was calmer than when he'd first arrived, thanks largely to the fact that he'd been neutered. But he could still be a complete maniac around the flat and would frequently tear around the place, playing with anything that he could lay his paws on. One day I watched him amuse himself for the best part of an hour with a bottle top, flipping it around the floor of the living room with his paws. Another time he found a bumblebee. It was obviously injured – it had one wing damaged – so it was struggling around on the coffee table in the living room. The bee was rolling around and every now and again it would fall off the table on to the carpet. Every time this happened, Bob would very gently pick it up with his teeth and put it back on the table. It was really impressive the way he could delicately pick the bee up by the wing and place it safely on the flat surface. He'd then watch it while it struggled around again. It was a really comical sight. He didn't want to eat it. He just wanted to play with it.

The street instinct was still apparent when it came to food as well. When I took him downstairs to do his toilet now, he made a beeline for the area at the back of the flats where the dustbins were kept. The large 'wheelie bins' were often left open and occasionally there were discarded black, plastic refuse sacks, that had been ripped open by urban foxes or stray dogs. Bob would always go and investigate them to see if there were any leftovers. On one occasion I'd caught him dragging a chicken drumstick that had somehow been overlooked by the other scavengers. Old habits die hard, I figured.

It was true, of course. Despite the fact I was feeding him on a regular basis, he still treated every meal as if it was going to be his last. At home in the flat, the moment I scooped some cat food into his bowl he would stick his face in it and start guzzling as if there was no tomorrow.

'Slow down and enjoy your food, Bob,' I'd tell him, but to no avail. Again, I figured he'd spent so long having to make the most of every eating opportunity that he hadn't adapted to living in a place where he was guaranteed a square meal twice a day. I knew how that felt. I'd spent large chunks of my life living the same way. I couldn't really blame him.

Bob and I had so much in common. Maybe that was why the bond had formed so fast – and was growing so deep.

The most irritating thing – literally – about him, however, was the fact that his fur had begun coating every corner of the flat.

It was perfectly natural, of course. Spring was here and he was getting rid of his winter coat. But he was starting to lose a hell of a lot of fur. To help the moulting process he was rubbing himself on anything and everything he could find in the flat. As a result he was covering it in a thick film of fur. It was a real pain.

It was a good sign that his coat – and the rest of his body – was returning to good health. He was still a bit scrawny, but there was no sign of his ribs as there had been when I'd first met him. His coat was naturally thin because of the environment he'd probably grown up in – the street. The medication had helped with his bald patches and the antibiotics had definitely done the trick in healing his old wound. That had almost disappeared now, in fact, if you didn't know it was there you would never have noticed it.

All in all he looked in a lot better nick than he had done a month or so earlier.

I didn't bathe him. Cats wash themselves, and he was a typical cat in that respect, regularly licking and washing himself. In fact, Bob was one of the most meticulous cats I'd ever seen. I'd watch him go through the ritual, methodically licking his paws. It fascinated me, especially the fact that it was linked so strongly to his ancient ancestors.

Bob's distant relatives originated from hot climates and didn't sweat, so licking themselves was their way of releasing saliva and cooling themselves down. It was also their version of the invisibility cloak.

Smell is bad for cats from a hunting point of view. Cats are stealth hunters and ambush their prey, so they have to be as unobtrusive as possible. Cat saliva contains a natural deodorant which is why they lick themselves a lot. It's been proven by zoologists that cats that lick the smell off themselves survive longer and have more successful offspring. It's also their way of hiding themselves from predators like large snakes, lizards and other larger carnivorous mammals.

Of course, the most important reason that Bob and his ancestors had always licked themselves was to establish and maintain good health. Cats effectively self-medicate. Licking cuts down the number of parasites, such as lice, mites and ticks that can potentially damage the cat. It also stops infection in any open wounds, as cats' saliva also contains an antiseptic agent. As I watched him one day, it occurred to me that this might be why Bob was licking himself so regularly. He knew his body had been in a bad way. This was his way of helping the healing process.

The other funny habit he'd developed was watching television. I first noticed that he watched things on screens one day when I was playing around on a computer in the local library. I often popped in there on the way to Covent Garden or when I wasn't busking. I'd taken Bob along for a walk. He had decided to sit on my lap and was staring at the screen with me. I noticed that as I was moving the mouse around he was trying to swat the cursor with his paw. So back at the flat, as an experiment one day, I'd just put the TV on and left the room to go and do something in the bedroom. I came back to find Bob ensconced on the sofa, watching.

I'd heard about cats watching TV from a friend whose cat loved *Star Trek: The Next Generation*. Whenever it heard that familiar music – Dah-Dah Dah Dah Dah-Dah Dah Dah – he'd come running into the room and jump on the sofa. I saw it happen a few times and it was hilarious. No joke.

Pretty soon, Bob had become a bit of a telly addict as well. If something caught his eye, then he suddenly was glued to the screen. I found it really funny watching him watching Channel Four racing. He really liked the horses. It wasn't something I watched but I got a real kick from watching him sitting there fascinated by it.

Chapter 8
Making It Official

One Thursday morning, a few weeks after we had started our busking partnership in Covent Garden, I got up earlier than usual, made us both some breakfast and headed out of the door with Bob. Rather than heading for central London as usual, we got off the bus near Islington Green.

I'd made a decision. With him accompanying me almost every day on the streets now, I needed to do the responsible thing and get Bob microchipped.

Microchipping cats and dogs used to be a complicated business but now it's simple. All it requires is a simple surgical procedure in which a vet injects a tiny chip into the cat's neck. The chip contains a serial number, which is then logged against their owner's details. That way if a stray cat is found people can scan the chip and find out where it belongs.

Given the life Bob and I led, I figured it was a good idea to get it done. If, God forbid, we ever got separated, we'd be able to find each other. If worse came to worst and something happened to me, at least the records would show that Bob wasn't a completely feral street cat; he had once been in a loving home.

When I'd first begun researching the microchipping process in the library I had quickly come to the conclusion that I couldn't afford it. Most vets were charging an extortionate sixty to eighty pounds to insert a chip. I just didn't have that kind of money and, even if I did, I wouldn't have paid that much on principle.

But then one day I got talking to the cat lady across the street.

'You should go along to the Blue Cross van in Islington Green on a Thursday,' she said. 'They just charge for the cost of the chip. But make sure you get there early. There's always a big queue.'

So I'd set off today nice and early to get to that morning's clinic, which I knew ran from 10a.m. to noon.

As the cat lady had predicted, we discovered a lengthy queue when we got to Islington Green. A long line stretched down towards the big Waterstone's bookshop. Luckily it was a bright, clear morning so it wasn't a problem hanging around.

There was the usual collection you find in a situation like that; people with their cats in posh carriers, dogs trying to sniff each other and being a general nuisance.

But it was quite sociable and it was certainly a smarter, more caring crowd than at the RSPCA where I'd first taken Bob to be checked out.

What was funny was that Bob was the only cat that wasn't in a carrier, so he attracted a lot of attention – as usual. There were a couple of elderly ladies who were absolutely smitten and kept fussing over him.

After about an hour and a half queuing, Bob and I reached the front of the line where we were greeted by a young veterinary nurse with short bobbed hair.

'How much will it cost to get him microchipped?' I asked her.

'It's fifteen pounds,' she replied.

It was pretty obvious from my appearance that I wasn't exactly rolling in money. So she quickly added, 'But you don't have to pay it all up front. You can pay it off over a few weeks. Say two pounds a week, how's that?'

'Cool,' I said, pleasantly surprised. 'I can do that.'

She gave Bob a quick check, presumably to make sure he was in decent-enough health, which he was. He was looking a lot healthier these days, especially now that he had fully shed his winter coat. He was lean and really athletic.

She led us into the surgery where the vet was waiting. He was a young guy, in his late twenties, probably.

'Morning,' he said to me before turning to chat to the nurse. They had a quiet confab in the corner and then started preparing for the chipping procedure. I watched as they got the stuff together. The nurse got out some paperwork while the vet produced the syringe and needle to inject the chip. The size of it slightly took my breath away. It was a big old needle. But then I realised it had to be if it was going to insert the chip, which was the size of a large grain of rice. It had to be large enough to get into the animal's skin.

Bob didn't like the look of it at all, and I couldn't really blame him. So the nurse and I got hold of him and tried to turn him away from the vet so that he couldn't see what he was doing.

Bob wasn't stupid, however, and knew something was up. He got quite agitated and tried to wriggle his way out of my grip. 'You'll be OK, mate,' I said, stroking his tummy and hind legs, while the vet closed in.

When the needle penetrated, Bob let out a loud squeal. It cut through me like a knife and for a moment I thought I was going to start blubbing when he began shaking in pain.

But the shaking soon dissipated and he calmed down. I gave him a little treat from my rucksack then carefully scooped him up and headed back to the reception area.

'Well done, mate,' I said.

The nurse asked me to go through a couple of complicated-looking forms. Fortunately the information she wanted was pretty straightforward.

'OK, we need to fill in your details so that they are on the database,' she said. 'We will need your name, address, age, phone number all that kind of stuff,' she smiled.

It was only as I watched the nurse filling in the form that it struck me. Did this mean that I was officially Bob's owner?

'So, legally speaking, does that mean I am now registered as his owner?' I asked the girl.

She just looked up from the paperwork and smiled. 'Yes, is that OK?' she said.

'Yeah, that's great,' I said slightly taken aback. 'Really great.'

By now Bob was settling down a little. I gave him a stroke on the front of the head. He was obviously still feeling the injection so I didn't go near his neck, he'd have scratched my arm off.

'Did you hear that, Bob?' I said. 'Looks like we're officially a family.'

I'm sure I drew even more looks than usual as we walked through Islington afterwards. I must have been wearing a smile as wide as the Thames.

Having Bob with me had already made a difference to the way I was living my life. He'd made me clean up my act in more ways than one.

As well as giving me more routine and a sense of responsibility, he had also made me take a good look at myself. I didn't like what I saw.

I wasn't proud of the fact I was a recovering addict and I certainly wasn't proud of the fact that I had to visit a clinic once a fortnight and collect medication from a pharmacy every day. So I made it a rule that, unless it was absolutely necessary, I wouldn't take him with me on those trips. I know it may sound crazy, but I didn't want him seeing that side of my past. That was something else he'd helped me with; I really did see it as my past. I saw my future as being clean, living a normal life. I just had to complete the long journey that led to that point.

There were still plenty of reminders of that past and of how far I had still to travel. A few days after I'd had him microchipped, I was rummaging around looking for the new Oyster card that had come through the post when I started emptying the contents of a cupboard in my bedroom.

There, at the back of the cupboard, under a pile of old newspapers and clothes, was a plastic Tupperware box. I recognised it immediately, although I hadn't seen it for a while. It contained all the paraphernalia I had collected when I was doing heroin. There were syringes, needles, everything I had needed to feed my habit. It was like seeing a ghost. It brought back a lot of bad memories. I saw images of myself that I really had hoped to banish from my mind forever.

I decided immediately that I didn't want that box in the house any more. I didn't want it there to remind and maybe even tempt me. And I definitely didn't want it around Bob, even though it was hidden away from view.

Bob was sitting next to the radiator as usual but got up when he saw me putting my coat on and getting ready to go downstairs. He followed me all the way down to the bin area and watched me as I threw the box into a recycling container for hazardous waste.

'There,' I said, turning to Bob who was now fixing me with one of his inquisitive stares. 'Just doing something I should have done a long time ago.'

Chapter 9

The Escape Artist

Life on the streets is never straightforward. You've always got to expect the unexpected. I learned that early on. Social workers always use the word 'chaotic' when they talk about people like me. They call our lives chaotic, because they don't conform to their idea of normality, but it is normality to us. So I wasn't surprised when, as that first summer with Bob drew to a close and autumn began, life around Covent Garden started to get more complicated. I knew it couldn't stay the same. Nothing ever did in my life.

Bob was still proving a real crowd-pleaser, especially with tourists. Wherever they came from, they would stop and talk to him. By now I think I'd heard every language under the sun – from Afrikaans to Welsh – and learned the word for cat in all of them. I knew the

Czech name, *kocka* and Russian, *koshka*; I knew the Turkish, *kedi* and my favourite, the Chinese, *mao*. I was really surprised when I discovered their great leader had been a cat!

But no matter what weird or wonderful tongue was being spoken, the message was almost always the same. Everyone loved Bob.

We also had a group of 'regulars', people who worked in the area and passed by on their way home in the evening. A few of them would always stop to say hello. One or two had even started giving Bob little presents.

It was the other 'locals' who were causing the problems.

To begin with I'd been getting a bit of hassle over at James Street from the Covent Guardians. I'd been continuing to play next to the tube station. On a couple of occasions a Guardian had come over and spoken to me. He'd laid down the law, explaining that the area was for painted statues. The fact that there didn't seem to be any around at that moment didn't bother him. 'You know the rules,' he kept telling me. I did. But I also knew rules were there to be bent a little when they could be. Again, that was life on the streets. If we were the kind of people who stuck to the rules, we wouldn't have been there.

So each time the Guardian moved me on, I'd head off elsewhere for a few hours then quietly slip back into James Street. It was a risk worth taking as far as I was concerned. I'd never heard of them calling in the police to deal with someone performing in the wrong place.

The people who were bothering me much more were the staff at the tube station who also now seemed to object to me busking outside their workplace. There were a couple of ticket inspectors in particular who had begun giving me a hard time. It had begun as dirty looks and the odd casual comment when I set myself up against the wall of the tube station. But then one really unpleasant inspector, a big, sweaty guy in a blue uniform, had come over to me one day and been quite threatening.

By now I had come to realise that Bob was a great reader of people. He could spot someone who wasn't quite right from a distance. He had spotted this guy the minute he started walking in our direction and had started squeezing himself closer to me as he approached.

'All right, mate?' I said.

'Not really. No. You had better piss off – or else,' he said.

'Or else what?' I said, standing my ground.

'You'll see,' he said obviously trying to intimidate me. 'I'm warning you.'

I knew he had no power outside the tube station and was just trying to spook me. But afterwards I'd made the decision that it might be smart to stay away for a while.

So at first I'd moved to the top of Neal Street, near the junction with Long Acre, still no more than a healthy stone's throw from the tube station but far enough to be out of sight of the staff. The volume of people passing there wasn't as great – or always as well-meaning – as the people around Covent Garden. Most times I worked there I'd get some idiot kicking my bag or trying to scare Bob. I could tell he wasn't comfortable there: he'd curl up in a defensive ball and narrow his eyes to a thin slit whenever I set up there. It was his way of saying: 'I don't like it here.'

So after a few days, rather than heading towards Covent Garden as usual, Bob and I climbed off the bus and walked through Soho in the direction of Piccadilly Circus instead.

Of course, we hadn't left central London – and the borough of Westminster – so there were still rules and regulations. Piccadilly worked in a similar way to Covent Garden; there were certain areas that were designated for buskers. This time I decided to stick to the rules. I knew that the area to the east of Piccadilly Circus on the road leading to Leicester Square was a good spot, specifically for buskers. So I headed there.

Arriving there with Bob, I picked a spot only a few yards away from one of the main entrances to the Piccadilly Circus tube station, outside the Ripley's Believe It Or Not exhibition.

It was a really busy late afternoon and evening with hundreds of tourists on the street, heading to the West

End's cinemas and theatres. We were soon doing all right, despite the fact that people move so fast around that area, running down the tube entrance. As usual, they slowed down and sometimes stopped when they saw Bob.

I could tell Bob was a little nervous because he curled himself up even tighter than usual around the bridge of my guitar. It was probably the number of people and the fact that he was in unfamiliar surroundings. He was definitely more comfortable when he was in a place that he recognised.

As usual, people from all over the world were milling around, taking in the sights of central London. There were a lot of Japanese tourists in particular, a lot of whom were fascinated by Bob. I'd soon learned another new word for cat: *neko*. Everything was fine until around six in the evening, when the crowds really thickened with the beginning of the rush hour. It was at that point that a promotions guy from Ripley's came out on to the street. He was wearing a big, inflatable outfit that made him look three times his normal size and was making big arm gestures encouraging people to visit Ripley's. I had no idea how it related to the exhibits inside the building. Maybe they had something on the world's fattest man? Or the world's most ridiculous job?

But I could tell immediately that Bob didn't like the look of him. I sensed him drawing in even closer to me when he first appeared. He was really unsure of the bloke and was staring at him with a look of slight trepidation. I knew exactly where he was coming from; he did look a bit freaky.

To my relief, after a while Bob settled down and seemed to forget about the man. For a while we just ignored him as he carried on trying to persuade people to step into Ripley's. He was having some success, so he stayed away from us. I was singing a Johnny Cash song, 'Ring of Fire', when, for no particular reason, the promotions guy suddenly approached us, pointing at Bob as if he wanted to come and stroke him. I didn't spot him until he was almost upon us, leaning down in his weird inflatable suit. And by then it was too late.

Bob's reaction was instantaneous. He just sprung up and bolted, running into the crowds with his new lead trailing behind him. Before I could even react, he'd disappeared, heading towards the entrance to the tube station.

Oh shit, I said to myself, my heart pumping. *He's gone. I've lost him.*

My instincts took over at once. I jumped up straight away and ran after him. I just left the guitar. I was much more worried about Bob than an instrument. I could find one of those anywhere.

I immediately found myself in a sea of people. There were weary-looking office workers heading down the tube at the end of a day's work, early evening revellers arriving for a night 'up West' and, as always, loads and loads of tourists, some with rucksacks, others clutching streetmaps, all looking a little overwhelmed at finding themselves at the beating heart of London. I had to bob and weave my way through them to even get to the entrance to the tube station. Inevitably, I bumped into a couple of people, almost knocking over one lady.

It was impossible to see anything through the constant wall of people that was moving towards me, but as I finally got to the bottom of the steps inside the concourse, things began to thin out a little bit. It was still heaving with people, but at least I could now stop and take a look around. I got down on my haunches and looked around at floor level. One or two people gave me strange looks but that didn't concern me.

'Bob, Bob, where are you, mate?' I shouted at one point, immediately realising how futile that was with all the noise in there.

I had to make a guess and head in one direction. Should I go towards the barriers that led to the escalators and down to the trains or move towards the various other exits? Which way would Bob go? My hunch was that he wouldn't go down the tube. We'd never been down there together and I had a feeling the moving escalators would frighten him.

So I moved towards the exits for the other side of Piccadilly Circus.

After a moment or two, I got a glimpse of something, just the faintest flash of ginger on one of the staircases. I then saw a lead trailing after it.

'Bob, Bob,' I shouted again, squeezing myself through the crowds once more as I headed in that direction.

I was now within thirty feet of him but I might as well have been a mile away, the crowds were so thick. There were streams of people coming down the staircase.

'Stop him, step on his lead,' I shouted out, catching another glimpse of ginger in the evening light above me.

But no one was taking any notice. No one was paying any attention.

Within moments the lead had disappeared and there was no sign of Bob. He must have reached the exit, which led to the bottom of Regent Street and run off from there.

By now a million thoughts were flashing through my head, none of them good ones. What if he had run out into the road at Piccadilly Circus? What if someone had seen him and picked him up? As I barged my way up the stairs and reached street level again I was in a real state.

Truth be told, I could have burst into tears, I was so convinced that I'd never see him again.

I knew it wasn't my fault, but I felt awful. Why the hell hadn't I fixed his lead to my rucksack or on to my belt so that he couldn't run any further than the length of his lead? Why hadn't I spotted his panic when the Ripley's guy had first appeared and moved somewhere else? I felt sick.

Again I had to make a choice. Which way would he have headed on hitting the streets? He could have turned left towards Piccadilly or even headed into the giant Tower Records store there. Again I trusted my instincts and guessed that he would have basically headed straight on – down the wider pavements of Regent Street.

Still in a complete panic, I began making my way down the street in the hope that someone had seen him.

I knew I must have been looking absolutely crazed because people were looking at me askance. Some were even moving out of my way, as if I was some deranged gunman on the rampage.

Fortunately, not everyone reacted that way.

After about thirty yards, I asked a young girl who was walking down the road with a bag from the Apple store at the Oxford Street end of Regent Street. She'd obviously walked all the way down the street, so I asked her if she'd seen a cat.

'Oh yeah,' she said. 'I saw a cat weaving along the street. Ginger. Had a lead hanging behind it. One bloke tried to stamp on the lead and catch it but the cat was too quick for him.'

My immediate reaction was joy. I could have kissed her. I just knew it was Bob. But that quickly gave way to paranoia. Who was that bloke who'd tried to catch him? What was he planning to do with him? Would that have frightened Bob even more? Was he now cowering somewhere where I'd never find him?

With all these new thoughts bouncing around in my head, I carried on down Regent Street, sticking my head into every shop I passed. Most of the shop assistants looked horrified to see this long-haired figure standing in their doorways and took a step back. Others just flashed me blank expressions and slow shakes of the head. I could see what they were thinking. They thought I was some piece of dirt that had just blown in off the street.

After about half a dozen shops, my mood began to swing again, this time back towards resignation. I had no idea how long it was since Bob had run off. Time had seemed to slow down. It was as if it was all happening in slow motion. I was close to giving up.

A couple of hundred yards down Regent Street, there was a side street ahead leading back down to Piccadilly. From there he could have headed in any one of a dozen directions: into Mayfair or even across the road down to St James's and Haymarket. If he'd gone that far then I knew he was lost.

I was about to give up and head down the side street, when I stuck my head into a ladies' clothes shop. There were a couple of shop assistants there looking a bit perplexed and looking towards the back of the shop.

They turned to see me and the moment I said the word 'cat' their faces lit up.

'A ginger tom?' one of them said.

'Yes, he's got a collar and lead.'

'He's round the back here,' one of them said, gesturing for me to come in and shut the door.

'That's why we shut the door,' the other one said. 'We didn't want him to get run over.'

'We figured someone was looking for him because of the lead.'

They led me towards a row of open wardrobes filled with fancy-looking clothes. I noticed the prices on some of them. Each one cost more money than I'd make in a month. But then, in the corner of one of the wardrobes, curled up in a ball, I saw Bob.

As time had slowed down during the past few minutes, a part of me had wondered whether he was trying to get away from me. Maybe he'd had enough of me? Maybe he didn't want the life I offered him any more? So when I approached him I was prepared for him to bolt again and run off. But he didn't.

I'd barely whispered softly, 'Hey Bob, it's me', before he jumped straight into my arms.

All my fears about him wanting rid of me evaporated as he purred deeply and rubbed himself against me.

'You gave me such a scare there, mate,' I said, stroking him. 'I thought I'd lost you.'

I looked up and saw that the two shopkeepers were standing nearby watching. One of them was dabbing her eyes, close to tears.

'I'm so glad you found him,' she said. 'He looked like such a lovely cat. We were wondering what we'd do with him if no one showed up before closing time.'

She came closer and stroked Bob for a moment as well. We then chatted for a couple of minutes as she and her colleague got ready to close the till and started preparing to shut up shop for the evening.

'Bye, Bob,' the pair said as we headed off back into the throng around Piccadilly Circus with Bob perched on my shoulder again.

When I got back to Ripley's I discovered – to my mild amazement – that my guitar was still there. Maybe the security guy at the door had kept an eye on it. Or perhaps one of the community support officers in the area had made sure it was safe. At the time there was a mobile police unit next to us. All the police and community support people loved Bob. He had become very popular with the police. I had no idea who the Good Samaritan was but to be honest I didn't care. I was just glad that Bob and I were reunited.

I wasted no time in gathering up my stuff and calling it a night. We'd not made enough money but that wasn't my biggest concern. I stopped at a general store and, with most of the cash I had on me, bought myself a little belt clip that I attached, first to me then to his lead. It would make sure that we remained connected all the time. On the bus rather than sitting on the seat next to me as usual, he sat on my lap. He could be an inscrutable chap but at other times I knew exactly what Bob was thinking. Tonight was one of those occasions. We were together, and neither of us wanted that to change.

Chapter 10

Santa Paws

During those first few days and weeks after the drama at Piccadilly, Bob and I clung to each other like two survivors hanging on to a life raft at sea. We'd both been badly shaken by the incident.

It made me think long and hard about our friendship. For a while I kept wondering whether his escape had been a signal that he wanted to put some distance between us. Deep down I knew that if he wanted to go back on to the streets – or wherever it was he came from – ultimately there was nothing I could, or should, do to stop him.

I'd even thought through what I should do if he showed any sign of wanting to run away again. If he did, and I managed to catch him before he disappeared altogether, I decided I'd give him away to the RSPCA or Battersea Dogs and Cats Home where they had a really nice cattery. I didn't want to be his gaoler. He had been too good a friend to me for me to curtail his freedom. He didn't deserve that.

Thankfully though, it hadn't come to that.

Once or twice since the incident, he had elected not to go out with me. When I had got the harness out in the morning he had run behind the sofa or hid under the table to tell me he wasn't up for it. I'd left him to it. But in the main he had been happy to come out every day. And when he had, he had been a slightly different character, more attentive to me but, in a strange way, also more relaxed.

Despite what had happened at Piccadilly Circus, he wasn't as frightened in crowds as he had been occasionally in the past. Maybe this was because I now had him clipped to my belt and kept a tighter hold on his lead when he was out. The truth was that I think he felt closer to me now. Our bond had been put to the test – and survived. I got the impression that now he wanted to stay by my side more strongly than ever.

Of course, it hadn't all been a bed of roses; working on the streets of London, there are bound to be moments when you feel threatened. A couple of weeks after we saw that strange inflated character at Piccadilly we were in Covent Garden when we saw a troupe of street performers on giant stilts. They were old-fashioned French performance artists and had really, garish, scary faces.

The instant he saw them tottering around above our heads, I could tell Bob felt threatened. He squeezed in close to me. I was trying to concentrate on singing, but every now and again he stopped me from playing the guitar as he flopped his tail over the fret board.

'Cut it out, Bob,' I said, apologising to the one or two tourists who'd stopped to listen.

Of course, they thought it was funny and part of the act. If only I could manage to get Bob to do what I wanted so easily.

As soon as the figures on stilts had disappeared it was a completely different story, of course. With them gone he was relaxed again and he moved away from me slightly. It was as if he knew that I was his safety net. I was glad to provide it.

As Christmas 2007 approached and our first calendar year together drew to a close, our life had settled into a real routine. Each morning I'd get up to find him waiting patiently by his bowl in the kitchen. He'd guzzle down his breakfast then give himself a good wash, licking his paws and face clean. Bob was still very reluctant to do his toilet inside the flat and most mornings I'd take him downstairs to relieve himself. On other occasions I'd leave him out and let him find his own way out to the grass. He'd find his way down and back up again without any trouble. I'd then get ready, pack up my rucksack, grab my guitar and head into town.

With Christmas only days away, the crowds in Covent Garden were getting bigger and bigger. So too were the number of treats and gifts Bob was getting. From the very early days, people had got into the habit of giving Bob little presents.

The first one came from a middle-aged lady who worked in an office not far from James Street and would regularly stop and talk to us. She'd had a ginger tom herself many years earlier and had told me that Bob reminded her of him.

She had arrived one evening with a big grin on her face and a smart bag from a fancy pet shop. 'I hope you don't mind but I bought Bob a little present,' she said.

'Of course not,' I said.

'It's not much,' she said, fishing out a little stuffed figure of a mouse.

'It's got a little catnip in it,' she smiled. 'Not a lot, don't worry.'

There was a part of me that felt awkward about it. Catnip was, after all, addictive to cats. I'd read all sorts of stuff about how it can drive them crazy if they get hooked on it. It was bad enough with me trying desperately to straighten myself out. I didn't want Bob developing a habit as well.

But she was too nice a lady to disappoint her. She stayed for a little while, relishing the sight of seeing Bob playing with the little mouse.

As the weather took a turn for the worse, people began to give Bob more practical presents.

One day another lady, a striking-looking Russian, sidled up to us smiling.

'Hope you don't mind, but with the weather turning cold, I thought I'd knit Bob something to keep him warm,' she said, producing a beautiful, light-blue knitted scarf from her shoulder bag.

'Wow,' I said, genuinely taken aback. 'That's great.'

I immediately wrapped it around Bob's neck. It fitted perfectly and looked fantastic. The lady was over the moon. She reappeared a week or two later with a matching blue waistcoat. I was no fashion expert, as anyone who met me would have been able to tell in an instant, but even I could tell that Bob looked amazing in it. People were soon queuing to take photographs of him in it. I should have charged; I would have made a fortune.

Since then at least half a dozen more people – well, women – had dropped off various items of knitted clothing for Bob.

One lady had even embroidered the name Bob into the little scarf that she had created for him. It struck me one day that Bob was becoming a fashion model. He was regularly modelling some new creation a kindly soul had made for him. It gave a new meaning to the word 'catwalk'.

It just underlined what I'd realised already: that I wasn't the only one who was forming a deep affection

for Bob. He seemed to make friends with almost everyone he met. It was a gift I wished I had myself. I'd never
found it that easy to bond with people.

No one had fallen more deeply in love with Bob than
my ex-girlfriend Belle. We were still close friends, probably better friends than when we were together and she
would pop round to the flat on a regular basis. It was
partly to see me and hang out but I was pretty sure that
she was also coming over to see Bob.

The two of them would play together for hours on the
sofa. Bob thought the world of her, I could tell.

It was about three weeks before Christmas that she
came round with a plastic shopping bag in her hand
and a big grin on her face.

'What have you got in there?' I said, sensing she was
up to something.

'It's not for you, it's for Bob,' she said, teasing me.

Bob was sitting in his usual spot under the radiator,
but perked up the minute he heard his name mentioned.

'Bob, come here, I've got a surprise for you,' Belle
said, flopping on to the sofa with the bag. He was soon
padding over, curious to find out what was inside.

Belle pulled out a couple of small animal T-shirts.
One just had a picture of a cute-looking kitten on it.
But the other one was red with green trim on it. It had
the words 'Santa Paws' in large white letters with a big
paw print underneath it.

'Oh, that's really cool Bob, isn't it?' I said. 'That's the
perfect thing to wear when we're in Covent Garden

close to Christmas. That will really put a smile on people's faces.'

It certainly did that.

I don't know if it was the Christmas spirit or simply seeing him in his outfit, but the effect was amazing.

'Ah, look it's Santa Paws,' I'd hear people say almost every few minutes.

A lot of people would stop and drop a bit of silver into my guitar case, others, however, wanted to give Bob something.

On one occasion this very well-heeled lady stopped and started cooing over Bob.

'He's fabulous,' she said. 'What would he like for Christmas?'

'I don't know, madam,' I replied.

'Well, put it this way, what does he need?' she said.

'He could do with a spare harness, I guess. Or something to keep him warm when the weather gets really cold. Or just get him some toys. Every boy likes toys at Christmas.'

'Jolly good,' she said, getting up and leaving.

I didn't think much more of it, but then, about an hour later, the lady reappeared. She had a big grin on her face and was carrying a smart-looking hand-knitted stocking, with cat designs on the front. I looked inside and could see it was stuffed with goodies: food, toys and stuff.

'You must promise me that you won't open it till Christmas,' she said. 'You must keep it under your tree until Christmas morning.'

I didn't have the heart to tell her that I didn't have enough money for a Christmas tree or any decorations in the flat. The best I'd been able to rustle up was a USB Christmas tree that plugged into the battered old Xbox I'd recently found at a charity shop.

In the days after that, however, I made a decision. She was right. I should have a decent Christmas for once. I had something to celebrate. I had Bob.

I suppose I'd become desensitised to Christmas because I hadn't had a decent one in years. I was one of those people who actively dreaded it.

During the past decade or so I'd spent most of them at places like Shelter, where they did a big Christmas lunch for homeless people. It was all very well meaning and I'd had a laugh or two there. But it just reminded me of what I didn't have: a normal life and a normal family. It just reminded me that I'd cocked up my life.

Once or twice I'd spent it on my own, trying to forget the fact that my family was on the other side of the world. Well, most of it. On a couple of occasions, I'd spent the day with my father. After going missing for a year when I first ended up on the streets, I'd stayed in contact, calling him very occasionally and he'd invited me down to his house in south London. But it hadn't been the greatest of experiences. He didn't really think much of me. I couldn't really blame him. I wasn't exactly a son to be proud about.

I'd been grateful for a nice lunch and a few drinks and, most of all, a bit of company. But it hadn't really been a great success and we hadn't done it again.

This year was different though. I invited Belle round on Christmas Eve for a drink. Then for Christmas Day I splashed out on a ready-made turkey breast with all the trimmings. I wasn't really into cooking and didn't have the equipment even if I had been. I got Bob some really nice treats including his favourite chicken meal.

When Christmas Day arrived we got up reasonably early and went out for a short walk so that Bob could do his business. There were other families from the block heading off to see relatives and friends. We all exchanged 'Happy Christmases' and smiles. Even that was more than I'd experienced in a long while.

Back up at the flat, I gave Bob his stocking. He had spotted it days earlier and had obviously guessed it was meant for him. I emptied the contents one by one. There were treats, toys, balls, and little soft things containing catnip. He absolutely loved it and was soon playing with his new toys like an excitable child on Christmas morning. It was pretty adorable.

I cooked our lunch early in the afternoon, then put a hat on each of us, had a can of beer and watched television for the rest of the afternoon and evening. It was the best Christmas I'd had in years.

Chapter 11
Mistaken Identity

By the spring and summer of 2008, being a busker on the streets of London was becoming more and more difficult, almost impossible at times.

There were a couple of reasons. I know people assume the economy doesn't affect people on the streets, but that's not the case at all. The recession – which at that point was only just gearing up – had hit me and people in my position quite hard. The kind-hearted folk who used to think nothing of dropping me and Bob a pound or two, were now holding on to their money. One or two regulars even told me as much. They said they were worried about losing their jobs. I couldn't really argue with them. So, as a result, I was having to work much longer hours often to make less money to feed me and Bob and keep us warm.

I could live with that, the bigger problem was the fact that the authorities had started coming down hard on street performers who didn't work in the designated spots. I wasn't sure why they'd decided to do this, especially now, but I did know that it had begun to make my life a real headache.

Most of the Covent Guardians had always been reasonable. I'd had trouble from the most aggressive of them, but in general they'd never been really heavy with me. But even they had started confiscating stuff if they felt you weren't taking what they said seriously. I don't think they had any new powers, they had just been told to get a bit more serious about what they were doing.

There were also a few, new faces among them. One of the more aggressive of the newcomers had threatened to take away my guitar a couple of times. I'd managed to dissuade him by promising to play in a designated area – or move out of the neighbourhood. I'd then sneaked around the corner for half an hour before returning to James Street.

It had become a constant game of hide and seek, but I was running out of places to hide. The new Guardians seemed to know where I was going to be. Most days now I'd be moved along or spoken to at some point. It was wearing me down. Deep down I knew that my time as a busker was drawing to an end. The straw that broke the camel's back came one afternoon in May that year.

Another of the reasons busking had become particularly hard for me was the staff at Covent Garden tube station. The bad vibe I'd been getting from there had become more and more unpleasant. I don't know why but they didn't want me busking there. There were now a number of ticket inspectors who would regularly wander across the road from the entrance to the tube station and give me a real mouthful of abuse.

I could handle that. I was well used to it. But they'd definitely been talking about me together and had come up with some kind of plan to campaign against me. Every now and again they would call up the British Transport Police, who would turn up and give me hassle. As if I needed any more of that. I'd learned to deal with them in the same way as the other authorities: I'd slope off, promising never to darken their doorstep again, then slink back into position when the coast was clear. I saw no harm in what I was doing. No one was getting hurt were they?

All that changed one afternoon.

I'd headed into Covent Garden as usual with Bob. I had a friend staying with me at the time, a guy called Dylan, who I'd met way back when I was with the band. He'd been kicked out of his previous accommodation when he'd refused to pay an extortionate new rent by some unscrupulous landlord. He needed a floor to sleep on for a couple of weeks. I'd been there myself, so I couldn't refuse him. He had begun sleeping on my sofa.

Bob hadn't taken too kindly to Dylan's arrival at first. I think he felt he was going to lose out in my affections. But as soon as he realised that Dylan was, in fact, another animal lover, and discovered that he was going to get more attention, then he was fine. Bob thrived on attention.

This particular afternoon Dylan decided he was going to come into London with us and hang around Covent Garden. It was a lovely, sunny day and he felt like enjoying it. He was playing with Bob as I set myself up on the corner of James Street. Looking back on it, I can't believe how fortunate it was that he was there.

I'd barely put the guitar strap over my shoulder when a British Transport Police van arrived at speed and pulled up alongside the pavement. Three officers jumped out and immediately started walking towards me.

'What's all this about?' Dylan said.

'Don't know. More of the usual stuff,' I said, fully expecting to have to go through the usual tap dance of promising to move away.

I was wrong.

'Right you, you're coming with us,' one of the officers said, pointing at me.

'What for?' I said.

'We're arresting you on suspicion of using threatening behaviour.'

'What? Threatening who? I don't know what the hell —'

Before I could finish my sentence they had grabbed me. While one of them read me my rights, another one stuck me in handcuffs.

'We'll explain at the station. Let's get your shit together and get in the van before we make things even worse for you,' he said.

'What about my cat?' I said gesturing at Bob.

'We've got some dog kennels at the station, we'll stick him in there,' another of the officers said. 'Unless you've got someone to take him.'

My head was spinning. I had no idea what was happening. But then, out of the corner of my eye, I saw Dylan. He was looking sheepish and didn't want to get involved.

'Dylan, will you look after Bob?' I said. 'Take him back to the flat. The keys are in my rucksack.'

He nodded and started moving towards Bob. I watched him scoop him up and reassure him. I could see the look on Bob's face; he was terrified by what was happening to me. Through the mesh windows at the back of the van, I watched as the figures of Dylan and Bob standing on the pavement disappeared from view.

We drove to the British Transport Police station. I still had no idea what was going on.

Within a few minutes I was standing in front of a desk clerk being asked to empty all my pockets and to answer all sorts of questions. I was then led into a cell where I was told to wait until I was seen by an officer. As I sat there in the barren cell, the walls gouged with graffiti and the floors smelling of stale urine, it brought awful memories flooding back.

I'd had run-ins with the police before, mostly for petty theft.

When you are homeless or have a drug habit you try to find easy options to make money. And, to be honest, few things are easier than shoplifting. My main thing was stealing meat. I'd lift legs of lamb and expensive steaks. Jamie Oliver steaks. Lamb shanks. Gammon joints. Never chicken, chicken is too low value. What I stole was the stuff with the highest price value. What you get is half the price on the label. If you go to a pub and sell the stuff that's what you could expect to get. Pubs are very solid ground for selling stolen goods. Everybody knows that.

The first time I did it to pay for my habit was in 2001 or 2002, something like that. Before that I'd been begging to feed my habit. Before *that* I'd been on a methadone course. I'd got clean but then I'd started using again because things were bad. I'd been moved into some dodgy accommodation where everyone was using and had spiralled back into bad habits.

I can still remember the first time I got busted. It was at the Marks and Spencer's at the Angel, Islington. I used to dress up smartly and tie my hair back, dress like a postman at the end of his daily rounds popping in for a snack or a pint of milk on the way home. It was all about appearance. You had to be clever about it. If I'd walked in with a rucksack or a shopping bag I'd never have stood a chance. I carried a postman's Royal Mail bag around with me. It's different today but back then nobody looked twice at you if you had one of those bags slung over your shoulders.

Anyhow, I got stopped one day. I had about one hundred and twenty pounds' worth of meat on me.

I was taken into police custody. At that time they gave me an on-the-spot fine of eight pounds for theft. I was lucky to get that because it was my first time.

Of course, it didn't stop me. I had a habit. I had to do what I had to do. I was on heroin and an occasional bit of crack. You take the risk. You have to.

When you get nicked it sucks. But you have got to bite the bullet. Obviously, you sit there feeling sorry for yourself, but you aren't going to fight the powers that be.

You try to get out of it, you make up lies but they don't believe you. They never really do. It's a vicious circle when you are down.

That was why busking had been so good for me. It was legal. It kept me straight. But now here I was back in the nick. It felt like a real kick in the stomach.

I'd been in the cell for about half an hour when the door opened suddenly and a white-shirted officer ushered me out.

'Come on,' he said.

'Where are you taking me now?' I asked.

'You'll see,' he said.

I was taken into a bare room with a few plastic chairs and a single table.

There were a couple of officers sitting opposite me. They looked disinterested, to be honest. But then one of them started questioning me.

'Where were you yesterday evening at around 6.30p.m.?' one of them asked.

'Um, I was busking in Covent Garden,' I said.

'Where?'

'On the corner of James Street, opposite the entrance to the tube,' I said, which was true.

'Did you go into the tube station at any time that evening?' the copper asked.

'No, I never go in there,' I said. 'I travel by bus.'

'Well, how come we've got at least two witnesses saying that you were in the station and that you verbally abused and spat at a female ticket attendant?'

'I've got absolutely no idea,' I said, bemused.

'They saw you come up the escalator from the tube and try to go through the automatic barrier without a ticket.'

'Well, as I say, that can't have been me,' I said.

'When you were challenged you verbally abused a female member of staff.'

I just sat there shaking my head. This was surreal.

'You were then led to the ticket booth and asked to buy a ticket,' he went on. 'When you did so, against your will, you then spat at the window of the ticket booth.'

That was it; I lost my cool.

'Look, this is bullshit,' I said. 'I told you I wasn't in the tube station last night. I'm never in there. And I never travel by tube. Me and my cat travel everywhere by bus.'

They just looked at me as if I was telling the biggest lies in the world.

They asked me if I wanted to make a statement, so I did, explaining that I'd been busking all night. I knew the CCTV footage would back this up. But at the back of my mind I was having all sorts of paranoid thoughts.

What if this was all a fit up? What if they had doctored the CCTV footage in the tube station? What if it went to court and it was my word against three or four London Underground officers?

Worst of all, I found myself anxiously wondering what would happen to Bob. Who would look after him? Would he stay with them or head back on to the street? And what would happen to him there? Thinking about it did my head in.

They kept me in for about another two or three hours. After a while I lost all track of time. There was no natural light in the room so I had no idea whether it was day or night outside. At one point a lady police officer came in, with a surly-looking male officer behind her.

'I need to do a DNA test,' she said as he took a position in the corner where he stood with his arms folded, glaring at me.

'OK,' I said, ignoring him. I figured I had nothing to lose. 'What do I have to do?' I asked the female officer.

'Just sit there and I'll take a swab of saliva from your mouth,' she said.

She produced a little kit, with loads of swabs and test tubes.

Suddenly I felt like I was at the dentist.

'Open wide,' she said.

She then stuck a long, cotton bud into my mouth, gave it a bit of a scrape around the inside of my cheek and that was that.

'All done,' she said, putting the bud in a test tube and packing her stuff away.

Eventually, I was let out of the cell and taken back to the desk at the front of the station where I signed for my stuff. I had to sign a form saying that I was released on bail and told that I had to return a couple of days later.

'When will I know if I am being formally charged?' I asked the duty officer, suspecting that he couldn't really tell me that. To my surprise he said that I'd probably know when I came back in a couple of days' time.

'Really?' I said.

'More than likely,' he said.

That was good and bad, I decided immediately. Good in the sense that I'd not have to wait months to find out if I was going to be charged, bad in the sense that if they were going to charge me I could find myself spending time inside very soon.

I really didn't relish that prospect.

After finally being let free, I emerged into the streets behind Warren Street in pitch darkness. There were already little groups of homeless people hunkering down for the night, hiding themselves away in alleyways.

It was approaching eleven o'clock. By the time I got back to Seven Sisters tube station it was close to midnight and the streets were full of drunks and people being turfed out of the pubs.

I breathed a huge sigh of relief when I got inside the flat.

Dylan was watching television with Bob curled up in his usual spot under the radiator. The minute I walked through the door, he jumped up and padded over to me, tilting his head to one side and looking up at me.

'Hello, mate, you all right?' I said, dropping to my knees and stroking him.

He immediately clambered up on to my knee and started rubbing against my face.

Dylan had headed off into the kitchen but soon reappeared with a cold tin of lager from the fridge.

'That's a life saver, thanks,' I said, ripping the ring off the tin and taking a slug of cold beer.

I sat up for a couple of hours with Dylan, trying to make sense of what had happened to me. I knew the ticket collectors at Covent Garden tube didn't like me – but I didn't think they'd go so far as to try and frame me for a crime I didn't commit.

'There's no way they can fix the DNA to match yours, mate,' Dylan reassured me.

I wish I could have been so certain.

I slept fitfully that night. I'd been really shaken by the experience. No matter how much I tried to tell myself it would work out fine, I couldn't erase the thought that my life could be about to take a terrible turn. I felt powerless, angry – and really scared.

I decided to give Covent Garden a wide berth the following day. Bob and I played around Neal Street and one or two other places towards Tottenham Court Road. But my heart wasn't in it. I was too worried about what was going to happen when I turned up at the police station the following day. Again that night I struggled to get much sleep.

I was due to report at the Transport Police station at midday but set off early to make sure I was on time. I didn't want to give them any excuses. I left Bob back at home – just in case I was going to be kept there for hours again. He had picked up on my anxiety as I'd paced around the flat eating my toast at breakfast.

'Don't worry, mate, I'll be back before you know it,' I reassured him as I left. If only I'd been as confident of that as I sounded.

It took me a while to find the station, which was hidden away on a backstreet off Tottenham Court Road. I'd arrived there in the back of a van and left after dark, so it wasn't surprising that I had trouble finding it.

When I did locate it, I had to sit and hang around for twenty minutes, during which time I found it hard to concentrate on anything. I was eventually called into a room where a couple of officers were waiting for me, one man and a younger woman.

They had files in front of them, which looked ominous. I wondered what they'd dug up about my past. God only knows what skeletons were hiding in that particular cupboard.

The male officer was the first to speak. He told me that I wasn't going to be charged with the offence of using threatening behaviour. I guessed why that was.

'The DNA didn't match the saliva on the ticket collector's booth did it?' I said, feeling suddenly empowered by what he'd told me.

He just looked at me with a tight-lipped smile. He couldn't say anything; I knew that. But he didn't need to. It seemed obvious to me that someone at the tube station had tried to fit me up, but had failed.

If that was the good news, the bad news wasn't long in following.

The lady told me that I was being charged with illegally busking, or 'touting for reward', to give it its formal title.

They shoved a piece of paper towards me and told me I was to report to court in a week's time.

I left the station relieved. 'Touting for reward' was a relatively minor offence, certainly compared to threatening behaviour. If I was lucky I'd get away with a small fine and a rap across the knuckles, nothing more.

Threatening behaviour would have been a completely different matter, of course. That would have left me open to a heavy punishment, maybe even imprisonment. I'd got off lightly.

Part of me wanted to fight back at the injustice of what had happened to me. The description of the person who spat on the window bore no relation to my appearance. I held on to the paperwork and thought I could do them for wrongful arrest.

But, to be honest, the main thought in my mind as I headed home that afternoon was relief and a sense that I'd turned some sort of corner. I wasn't sure yet what it was.

I still had to get past the court hearing. I went to the local Citizens Advice centre and got a bit of legal advice. I should probably have done that earlier, but I'd been too messed up to think of it.

It turned out that because I was on a drug rehab programme and living in sheltered accommodation, I was eligible for legal aid. But the truth was I didn't think I needed a solicitor representing me in court, so I simply got some advice about what to say.

It was pretty straightforward. I needed to front up and admit that I was guilty of busking: plain and simple. I simply had to go along, plead accordingly and hope the magistrate wasn't some kind of sadist with a hatred for street musicians.

When the day came I put on a clean shirt (over the top of a T-shirt bearing the slogan 'Extremely Unhappy') and had a shave before heading to court. The waiting area was full of all sorts of people, from some really scary-looking guys with shaven heads and Eastern European accents to a couple of middle-aged guys in grey suits who were up on driving offences.

'James Bowen. The court calls Mr James Bowen,' a plummy-sounding voice eventually announced. I took a deep breath and headed in.

The magistrates looked at me like I was a piece of dirt that had been blown in off the street. But under the law there wasn't too much they could do to me, especially as it was my first offence for busking.

I got a three-month conditional discharge. I wasn't fined.

But they made it clear that if I did reoffend I could face a fine – and even worse.

Belle and Bob were waiting for me outside the court-house after the hearing was over. Bob immediately jumped off her lap and walked over to me. He didn't want to be too melodramatic about it all, but it was clear he was pleased to see me.

'How did it go?' Belle asked.

'Three-month conditional discharge, but if I get caught again I'm for the high jump,' I said.

'So what are you going to do?' she said.

I looked at her, then looked down at Bob. The answer must have been written all over my face.

I had reached the end of the road. I'd been busking on and off now for almost a decade. Times had changed – and my life had changed, certainly since Bob had come into it. So it was becoming more and more clear to me that I couldn't carry on busking, it didn't make any sense on any level. There were times when it didn't earn me enough money to make ends meet. There were times when it put me – and more importantly, Bob – in dangerous situations. And now there was a real danger that if I was caught busking in the wrong place again, I could get banged up in prison. It just wasn't worth it.

'I don't know what I'm going to do, Belle,' I said. 'But the one thing I know I'm not going to do is carry on busking.'

Chapter 12

Number 683

My head was spinning for the next few days. I felt a real mixture of emotions.

Part of me was still angry at the unfairness of what had happened. I felt like I'd lost my livelihood simply because a few people had taken against me. At the same time, however, another part of me had begun to see it might have been a blessing in disguise.

Deep down I knew I couldn't carry on busking all my life. I wasn't going to turn my life around singing Johnny Cash and Oasis songs on street corners. I wasn't going to build up the strength to get myself totally clean by relying on my guitar. It began to dawn on me that I was at a big crossroads, that I had an opportunity to put the past behind me. I'd been there before, but for the first time in years, I felt like I was ready to take it.

That was all very well in theory, of course. I also knew the brutal truth: my options were pretty limited. How was I now going to earn money? No one was going to give me a job.

It wasn't because I was stupid; I knew that. Thanks to the IT work I'd done when I was a teenager back in Australia I was fairly knowledgeable when it came to computers. I spent as much time as I could on friends' laptops or on the free computers at the local library and had taught myself a fair bit about the subject. But I didn't have any references or relevant experience in the UK to rely on and when a prospective employer asked me where I'd spent the past ten years I couldn't exactly say I'd been working for Google or Microsoft. So I had to forget that.

There wasn't even any point in me applying to do a training course in computing because they wouldn't accept me. Officially I was still on a drug rehabilitation programme. I was living in sheltered accommodation and didn't even have an O level to my name. They wouldn't – and probably couldn't – touch me with a bargepole. All in all, I was a non-starter when it came to getting a normal job. Whatever normal is.

I realised quickly that there was only one realistic alternative. I didn't have the luxury of being able to wait for something to turn up. I needed to make money to look after myself and Bob. So a couple of days after the court hearing I set off with Bob for Covent Garden – for the first time in years, without my guitar on my back. When I got to the piazza I headed straight for the spot where I knew I'd probably find a girl called Sam, the area's *Big Issue* coordinator.

I had tried selling the *Big Issue* before, back in 1998 and 1999 when I first ended up on the streets. I'd got myself accredited and worked the streets around Charing Cross and Trafalgar Square. It hadn't worked out. I'd lasted less than a year before I gave it up.

I could still remember how difficult it was.

When I was selling the *Big Issue*, so many people used to come up to me and snarl 'get a job'. That used to really upset me. They didn't realise that selling the *Big Issue* is a job. In fact, being a *Big Issue* seller effectively means you are running your own business. When I was selling the magazine I had overheads. I had to buy copies to sell. So each day I turned up at the coordinator's stand I had to have at least a few quid in order to buy a few copies of the magazine. That old saying is as true for *Big Issue* sellers as it is for anyone else: you have to have money, to make money.

So many people think it's a complete charity job and that they give the magazines to the sellers for free. That's just not the case. If it was, people would be selling a lot more than they do. The *Big Issue* philosophy is that it is helping people to help themselves. But back then I wasn't really sure I wanted any help. I wasn't ready for it.

I could still remember some of the grim, soul-destroying days I'd spent sitting on a wet and windy street-corner pitch trying to coax and cajole Londoners to part with their cash in return for a magazine. It was really hard, especially as back then my life was still ruled by drugs. All I usually got for my trouble was a load of abuse or a kick in the ribs.

Most of all it had been hard because I had been invisible. Most people just didn't give me the time of day. They would do all they could to avoid me, in fact. That's why I had turned to busking, at least then I had my music to attract people's attention and let them know I was actually a living, breathing creature. And even then most of them ignored me.

I wouldn't have even contemplated going back to selling the *Big Issue* if it hadn't been for Bob. The way he'd transformed my fortunes – and my spirits – on the streets had been amazing. If I could do as well selling the *Big Issue* as I'd done busking with Bob then maybe I could take that big step forward. Of course there was only one problem: I had to get them to accept me first.

I found Sam at the spot where the area's *Big Issue* sellers gathered to buy their magazines, on a side street off the main piazza of Covent Garden. There were a few vendors there, all men. I recognised one or two of the faces. One of them was a guy called Steve, who I knew was a driver for the magazine. I'd seen him around the place, delivering the magazines on Mondays when the new issues came out.

We'd registered each other's presence around Covent Garden a couple of times and were a bit wary of each other. I got the distinct impression he wasn't very pleased to see me, but I didn't care. I hadn't come to see him; it was Sam I needed to talk to.

'Hello, you two not busking today?' she said, recognising me and Bob and giving him a friendly pat.

'No, I'm going to have to knock that on the head,' I said. 'Bit of trouble with the cops. If I get caught doing it illegally again I'm going to be in big trouble. Can't risk it now I've got Bob to look after. Can I, mate?'

'OK,' Sam said, her face immediately signalling that she could see what was coming next.

'So,' I said, rocking up and down on my heels. 'I was wondering—'

Sam smiled and cut me off. 'Well, it all depends on whether you meet the criteria,' she said.

'Oh yeah, I do,' I said, knowing that as a person in what was known as 'vulnerable housing' I was eligible to sell the magazine.

'But you are going to have to go through all the red tape and go down to Vauxhall to sign up,' she said.

'Right.'

'You know where the offices are?' she said, reaching for a card.

'Not sure,' I said. I was sure the offices had been somewhere else when I'd signed up years ago.

'Get a bus to Vauxhall and get off by the train station. It's across the road from there not far from the river on the one-way system,' she said. 'Once you're badged

157

up, just come back here and see me and we can get you going.'

I took the card and headed home with Bob. 'Better get ourselves organised, Bob,' I said. 'We're going for a job interview.'

I needed to get some paperwork sorted before I could go to the *Big Issue* office, so the next day I went to see my housing worker. In any case, I was supposed to see her regularly. I explained my current situation and what had happened with the Transport Police. She happily gave me a letter saying that I was living in 'vulnerable housing' and that selling the *Big Issue* would be a good way of helping me get my life back together again.

The day after that I made myself look respectable, got my hair tied back, put on a decent shirt and set off for Vauxhall with all the bits and pieces I needed.

I also took Bob with me. Part of my thinking was that Bob might help me sell magazines in the way that he'd helped me make money busking. He was going to be part of my team, so I wanted to get him registered as well, if that was at all possible.

The *Big Issue* offices are in an ordinary-looking office block on the south side of the Thames, near Vauxhall Bridge and the MI6 building.

The first thing I noticed when I arrived in the reception area was a large sign saying 'No Dogs Allowed'. Apparently they used to allow dogs in there but they had banned them as so many dogs had started fighting with each other. It didn't say anything about cats, however.

After filling in a few bits of paper, I was told to take a seat and wait. After a while I was called in to have an interview with a guy in one of the offices. He was a decent bloke and we chatted for a while. He'd been on the streets himself years ago and had used the *Big Issue* as a stepping-stone to help get his life together.

I explained my circumstances. He was sympathetic.

'I know what it's like out there, James, believe me,' he said.

It took just a few minutes before he gave me a thumbs-up sign and told me to go and get badged up in another office.

I had to have my photo taken and then wait to get a laminated badge with my vendor number on it. I asked the guy who was issuing the badges whether Bob could have an ID card as well.

'Sorry,' he said, shaking his head. 'Pets aren't allowed to have their own badges. We've had this before with dogs. Never with a cat, though.'

'Well, what about if he is in the picture with me?' I asked.

He pulled a face, as if to say, I'm not sure about that. But in the end he relented.

'Go on then,' he said.

'Smile, Bob,' I said, as we sat in front of the camera.

As he waited for the photo to be processed, the guy got on with the rest of the registration process. When you become a *Big Issue* seller you get assigned a random number. They are not issued in sequence. If they did that the numbers would now be running into the thousands because so many people have signed up to sell the *Big Issue* over the years then just disappeared off the face of the earth. So when someone fails to show up on the records for a while the number comes back into circulation. They have to do that.

After waiting about a quarter of an hour, the guy reappeared at the desk.

'Here you go, Mr Bowen,' he said, handing me the laminated badge.

I couldn't help breaking into a big grin at the picture. Bob was on the left-hand side. We were a team. *Big Issue* Vendors Number 683.

It was a long journey back to Tottenham, involving two buses. So I whiled away the hour and a half it took us reading through the little booklet they gave me. I'd read something similar ten years earlier but hadn't really retained any of it. If I was honest, I'd not really taken it seriously. I'd been too out of it a lot of the time. This time around I was determined to take it more seriously.

It began with the magazine's main philosophy:

'The *Big Issue* exists to offer homeless and vulnerably housed people the opportunity to earn a legitimate income by selling a magazine to the general public.

We believe in offering "a hand up, not a hand out" and in enabling individuals to take control of their lives.'

That's exactly what I want, I said to myself, *a hand up. And this time I'll accept it.*

The next bit stated that I had to 'undergo an induction process and sign up to the code of conduct'. I knew the first bit meant that I'd have to work at a 'trial pitch', where my performance would be watched and assessed by the local organisers.

If that went well I'd be allocated a fixed pitch, it went on. I'd also get ten free copies of the magazine to get me started. It made it clear that it was then down to me. 'Once they have sold these magazines they can purchase further copies, which they buy for £1 and sell for £2, thereby making £1 per copy.'

The rules went on to explain that vendors were employed by the *Big Issue*. 'We do not reimburse them for magazines which they fail to sell, hence each individual must manage their sales and finances carefully. These skills, along with the confidence and self-esteem they build through selling the magazine, are crucial in helping homeless people reintegrate into mainstream society.'

That was the simple economics of it. But there was a lot more to it than that, as I would soon discover.

The next morning I headed back down to Covent Garden to see Sam, the coordinator. I was keen to get on with my 'induction'.

'All go OK down at Vauxhall?' she said, as Bob and I approached her.

'I guess it must have done. They gave me one of these,' I grinned, proudly producing my laminated badge from under my coat.

'Great,' Sam said, smiling at the photo of me and Bob. 'I'd better get you started then.'

She began by counting out my ten free copies of the magazine.

'There you go,' she said. 'You know you'll have to buy them after this?'

'Yep, I understand,' I said.

For a few minutes she studied a sheet of papers.

'Just trying to work out where to put your trial pitch,' she said, apologetically.

A moment or two later I could see she'd made up her mind.

'Found somewhere?' I asked, feeling quite excited about it.

'Think so,' Sam said.

I couldn't believe what she said next.

'OK, we'll give you the training pitch just here,' she said, pointing in the direction of Covent Garden tube station, a few yards further up James Street.

I couldn't stop myself from bursting out laughing.

'Are you OK? Is that a problem?' she said, looking

confused. 'I can look to see if there's somewhere else.'

'No, it's not a problem at all,' I said. 'It'll be great there. It'll be a real walk down memory lane. I'll get started right away.'

I wasted no time and set up immediately. It was mid-morning, a few hours before I'd normally have set up busking, but there were lots of people milling around, mostly tourists. It was a bright, sunny morning, which, I knew from experience, always puts people in a better and more generous mood.

When I'd been busking I'd always felt like I was running the gauntlet of the authorities by playing here. Selling the *Big Issue* was a totally different prospect. I was officially licensed to be there. So I placed myself as close to the station as possible without actually being inside the concourse.

I couldn't resist looking inside to see if there was any sign of the ticket officers who'd given me grief in the past. Sure enough, I saw one of them, a big, sweaty fat guy in a blue shirt. He was too tied up to notice me at this stage but I knew that he would at some point.

In the meantime, I got on with the job of trying to shift my ten copies of the *Big Issue*.

I knew they'd given me this pitch because, as far as normal *Big Issue* sellers were concerned, it was a nightmare. The entrance and exit of a tube station is not a place where people usually have the time to slow down and engage with someone trying to sell them something. They are in a hurry, they have got places to go, people to see. A normal *Big Issue* seller would have done well to stop one in every thousand people that raced past him or her. It would have been a thankless task. During my time busking across the street, I'd spent enough time watching a succession of vendors try and fail to catch people's attention there to know the reality.

But I also knew that I wasn't a normal *Big Issue* seller. I had a secret weapon, one that had already cast his spell on Covent Garden. And he was soon weaving his magic.

I'd put Bob down on the pavement next to me where he was sitting contentedly watching the world go by. A lot of people didn't notice him as they flew past on their mobile phones, fishing inside their pockets for their tickets. But a lot of people did.

Within moments of me setting up, a couple of young American tourists had pulled up to a halt and started pointing at Bob.

'Aaaah,' one of them said, immediately reaching for her camera.

'Do you mind if we take a picture of your cat?' the other one asked.

'Sure, why not?' I said, pleased that, unlike so many people, they'd had the decency to ask. 'Would you like to buy a copy of the *Big Issue* while you're at it. It will help him and me get some dinner tonight.'

'Oh sure,' the second girl said, looking almost ashamed that she'd not thought of it.

'It's no problem if you don't have the money,' I said. 'It's not compulsory.'

But before I could say anything else she'd given me a five-pound note.

'Oh, I'm not sure I've got any change. I've literally just started,' I said, feeling flustered myself now. I know a lot of people think *Big Issue* sellers routinely say this, but I genuinely didn't have much in my pockets. When I counted it out, I had just under a pound in shrapnel in my pocket and handed that over to her.

'That's fine,' she said. 'Keep the change and buy your cat something nice to eat.'

As the American girls left, another group of tourists passed by, this time Germans. Again, they started cooing over Bob. They didn't buy a magazine, but it didn't matter.

I knew already that I'd have no trouble selling the ten copies. In fact, I might even be heading back to Sam for some more stock before the end of the day.

Sure enough I sold six copies within the first hour. Most people gave me the correct money but one elderly gent in a smart, tweed suit, gave me a fiver. I was already feeling vindicated in making this move. I knew I wouldn't always fare this well and that there would be ups and downs. But I already felt like I'd taken a big step in a new direction.

It had been a pretty good day already, but the icing on the cake came after I'd been there for about two and a half hours. By now I was down to my last two magazines. I was suddenly aware of a bit of a commotion inside the station. All of a sudden a small group of London Underground staff appeared in the concourse in full view of me. They seemed to be deep in conversation about something and one or two of them were on walkie-talkies.

My mind couldn't help going back to what had recently happened to me. I wondered whether there had been another incident and whether some other poor sap was going to be fitted up for a crime that he hadn't committed.

Whatever the panic was, however, it soon passed and they began to disperse. It was then that the large, sweaty figure of the ticket attendant spotted me and Bob outside the station. He immediately marched in our direction.

He looked hassled and hot tempered and was as red as a beetroot in the face. They say that revenge is a dish best eaten cold, so I decided to stay cool.

'What the f*** are you doing here?' he said. 'I thought you'd been locked up. You know you're not supposed to be here.'

166

I didn't say anything at first. Instead, very slowly and deliberately, I flashed him my *Big Issue* badge.

'I'm just doing my job, mate,' I said, savouring the mixture of bewilderment and anger that immediately began spreading across his face. 'I suggest you get on with yours.'

Chapter 13

Pitch Perfect

I hadn't got many decisions right in my life. Whenever I'd been given an opportunity in the past ten years I'd screwed things up big time. Within a couple of days of deciding to become a *Big Issue* seller, however, I was pretty sure that I'd taken a step in the right direction for once.

It had an immediate impact on life for me and Bob. For a start it gave us more structure. I effectively had a Monday to Friday job, well, a Monday to Saturday one, in fact.

For those first two weeks, Bob and I worked at Covent Garden from Monday to Saturday, which tied in with the publication of the magazine. The new edition would come out each Monday morning.

We'd be there from sometime in the middle of the morning, and often finish at the end of the early evening rush hour, which was around 7p.m. We stayed for as long as it took us to sell a batch of papers.

Being with Bob had already taught me a lot about responsibility but the *Big Issue* took that to another level. If I wasn't responsible and organised I didn't earn money. And if I didn't earn money Bob and I didn't eat. So from that very first fortnight, I had to grasp how to run my *Big Issue* pitch as a business.

For someone whose life had been completely disorganised for the best part of ten years, this was a huge leap. I'd never been great with money, and had to live from hand to mouth. I surprised myself with the way I adapted to the new demands.

There were downsides, of course, there were bound to be. There is no sale or return with the *Big Issue* so I learned quickly that if you miscalculated the amount of magazines, you could lose out quite badly. You can take a serious blow if you are stuck with fifty papers on Saturday night. Come Monday, you get no credit against the next purchase from the old magazines, so the old papers are pulp. At the same time, you didn't want to under buy. Too few and you'd sell out too quickly and miss out on willing buyers. It was no different from running Marks and Spencer's – well, in theory.

The other thing you had to factor in was that there was a huge difference in the quality of the magazines from week to week. Some weeks it would be a good issue packed with interesting stuff. Other weeks it would be quite dull and really hard to sell, especially if the cover didn't have some famous film or rock star on it. It could be a bit unfair.

It took a while to get the balance right.

While I was working out the best way to sell the *Big Issue*, I still lived from hand to mouth. What I earned between Monday and Saturday evening was generally gone by Monday morning. Sometimes at the start of each week I'd turn up at the coordinator's stand with only a few quid. If Sam was there I'd ask her to do me a favour and buy ten papers for me on the understanding I'd pay her back as soon as I had some money. She would usually do this for vendors who she knew she could trust to repay her and I had done this once or twice before when I was desperate and always repaid her within hours. I knew the money was coming out of her pocket, not the *Big Issue*'s, so it was only fair.

Then when I had sold those copies I'd go back and pay off what I owed and get some more papers. I'd build it up that way from there.

As a result of this, in real terms, I was actually making less money than I had been busking with Bob. But as I settled down into this new routine, I decided it was a price worth paying. The fact that I was working legitimately on the streets made a huge difference to me. If I got stopped by a policeman, I could produce my badge and be left in peace. After the experience with the Transport Police that meant a lot.

The next couple of months working at the tube station flew by. In many ways it was similar to busking. We'd attract the same sort of people: a lot of middle-aged and elderly ladies, groups of female students, gay guys but also people from all walks of life.

One day during the early part of the autumn of 2008 we were approached by a very flamboyant-looking guy. He had bleached-blond hair and was wearing jeans, cowboy boots and I could tell that the leather jacket and jeans must have cost a fortune. I was sure he was an American rock star; he certainly looked like one.

As he'd walked along, he had immediately spotted Bob. He stopped in his tracks and smiled.

'That's one cool cat,' he said, in a sort of transatlantic drawl.

He looked really familiar but I couldn't for the life of me place him. I was dying to ask him who he was, but thought it was rude. I was glad I didn't.

He spent a minute on his knees just stroking Bob.

'You guys been together long?' he asked.

'Uhhmm, gosh, let me think,' I said, having to work it out. 'Well we got together in the spring of last year, so it's about a year and a half now.'

'Cool. You look like real soul brothers,' he smiled. 'Like you belong together.'

'Thanks,' I said, by now desperate to know who the hell this guy was.

Before I could ask him he got up and looked at his watch.

'Hey, gotta go, see you guys around,' he said, reaching into a pocket in his jacket and producing a wad of cash.

He then dropped a tenner into my hand.

'Keep it,' he said, as I began to rummage around for change. 'You guys have a good day.'

'We will,' I promised him. And we did.

It made such a difference that I was now working outside the tube station legitimately. I'd had a couple of moments with some of the familiar faces from the tube station again, one or two of whom had given me some filthy looks. I'd ignored them. The rest of the staff there were actually fine. They knew I was getting on with my job and as long as I didn't offend or harass anyone, that was fine.

Inevitably, Bob and I had also got a bit of attention from other *Big Issue* vendors in the area.

I wasn't so naive as to think that everything was going to be all sweetness and light with the other vendors and assorted street workers. Life on the streets wasn't like that. It wasn't a community built on caring for each other, it was a world in which everyone looked after number one. But, to begin with, at least, most of the other *Big Issue* sellers reacted warmly to the sight of the new guy with a cat on his shoulders.

There had always been vendors around with dogs. One or two of them had been real characters. But, as far as I was aware, there had never been a *Big Issue* seller with a cat in Covent Garden – or anywhere else in London – before.

Some of the vendors were rather sweet about it. A few of them came up and started stroking him and asking questions about how we met and what I knew about his background. The answer, of course, was nothing. He was a blank slate, a mystery cat, which seemed to endear everyone to him even more.

No one was interested in me, of course. The first thing they'd say when they saw us again was 'How's Bob today?' No one ever asked how I was. But that was OK, that was to be expected. I knew the air of bonhomie wouldn't last. It never did on the streets.

With Bob at my side I discovered that I could sell as many as thirty or even fifty papers on a good day. At £2 a paper, as they were priced back then, it could add up quite well, especially with the tips that some people gave me – or, more usually, Bob.

One early autumn evening, Bob was sitting on my rucksack, soaking up the last of the day's sun, when a very well-heeled couple walked past the tube station. To judge by their outfits they were heading for the theatre or maybe even the opera. He was wearing a tuxedo and a bow tie and she had a black silk dress on.

'You two look very smart,' I said, as they stopped and started drooling over Bob.

The lady smiled at me but the guy ignored me.

'He's gorgeous,' the lady said. 'Have you been together for a long time?'

'Quite a while,' I said. 'We kind of found each other on the streets.'

'Here you go,' the guy said, suddenly pulling out his wallet and removing a twenty-pound note.

Before I could even reach into my coat to fish out some change, he'd waved me away. 'No that's fine, keep it,' he said, smiling at his companion.

The look she gave him spoke volumes. I had a feeling they were on a first date. She had clearly been impressed by him giving me that much money.

As they walked off I noticed her leaning into him and wrapping her arm into his.

I didn't care whether it was genuine or not. It was the first time I'd ever been given a twenty-pound drop.

After a few more weeks of trying out the spot at the tube station, I realised that – far from being a 'bad' pitch – the tube station was actually ideal for me and Bob. So I was disappointed when Sam told me that having finished my probation period I would be moving to another pitch at the end of the fortnight.

It wasn't exactly a surprise. The thing about being a member of the *Big Issue* vendor community is that everyone can see how well each other is doing. When the vendors go to the coordinator they can see who has been buying what quantities on a list that's there for everyone to see. You can read it and spot who has been buying papers in batches of tens and twenties and how many batches they are buying. So during that first fortnight, they would have seen that I was buying a lot of magazines.

It soon became obvious that it was something that had been spotted by some of the other vendors. In that second week I noticed a subtle but definite change in the attitude towards me.

I wasn't at all surprised when Sam told me that I'd ended my probation and would now be moved to a different pitch. Our new location wasn't a long way from the tube station, on the corner of Neal Street and Short's Gardens, outside a shoe shop called Size.

I got the distinct feeling that the older hands had taken a dislike to me and Bob and hadn't taken too kindly to us doing so well out of what was supposed to be a bad pitch. For once, however, I buttoned my lip and accepted it. *Choose your battles, James,* I counselled myself.

It turned out to be good advice.

Chapter 14
Under the Weather

It was a cold and wet autumn that year. The trees were soon being stripped of their foliage as the cold winds and heavy rains began to build. On one particular morning, as Bob and I left the block of flats and set off for the bus stop, the sun was once more nowhere to be seen and a light, fine drizzle was falling.

Bob wasn't a big fan of the rain so at first I assumed it was to blame for the lethargic way in which he began padding his way along the path. He seemed to be taking each step at a time, almost walking in slow motion. *Maybe he's got second thoughts about joining me today*, I said to myself. *Or maybe it was true what they said about cats being able to sense bad weather in the air.* As I cast an eye up to the sky, a giant bank of steely, grey clouds were hovering over north London like some vast, alien spaceship.

It was probably going to be like this all day. There was almost certainly some heavier rain on its way. Maybe Bob was right and we should turn around, I thought for a second. But then I remembered the weekend was coming and we didn't have enough money to get through it. *Beggars can't be choosers – even if they have been cleared of all charges*, I said to myself, trying to make light of the predicament.

I was never happy to be working on the streets of London but today it seemed an even bigger pain in the butt than usual.

Bob was still moving at a snail's pace and it had taken us a couple of minutes to get a hundred yards down the road.

'Come on, mate, climb aboard,' I said, turning around and ushering him up into his normal position.

He draped himself on my shoulder and we trudged off towards Tottenham High Road and the bus. The rain was already intensifying. Fat, heavy drops of water were bouncing off the pavement. Bob seemed fine as we sploshed our way along, ducking under any available shelter as we went. But as we settled into our bus journey I realised there was more to his low spirits than just the weather.

The ride was normally one of his favourite parts of the day. Bob was a curious cat. Normally the world was an endlessly interesting place to him. No matter how often we did it, he would never tire of pressing himself against the glass. But today he wasn't even bothered about taking the window seat – not that he'd have seen much through the condensation and streaks of rain that obscured our view of the outside world. Instead he curled up on my lap. He seemed tired. His body language was droopy. Looking at his eyes he seemed a bit drowsy, as if he was half asleep. He was definitely not his normal, alert self.

It was when we got off at Tottenham Court Road that he took a distinct turn for the worse. Luckily the rain had eased off a bit by now and I was able to splash my way through the backstreets in the direction of Covent Garden. It wasn't an easy process and I kept hopping around to sidestep the bigger puddles and the giant umbrellas that flew at me every now and then.

As we walked down Neal Street I was suddenly aware that Bob was behaving oddly on my shoulder. Rather than sitting there impassively as normal, he was twitching and rocking around.

'You all right there, mate?' I said, slowing down.

All of a sudden he began moving in a really agitated way, making weird retching noises as if he was choking or trying to clear his throat. I was convinced he was going to jump or fall off so I placed him down on the street to see what was wrong. But before I could even kneel down he began to vomit. It was nothing solid, just bile. But it just kept coming. I could see his body convulsing as he retched and fought to expel whatever it was that was making him sick. For a moment or two

I wondered whether it was my fault and he felt queasy because of all the motion today.

But then he was sick again, retching away and producing more bile. It was clearly more than motion sickness. Pretty soon he didn't have anything left to bring up, which was puzzling because he'd eaten well the night before and at breakfast. That was when I realised there must be more to it than this. He must have been sick already today, even before we left the flats, probably when he'd been in the garden doing his business. He must have been feeling sick during the bus journey too, I could now see. I blamed myself for not spotting it sooner.

It's weird how you react in a situation like that. I'm sure my instincts were the same as any parent or pet owner. All sorts of crazy, sometimes conflicting thoughts rushed through my mind. Had he simply eaten something that disagreed with him this morning? Had he swallowed something in the flat that had set him off? Or was this something more serious? Was he going to drop dead in front of me? I'd heard stories about cats collapsing in front of their owners after drinking cleaning fluids or choking on bits of plastic. For a split second, an image of Bob dying flashed through my head. I managed to pull myself together before my imagination ran riot.

Come on, James, let's deal with this sensibly, I told myself.

I knew that all the retching and the fact that he no longer had any liquid to bring up meant that he was getting dehydrated. If I didn't do anything he could do damage to one of his organs. I decided that some food and, more importantly, some water, would be a good idea. So I scraped him up and held him in my arms as we walked on to Covent Garden and a general store I knew nearby. I didn't have much cash on me at all, but I cobbled together enough to buy a liquidised chicken meal that Bob usually loved and some good, mineral water. I didn't want to risk giving him contaminated tap water. That might make matters even worse.

I carried him to Covent Garden and placed it down on the pavement near our normal pitch. I got out Bob's bowl and spooned the chicken into it.

'Here we go, mate,' I said, stroking him as I placed the bowl in front of him.

Ordinarily he would have pounced immediately and guzzled down a bowl of food at a rate of knots, but not today. Instead he stood and looked at it for a while before he decided to tuck in. Even then he was very tentative about it, only picking at the bowl. He only ate the jelly. He didn't touch a bit of the meat. Again, it set the alarm bells ringing. This wasn't the Bob I knew and loved. Something was definitely wrong.

I half-heartedly set myself up to start selling the magazine. We needed some money to get us through the next few days, especially if I was going to have to take Bob to a vet and pay for some drugs. But my heart really wasn't in it. I was far more concerned with watching Bob than trying to capture the attention of passers-by. He lay there, impassive, uninterested in anything. Unsurprisingly, not too many people stopped to make a donation. I cut the day short after less than two hours. Bob hadn't been sick again, but he definitely wasn't right. I had to get him home to the warmth – and dryness – of the flat.

I guess I'd been lucky with Bob until now. Ever since I'd taken him under my wing, he had been in perfect health, 100 per cent tip top. He'd had fleas early on but that was to be expected of a street cat. Since I'd treated him for that and given him an early worming treatment, he'd suffered no health problems at all.

Every now and again I had taken him to the Blue Cross van on Islington Green where he'd been microchipped. The vets and vet nurses there knew him well by now and always commented on what good condition he was in. So this was alien territory for me. I was terrified that it might be something serious. As he lay on my lap on the bus returning to Tottenham, I felt the emotions welling up every now and again. It was all I could do to stop myself from bursting into tears. Bob was the best thing in my life. The thought of losing him was terrifying .I couldn't keep that thought out of my head.

When we got home Bob just headed straight for the radiator where he just curled up and went straight to sleep. He stayed there for hours. That night I didn't sleep much, worrying about him. He'd been too out of it to even follow me to bed and was snoozing under the radiator in the front room. I kept hauling myself out of bed to check on him. I'd creep up in the gloom and listen for the sound of his breathing. One time I was convinced he wasn't and had to kneel down to place my hand on his diaphragm to make sure it was moving. I couldn't believe how relieved I was when I found he was purring gently.

Money was so tight I simply had to go out again the following day. That presented me with a real dilemma. Should I leave Bob in the flat on his own? Or should I wrap him up warm and take him into central London with me so that I could keep an eagle eye on him.

Luckily the weather was a lot better today. The sun had decided to make an appearance. And when I wandered out of the kitchen with my cereal bowl in my hands, I saw Bob looking up at me. He looked a little perkier today. And when I offered him a little food he nibbled at it a lot more enthusiastically.

I decided to take him with me. It was still early in the week, so I'd have to wait a few days before I could get him looked at by the Blue Cross van. So, in advance of that, I decided to do some research and headed for the local library where I logged on to a computer and started researching Bob's symptoms.

I'd forgotten what a bad idea it is to search through medical websites. They always give you the worst possible scenario.

I punched in a few key words and came across a couple of informative-looking sites. When I entered the main symptoms – lethargic, vomiting, appetite loss and a few others – a whole swathe of possible illnesses popped up.

Some weren't too bad, for instance, it could have been down to hairballs or maybe even a bad case of flatulence. But then I started looking at other possibilities. Just the As in the list were bad enough. They included Addison's disease, acute kidney disease and arsenic poisoning. As if they weren't scary enough, other options on the long list included feline leukaemia, colitis, diabetes, lead poisoning, salmonella and tonsillitis. Worst of all, as far as I was concerned, one of the sites said it could be an early sign of bowel cancer.

By the time I'd been reading for fifteen minutes or so I was a nervous wreck.

I decided to switch tack and look at the best treatments for vomiting. That was more positive. The sites I looked at suggested plenty of water, rest and supervision. So that was my plan for the next twenty-four to forty-eight hours. I'd basically keep an eye on him around the clock. If he started vomiting again, obviously, I'd head for the vets immediately. If not, I'd go to the Blue Cross on Thursday.

The next day I decided to stay at home until late in the afternoon to give Bob a good chance to rest. He slept like a log, curled up in his favourite spot. I wanted to keep an eye on him. He seemed OK, so I decided to leave him for three or four hours and try and squeeze in some selling. I didn't have much option.

Trudging through the streets that led from Tottenham Court Road to Covent Garden I was aware of my invisibility again. When I got to Covent Garden all everyone could ask was 'Where's Bob?' When I told people that he was ill they were all really concerned. 'Is he going to be all right?'; 'Is it serious?'; 'Is he going to see a vet?'; 'Is he OK on his own at home?'

It was then that an idea struck me. I had come across a vet nurse called Rosemary. Her boyfriend, Steve, worked at a comic-book shop near where we sometimes set up. Bob and I would pop in there every now and again and we had become friends. Rosemary had been in there with Steve one day and we'd struck up a conversation about Bob.

I decided to stick my head in there to see if either of them was around. Luckily Steve was there and gave me a phone number for Rosemary.

'She won't mind you ringing her,' he said. 'Especially as it's about Bob. She loves Bob.'

When I spoke to Rosemary she asked me a load of questions.

'What does he eat? Does he ever eat anything else when he's out and about?'

'Well, he rummages around in the bins,' I said.

It was a habit he had never shaken off. He was an absolute terror. I'd seen him tear the garbage bags to pieces in the kitchen. I'd have to put them outside the front door. He was a street cat. You can take the cat off the street, but you can't take the street out of the cat.

I could hear it in her voice, it was as if a light bulb had been switched on.

'Hmmm,' she said. 'That might explain it.'

She prescribed some probiotic medication, some antibiotics and some special liquid to settle the stomach.

'What's your address?' she said. 'I'll get it biked over to you.'

I was taken aback.

'Oh, I'm not sure that I can afford that, Rosemary,' I said.

'No, don't worry, it won't cost you anything. I'll just add it to another delivery in the area,' she said. 'This evening OK?'

'Yes, great,' I said.

I was overwhelmed. Such spontaneous acts of generosity hadn't exactly been a part of my life in the past few years. Random acts of violence, yes; kindness, no. It was one of the biggest changes that Bob had brought with him. Thanks to him I'd rediscovered the good side of human nature. I had begun to place my trust – and faith – in people again.

Rosemary was as good as her word. I had no doubt she would be. The bike arrived early that evening and I administered the first doses of the medicine straight away.

Bob didn't like the taste of the probiotic. He screwed his face up and recoiled half a step when I gave him his first spoonful of it.

'Tough luck, mate,' I said. 'If you didn't stick your face in rubbish bins, you wouldn't have to take this stuff.'

The medicine had an almost immediate impact. That night he slept soundly and was a lot friskier the following morning. I had to hold his head in my hand to make sure he swallowed the probiotic.

By the Thursday he was well on the road to recovery. But, just as a precaution, I decided to pop along to see the Blue Cross van on Islington Green.

The nurse on duty recognised him immediately and looked concerned when I told her Bob had been under the weather.

'Let's give him a quick check up, shall we?' she said.

She checked his weight and inside his mouth and had a good feel around his body.

'All seems well,' she said. 'I think he's on the road to recovery.'

We chatted for a couple of minutes before I headed off.

'Just don't go rummaging in those bins any more, Bob,' the nurse said as we left the makeshift surgery.

Seeing Bob sick had a profound effect on me. He had seemed to be such an indestructible cat. I'd never imagined him getting ill. Discovering that he was mortal really shook me.

It underlined the feeling that had been building inside me for a while now. It was time for me to get myself clean.

I was fed up with my lifestyle. I was tired of the mind-numbing routing of having to go to the DDU unit every fortnight and the chemist every day. I was tired of feeling like I could slip back into addiction at any time.

So the next time I went to see my counsellor I asked him about coming off methadone and taking the final step towards becoming completely clean. We'd talked about it before, but I don't think he'd ever really taken me at my word. Today, he could tell I was serious.

'Won't be easy, James,' he said.

'Yeah, I know that.'

'You'll need to take a drug called Subutex. We can then slowly decrease the dosage of that so that you don't need to take anything,' he said.

'OK,' I said.

'The transition can be hard, you can have quite severe withdrawal symptoms,' he said, leaning forward.

'That's my problem,' I said. 'But I want to do it. I want to do it for myself and for Bob.'

'OK, well, I will get things moving and we will look at beginning the process in a few weeks' time.'

For the first time in years, I felt like I could see the tiniest light at the end of a very dark tunnel.

Chapter 15
The Naughty List

I could sense there was something wrong the moment I arrived at the Covent Garden coordinators' stand one damp, cold Monday morning. A few other vendors were hanging around, stamping their feet to keep warm and sipping at Styrofoam cups of tea. When they noticed me and Bob, a couple of them muttered to each other and threw me dirty looks, as if I was an unwelcome guest.

When Sam, the coordinator appeared from the other side of the distribution trolley where she'd been collecting a new batch of papers, she immediately jabbed a finger at me.

'James, I need to have a word with you,' she said, looking stern.

'Sure, what's the problem?' I said, approaching her with Bob on my shoulder.

She almost always said hello to him and gave him a stroke, but not today.

'I've had a complaint. In fact, I've had a couple of complaints.'

'What about?' I said.

'A couple of vendors are saying that you are floating. You've been spotted doing it a few times around Covent Garden. You know floating is against the rules.'

'It's not true,' I said, but she just put her palm up in classic 'talk to the hand' fashion.

'There's no point arguing about it. The office wants you to go in for a talk.'

I assumed that was that and headed towards the stacks of papers that had just arrived.

'Sorry, no, you can't buy any more magazines until you go into Vauxhall and sort it out.'

'What? I can't get any more magazines today?' I protested. 'How am I going to make any money for Bob and me?'

'Sorry, but you are suspended until you sort it out with head office.'

I was upset, but not entirely surprised. Things had been building up to this for a while.

One of the many rules that you have to follow as a *Big Issue* seller is that you stick to selling your papers at your designated spot. You aren't supposed to sell at someone else's pitch. And you aren't supposed to 'float', that is, to sell while you are walking around the streets. I was 100 per cent in agreement with the rule. I wouldn't have liked it if someone started walking around next to my pitch waving *Big Issue*s around. It was the fairest and simplest way of policing London's army of vendors.

But during the past month or two I'd had a couple of vendors come up to me to complain that I was 'floating'. They reckoned they'd seen me selling papers while I was walking around with Bob. It wasn't true, but I could see why they might have thought it.

Walking around with Bob had always been a stop-start process. Wherever we went around London, we were stopped every few yards by people wanting to stroke him and talk to him or have a photograph taken.

The only difference now was that people would sometimes ask to buy a copy of the *Big Issue* as well.

As I explained to the other vendors, it put me in a really tricky spot. What I should technically say was, 'Sorry, you'll have to come to my pitch or buy one from the nearest vendor.' But I knew what the end result of that would be: no sale, which wouldn't benefit anyone.

A few of the vendors I'd spoken to had sympathised and understood. Quite a few others didn't, however.

I guessed immediately who had reported me. It didn't take a genius to work it out.

A month or so before Sam had issued the suspension, I'd been walking down Long Acre, past the Body Shop where a guy called Geoff had a *Big Issue* pitch. Gordon Roddick, whose wife Anita had founded the Body Shop, had strong links with the *Big Issue* so there were always vendors outside their stores. I knew him a little bit and

I'd acknowledged him as I walked past. But then, a few moments later, an elderly American couple had stopped me and Bob in the street.

They were incredibly polite, your classic stereotype Midwestern husband and wife.

'Excuse me, sir,' the husband said, 'but could I just take a picture of you and your companion? Our daughter loves cats and it would make her day to see this.'

I'd been more than happy to oblige. No one had called me 'sir' for years – if ever!

I'd got so used to posing for tourists that I'd perfected a couple of poses for Bob that seemed to work best for photographs. I would get him on my right shoulder and turn him to face forward with his face right next to mine. I did this again this morning.

The American couple was delighted with this. 'Oh, gee, I can't thank you enough. She will be thrilled to pieces with that,' the wife said.

They couldn't stop saying thank you and offered to buy a copy of the magazine. I said no and pointed to Geoff a few yards away.

'He is the official *Big Issue* vendor in this area so you should go and buy it from him,' I said.

They'd decided not to and moved on. But then just as they'd been walking off, the wife had leant towards me and squeezed a fiver into my hand.

'Here you go,' she said. 'Give yourself and your lovely cat a treat.'

It was one of those classic situations where perception and reality were the complete opposite of each other. Anyone who had been there would have seen I hadn't solicited money and had actively tried to push them towards Geoff. To Geoff, on the other hand, it looked like I'd not just taken money without handing over a magazine, something else which was forbidden, but I'd compounded the crime by telling them to ignore him.

I knew immediately that it would look bad so I headed towards him to try and explain. But I was already too late. He was shouting obscenities at me and Bob before I got within ten yards. I knew Geoff had a fiery temper and had a reputation for being punchy with it. I decided not to risk it. He was in such a rage, I didn't even try to reason with him and headed off to leave him in peace.

It was soon pretty obvious that the incident must have become, well, a big issue among the *Big Issue* vendors. After that there must have been some kind of whispering campaign against me.

It started with snide remarks.

'Floating around again today,' one vendor said to me sarcastically as I passed his pitch one morning. At least he was vaguely civil about it.

Another vendor, around St Martin's Lane, had been much more direct.

'Whose sales are you and that mangy moggie going to steal today?' he had snarled at me.

Again, I tried to explain the situation but I might as well have been talking to the wall. It was clear that vendors were gossiping to each other, putting two and two together and coming up with five.

I hadn't worried about it that much at first, but it had then escalated a little.

Not long after the incident with Geoff, I started getting threats from the drunk vendors. *Big Issue* vendors aren't supposed to drink on the job. That is one of the most fundamental rules. But the truth is that a lot of vendors are alcoholics and carry a can of extra-strength lager with them in their pockets. Others keep a flask of something stronger and take a little nip from it every now and again to keep them going. I have to hold my hands up: I'd done it myself once, on a particularly cold day. But these guys were different. They were blind drunk.

One day Bob and I were walking through the piazza when one of them lurched at us, slurring his words and waving his arms.

'You f***ing bastard, we'll f***ing get you,' he said. I wish I could say that this only happened once, but it became almost a weekly event.

The final clue that all was not well had come one afternoon when I'd been hanging around the coordinator's pitch in Covent Garden. Sam's colleague Steve would often do her afternoon shift for her.

He was always good to Bob. I don't think Steve liked me much, but he would always make a fuss of Bob. On this particular day, however, he had been in a foul mood towards us both.

I was sitting on a bench minding my own business when Steve came over to me.

'If it was up to me you wouldn't be selling,' he said, real venom in his voice. 'As far as I'm concerned you're a beggar. That's what you and that cat are doing.'

I was really upset by this. I'd come such a long way. I'd made such a huge effort to fit into the *Big Issue* family in Covent Garden. I'd explained time and again what was happening with Bob, but it made no difference. It would go in one ear and straight back out the other.

So, as I say, I wasn't entirely surprised when Sam broke the news about my having to go to head office. But it still left me reeling.

I walked away from Covent Garden dazed and not a little confused. I really didn't know what to do now that I was on the 'Naughty List'.

That night me and Bob ate our dinners then went to bed early. It was getting cold and, with the financial situation looking bleak, I didn't want to waste too much electricity. So while Bob curled up at the foot of the bed, I huddled under the covers trying desperately to work out what to do next.

I had no idea what the suspension meant. Could it mean that I would be banned for good? Or was it simply a slap on the wrists? I had no idea.

As I lay there, memories came flooding back of how my busking had been unfairly brought to an end. I couldn't bear the thought of being denied a livelihood by other people's lies a second time.

It seemed even more unfair this time. I hadn't got into any trouble until now, unlike a lot of the *Big Issue* vendors I'd seen around Covent Garden who were often breaking rules and getting told off by Sam and the other coordinators.

I knew about one guy who was notorious with all the sellers. He was this big, brash cockney geezer, a very intimidating character; he would growl at people in a really threatening voice. He'd frighten women, in particular, by going up to them and saying: 'Come on, darling, buy a magazine.' It was almost as if he was threatening them. 'Buy one, or else . . .'

Apparently he used to roll the magazine up and then slip it into people's bags as they were walking past. I'd also heard that he would then stop them and say: 'That will be two pounds, please' and then follow them until they gave him money to go away. That kind of thing doesn't help anyone. Most of the time the victims would simply toss the papers into the nearest bin. It wasn't even as if the money was going to a good cause. This brute of a man was said to be a gambling addict and other sellers said that all he did was pump it straight back into fruit machines.

He had obviously broken so many of the basic rules it was ridiculous, yet as far as I knew, he'd never been disciplined.

Whatever misdemeanours I had supposedly committed, it didn't compare to that. And it was the first time I'd been accused of anything. Surely that would count in my favour? Surely it wasn't a question of one strike and you're out? I simply didn't know. Which was why I was beginning to panic.

The more I thought about it, the more confused and helpless I felt. But I knew I couldn't just do nothing. So the following morning I decided to head out as normal and simply try another coordinator in a different part of London. It was a risk, I knew that, but I figured it was one that was worth taking.

As a *Big Issue* seller you learn that there are coordinators all over town, around Oxford Street, King's Cross and Liverpool Street, in particular. You get to know the whole network. So I decided to chance my arm over at Oxford Street where I'd met a couple of people in the past.

I arrived at the stall mid-morning and tried to make the situation as low-key as possible. I flashed my badge and bought a pile of twenty papers. The guy there was wrapped up in other things so barely registered me. I didn't hang around long enough to give him the chance. I simply headed for a spot where there was no sign of anyone else selling and took my chances.

I felt sorry for Bob in all this. He was quite nervous and seemed disoriented, and understandably so. He liked routine, he thrived on stability and predictability. He didn't take kindly to chaos once more re-entering his life. Nor did I, to be honest. He must have been wondering why our normal routine had been so suddenly and inexplicably changed.

I managed to sell a decent number of magazines that day – and did the same the following day. I moved locations all the time, imagining that the *Big Issue* outreach team was on the lookout for me. I knew it was illogical and slightly mad, but I was paranoid, terrified that I was going to lose my job.

I had images of me being hauled in front of some committee and being stripped of my badge and cast out. 'Why is this happening to us?' I said to Bob as we headed back on the bus one evening. 'We didn't do anything wrong. Why can't we get a break?' I resigned myself to having to spend the next few weeks taking my chances in other parts of London, hoping that the coordinators didn't know I was persona non grata.

I was sitting under a battered old umbrella on a street somewhere near Victoria Station late on a Saturday afternoon when I finally told myself that I had made a mistake. Well, to be honest, it was Bob who told me.

It had been hammering down with rain for about four hours and barely a person had slowed down to stop and buy a magazine. I couldn't blame them. They just wanted to get out of the deluge.

Since we'd started selling early in the afternoon, the only people who had shown an interest in me and Bob had been the security staff of the various buildings where we'd stopped to try and take shelter.

'Sorry, mate, you can't stay here,' they'd said to me with monotonous regularity.

I'd found the umbrella discarded in a bin and had decided to use it in one last attempt to avert another mini-disaster of a day. It wasn't working.

I had been managing to get hold of papers from various vendors around London for about a month now. I had been careful about who I approached and wherever I could I got other vendors to buy papers for me. A lot of people knew who I was. But there were enough who didn't know I was on the suspended list who picked up batches of ten or twenty papers for me, to get me by. I didn't want to get them into trouble, but if they didn't know I was banned then no one could criticise them. I figured it was safe and after everything I had been through over the past few months, I just wanted to make a living and take care of myself and Bob.

It hadn't been going well though. Finding the right pitch was a real problem, mainly because most of the places I'd set up shop weren't actually licensed. Bob and I had been moved on from various street corners around Oxford Street, Paddington, King's Cross, Euston and other stations. One day, after being asked to move on three times by the same policeman, I got a semi-official warning that next time I'd be arrested. I didn't want to go through that again.

It was a real catch-22 situation. I'd made sure to steer clear of the main pitches and tried to pick places that were a bit off the beaten track. But as a result I'd found it really hard to sell the magazine, even with Bob. The *Big Issue* hadn't designated its prime sales spots by accident. They knew exactly where papers would sell – and where they wouldn't. These were the spots I'd found myself occupying.

People were still drawn to Bob, of course, but the locations just weren't right. Inevitably, this had hit me in the pocket, and it had become much harder for me to manage the business side of the *Big Issue*. Tonight I was going to hit rock bottom in that respect. I had about fifteen papers left. I knew I wasn't going to sell them and by Monday they would be out of date when a new edition came out. I was in trouble.

As the light faded and the rain continued to fall, I told myself that I'd try a couple more pitches in the hope of shifting these papers. I hadn't figured on Bob, though.

Until now he'd been as good as gold, a real stoic even on the most desperately grim day. He'd even put up with the regular splashings he got from passing cars and people, even though I knew he hated getting soaked in the cold. But when I tried to stop and sit down at the first street corner I'd spotted, he refused to stop walking. It was extremely rare that he pulled on the lead like a dog, but that's exactly what he was doing now.

'OK, Bob, I get the message, you don't want to stop there,' I said, simply thinking that he didn't fancy that particular location. But when he did exactly the same thing at the next spot and then again at the next spot after that, the penny finally dropped.

'You want to go home, don't you, Bob?' I said. He was still walking along on the lead, but on hearing this he slowed down and tilted his head almost imperceptibly in my direction, giving me what for all the world looked like a raised eyebrow. He then stopped and gave me the familiar look that said he wanted to be picked up.

In that instant I made the decision. Until now, Bob had been a rock, sticking loyally by my side despite the fact that business hadn't been so good and his bowl had consequently been a little less full of food. It just underlined to me how loyal he was. Now I had to be loyal to him and get us back on track with the *Big Issue* management.

I knew it was the right thing to do. The *Big Issue* had been a great step forward for me. It had given me the biggest boost I'd had for a long time, well, since Bob had come into my life, in fact. I just needed to clear up the situation with them. I couldn't avoid facing the music any longer. For Bob's sake as much as mine. I couldn't keep doing this to him.

And so it was that the following Monday morning I had a good wash and put on a decent shirt and set off for Vauxhall. I took Bob with me, to help explain the case.

I really wasn't sure what to expect when I got there. The worst-case scenario, obviously, would be that I'd be stripped of my badge and banned from selling the magazine. That would have been grossly unfair. But I knew there would have to be some kind of punishment if they found me guilty of 'floating'. My best hope was to convince them that I hadn't been doing that.

Arriving at the *Big Issue* office I explained the situation and was told to wait.

Bob and I sat there for about twenty minutes before we got to see someone. A youngish guy and an older woman led me into a non-descript office and asked me to shut the door behind me. I held my breath and waited for the worst.

They gave me a real dressing down. They claimed I'd broken a couple of the cardinal rules.

'We've had complaints that you've been floating and begging,' they said.

I knew who had made the complaints but didn't let on. I knew I mustn't turn it into a personality clash. *Big Issue* vendors were supposed to get on with each other and if I sat there slagging off a list of other vendors it wasn't going to do me any good. Instead I tried to explain to them how difficult it was to walk around Covent Garden with Bob without being offered money for the magazine.

I gave them a couple of examples, one involving some blokes outside a pub who had stopped to admire Bob and offered me a fiver for three copies. There was an interview in there with an actress they all fancied, they told me.

'Things like that happen all the time,' I told them. 'If someone stops me outside a pub, to refuse to sell them a paper would just be rude.'

They listened sympathetically and nodded at some of the points I made.

'We can see that Bob attracts attention. We've spoken to a few vendors who have confirmed that he's a bit of a crowd puller,' the young guy said, with more than a hint of sympathy in his voice.

But when I'd finished defending myself, he leaned forward and broke the bad(ish) news. 'Well, we're still going to have to give you a verbal warning.'

'Oh, OK. A verbal warning, what does that mean?' I asked, genuinely surprised.

He explained that it wouldn't prevent me from selling, but that the situation might change if I was found guilty of floating again.

I felt a bit silly afterwards. A verbal warning was neither here nor there. I realised that I'd panicked completely and, typically, jumped to the worst possible conclusion. I hadn't understood what was going to happen. I had been terrified that I was going to lose my job. The images I had of me being hauled in front of some committee and being stripped of my badge and cast out were just a figment of my imagination. I didn't realise it was not that serious.

I headed back to Covent Garden to see Sam, feeling slightly sheepish about what had been happening.

When she saw me and Bob, she smiled at us knowingly.

'Wasn't sure whether we'd see you two again,' she said. 'Been into the office to sort it out?'

I explained what had happened. I then gave her the piece of paper that I'd been given at the end of the meeting.

'Looks like you are back on probation for a bit,' she said. 'You can only work after 4.30p.m. and on Sundays for a few weeks. Then we can put you back on a normal shift. Just make sure to keep yourself clean. If someone comes up to you and Bob and offers to buy a magazine, say you haven't got one, or if it's obvious you have, say they are promised for regular customers. And don't get involved.'

It was all good advice, of course. The problem was that other people might want to 'get involved'. And so they did.

One Sunday afternoon Bob and I had headed to Covent Garden to do a couple of hours' work. Given the restrictions on us, we had to take whatever chances we could get.

We were sitting near the coordinators' spot on James Street when I was suddenly aware of a large and rather threatening presence. It was a guy called Stan.

Stan was a well-known figure in *Big Issue* circles. He'd worked for the company for years. The problem was that he was a bit unpredictable. When he was in the right frame of mind he could be the nicest guy you'd ever met. He would do anything for you, and frequently did.

He'd bailed me out and given me a couple of free papers on a couple of occasions.

However, when Stan was in a bad mood or, even worse, drunk, he could be the most objectionable, argumentative and aggressive pain in the arse in the world.

I quickly spotted that it was the latter Stan who was now standing in front of me.

Stan was a big guy, all of six feet four. He leaned down over me and bellowed: 'You aren't supposed to be here, you are banned from the area.'

I could smell his breath; it was like a distillery.

I had to stand my ground.

'No, Sam said I could come over here on Sunday or after 4.30p.m.,' I said.

Fortunately another guy who worked with Sam, Peter, was there as well and he backed me up, much to Stan's annoyance.

He lurched back for a moment then move backed in, breathing whisky fumes all over me once more. He was looking at Bob now, and not in a friendly way.

'If it was up to me I'd strangle your cat right now,' he said. His words really freaked me out.

If he'd made a move towards Bob I would have attacked him. I would have defended him like a mother defending her child. It's the same thing. He was my baby. But I knew that would be fatal, from the *Big Issue*'s point of view. It would be the end.

So I made two decisions there and then. I picked up Bob and headed elsewhere for the afternoon. I wasn't going to work anywhere near Stan when he was in this mood. But I also made the decision to move away from Covent Garden.

It would be a wrench. Bob and I had a loyal customer base there and, besides anything else, it was a fun place to work. The inescapable truth, however, was that it was becoming an unpleasant and even a dangerous place to work. Bob and I needed to move to a less competitive part of London, somewhere where I wasn't so well known. There was one obvious candidate.

I used to busk around the Angel tube station in Islington before I went to Covent Garden. It was a good area, less lucrative than Covent Garden but still worthwhile. So I decided the next day to take a visit to the coordinator there, a great guy called Lee, who I knew a little bit.

'What are the chances of me getting a good pitch here?' I asked him.

'Well, Camden Passage is pretty busy, as is the Green, but you could do outside the tube station if you like,' he said. 'No one fancies it much.'

I had a feeling of déjà vu. It was Covent Garden all over again. For other *Big Issue* sellers in London, tube stations were reckoned to be a complete nightmare, the worst possible places to try and sell the paper. The way the theory went was that people in London are simply moving too fast, they don't have time to slow down, make the decision to buy one and dip into their pockets. They've got to be somewhere else, they are always in a hurry.

As I'd discovered at Covent Garden, however, Bob had the magical ability to slow them down. People would see him and suddenly they weren't in quite such a rush. It was as if he was providing them with a little bit of light relief, a little bit of warmth and friendliness in their otherwise frantic, impersonal lives. I'm sure a lot of people bought a *Big Issue* as a thank you for me giving them that little moment. So I was more than happy to take what was supposed to be a 'difficult' pitch right outside Angel tube.

We started that same week. I left the Covent Garden vendors to it.

Almost immediately we began to get people slowing down to say hello to Bob. We had soon picked up where we had left off in Covent Garden.

One or two people recognised us.

One evening, a well-dressed lady in a business suit stopped and did a sort of double take.

'Don't you two work in Covent Garden?' she said.

'Not any more, madam,' I said with a smile, 'not any more.'

Chapter 16
Angel Hearts

The move to Angel had definitely met with Bob's seal of approval; I only had to look at his body language each day as we headed to work.

When we got off the bus at Islington Green, he wouldn't ask to climb on my shoulders in the way he tended to do when we'd been in central London. Instead, most mornings he would take the lead and march purposefully ahead of me, down Camden Passage, past all the antique stores, cafés, pubs and restaurants, and along towards the end of Islington High Street and the large paved area around the tube station entrance.

Sometimes we'd need to head to the *Big Issue* coordinator on the north side of the Green, so we'd take a different route. If that was the case, he'd always make a beeline for the enclosed garden area at the heart of the

Green. I'd wait and watch while he rummaged around in the overgrowth, sniffing for rodents, birds or any other poor unsuspecting creature upon which he could test his scavenging skills. So far, he'd drawn a blank, but it didn't seem to dampen his enthusiasm for sticking his head into every nook and cranny in the area.

When we eventually arrived at his favourite spot, facing the flower stall and the newspaper stand near one of the benches by the entrance to the Angel tube station, he would stand there and watch me go through the arrival ritual, placing my bag down on the pavement and putting a copy of the *Big Issue* in front of it. Once all this was done, he would sit himself down, lick himself clean from the journey and get ready for the day.

I felt the same way about our new stamping ground. After all the trouble I'd had at Covent Garden over the years, Islington seemed like another fresh start for us both. I felt like we were starting a new era, and that this time it was going to last.

The Angel was different from Covent Garden and the streets around the West End in lots of subtle ways. In central London, the streets were mostly crammed with tourists and, in the evenings, West End revellers and theatregoers. The Angel wasn't quite as busy, but the tube station still saw a mass of humanity pouring in and out each day.

It was a distinctively different type of person, though. There were still a lot of tourists, of course, many of them drawn to the restaurants and arty venues like Sadler's Wells and the Islington Business Design Centre.

But it was also a more professional and, for want of a better word, more 'upmarket' place. Each evening I'd notice hordes of people in business suits heading in and out of the tube station. The bad news was that most of them barely even registered the fact that there was a ginger cat sitting outside the station. The good news was that a large proportion of those who did slow down and spot him took an instant shine to Bob. They were also really generous. I noticed immediately that the average purchase and tip at Islington was just that little bit bigger than in Covent Garden.

The Angel locals were also generous in a different kind of way to those in Covent Garden. Almost as soon as we began selling the *Big Issue* there, people began giving Bob bits of food.

The first time it happened was on our second or third day. A very smartly dressed lady stopped for a chat. She asked me whether we were going to be there every day from now on, which struck me as a bit suspicious. Was she going to make some sort of complaint? I was completely off the mark, however. The following day she appeared with a small Sainsbury's bag containing some cat milk and a pouch of Sheba.

'There you go, Bob,' she said happily, placing them on the pavement in front of Bob.

'He'll probably have that at home tonight if that's OK,' I said, thanking her.

'Of course,' she said. 'As long as he enjoys it that's the main thing.'

After that, more and more locals started donating titbits for him.

Our pitch was down the road from a large Sainsbury's supermarket. It soon became obvious that people were going in there to do their normal shopping and were picking up a little treat for Bob on their way round. They would then drop their presents off on their way back home.

One day, just a few weeks after we began at Angel, about half a dozen different people did this. By the end of the day, I couldn't fit all the tins of cat milk, pouches of food and tins of tuna and other fish that had been piling up all day into my rucksack. I had to keep it all in a large Sainsbury's bag. When I got back to the flat, it filled up an entire shelf in one of the kitchen cupboards. It kept us going for almost a week.

The other thing that was a world apart from Covent Garden was the attitude of the staff at the tube station. At Covent Garden I was the Antichrist, a hate figure almost. I could count the number of people with whom I'd forged a good friendship in the years I'd been busking or selling the *Big Issue* there on the fingers of one hand. In fact I didn't even need that. I could think of two at most.

By contrast, the staff at Angel were really warm and generous towards Bob from the very beginning. One day, for instance, the sun had been blazingly hot. The mercury must have been up in the 90s at one point. Everyone was walking around in shirt sleeves even though, technically, it was autumn. I was sweating like crazy in my black jeans and black T-shirt.

I deliberately placed Bob in the shade of the building behind us so that he didn't get too hot. I knew that heat was bad for cats. An hour or so after we'd set up our pitch, it became clear to me that I'd soon need to get some water for Bob. But before I was able to do something, a figure appeared from inside the tube station with a nice clean, steel bowl brimming with clear water. I recognised the lady immediately. Her name was Davika, one of the ticket attendants, she'd stopped to talk to Bob on numerous occasions already.

'Here you go, Bob,' she said, stroking him on the back of the neck as she placed the bowl in front of him. 'Don't want you getting dehydrated now, do we?' she said.

He wasted no time in diving in and lapped it up in no time whatsoever.

Bob had always had this ability to endear himself to people, but it never ceased to amaze me just how many seemed to become devoted to him. He had won the Islington crowd over in a matter of weeks. It was amazing really.

Of course, it wasn't perfect at the Angel. This was London after all. It could never have been all sweetness and light. The biggest problem was the concentration of people working the area around the tube station.

Unlike Covent Garden where all the surrounding streets were alive with activity, at the Angel things tended to be concentrated around the tube. So as a result there were a lot of other people operating on the streets, from people dishing out free magazines to charity workers – or 'chuggers', as they were known.

This was one of the biggest changes that I'd noticed since I'd started working on the streets a decade earlier. The streets were very much more competitive than they used to be. The 'chuggers' were mostly hyper-enthusiastic young people working for charities. Their job was to collar well-heeled commuters and tourists and get them to listen to a spiel about their charity. They would then try to persuade them to sign up for direct debits to be taken from their bank accounts. It was like being mugged by a charity – hence their nickname: chuggers.

Some were third world charities others were health related, to do with cancer or other illnesses like cystic fibrosis and Alzheimer's. I didn't have a problem with them being there but it was the way they hassled people that annoyed me. I had my own sales spiel for the *Big Issue*, of course. But I wasn't as intrusive or as nagging as some of these. They would follow people down the road engaging them in conversations they didn't want to have.

As a result of this, I would see people emerge from the tube station, see a wall of these enthusiastic canvassers, usually in their loud coloured T-shirts, and make a run for it. A lot of them were potential *Big Issue* buyers so it was very annoying.

If someone was really driving people away I would have a word. Some of the canvassers were fine about it. They respected me and gave me my space. But others didn't.

One day I got into a heated argument with a young student with a mop of Marc Bolan-like curls. He'd been really irritating people by bouncing around and walking alongside them as they tried to get away. I decided to have a word.

'Hey, mate, you're making life difficult for the rest of us who are working here,' I said, trying to be civil about it. 'Can you just move along the road a few yards and give us some space?'

He'd got really antsy about it. 'I've got every right to be here,' he said. 'You can't tell me what to do and I will do what I want.'

If you want to get someone's back up, you just need to say something like that. So I put him straight on the fact that while he was trying to make pocket money to fund his 'gap year', I was trying to make money to pay for my electricity and gas and to keep a roof over my and Bob's head.

His face kind of sank when I put it in those terms.

The other people who were a real irritant for me were the people who sold the assorted free magazines that were being published now. Some of them – like *StyleList* and *ShortList*– were actually good-quality magazines, so they caused me no end of problems, the simplest of which boiled down to a question: why were people going to pay for my magazine when they could get a free one from these people?

So whenever one strayed into my area I'd try to explain it to them. I'd say to them straight up: 'We all need to work, so you need to give me some space to do my job, you need to be at least twenty feet away.' It didn't always work, however, often because a lot of the vendors who gave away these magazines didn't speak English. I would try to explain the situation to them but they didn't understand what I was trying to say to them. Others simply didn't want to listen to my complaints.

By far the most annoying people to work the streets around me, however, were the bucket rattlers: the charity workers who would turn up with large plastic buckets collecting for the latest cause.

Again, I sympathised with a lot of the things for which they were trying to raise money: Africa, environmental issues, animal rights. They were all great, worthwhile charities. But if the stories I had heard about how much of the money disappeared into the pockets of some of these bucket shakers were true, I didn't have much sympathy. A lot of them didn't have licences or any kind of meaningful accreditation. If you looked at the laminated badges around their necks, they could have been something from a kid's birthday party. They looked amateurish.

Yet, despite this, they were allowed inside the tube stations, a place that was an absolute no-go zone for a *Big Issue* seller. It would really nark me when I saw a bucket rattler inside the concourse hassling people. Sometimes they would be standing right up against the turnstiles. By the time they emerged out of the station the commuters and visitors were usually in no mood to be persuaded to buy the *Big Issue*.

It was, I suppose, a bit of a reversal of roles. In Covent Garden I had been the maverick who hadn't stuck to the designated areas and bent the laws a bit. Now I was on the receiving end of that.

I was the only licensed vendor in the area outside the tube station. And I'd worked out the areas that I could and couldn't stray into with the other main sellers there – the newspaper vendor and the florist in particular. The chuggers, hawkers and bucket rattlers ran rough-shod over those rules. I guess some people would have thought it was ironic, but there were times when I failed to see the funny side of it, I have to admit.

Chapter 17

Forty-eight Hours

The young doctor at the DDU – the drug dependency unit – scribbled his signature at the bottom of the prescription and handed it over to me with a stern expression on his face.

'Remember, take this, then come back to me at least forty-eight hours later when you can feel the withdrawal symptoms have really kicked in,' he said, holding my gaze. 'It's going to be tough, but it will be a lot tougher if you don't stick to what I've said. OK?'

'OK, I understand,' I nodded, picking myself up and heading out of his treatment room. 'Just hope I can do it. See you in a couple of days.'

I'd been turning up at my fortnightly consultations for a couple of months since we'd first talked about coming off methadone. I thought I was ready for it, but my counsellors and doctors obviously didn't share that opinion. Each time I'd come in they had kept postponing it. I'd not got any kind of explanation as to why this was. Now, at last, they had decided it was time: I was going to make the final step towards being clean.

The prescription the counsellor had just given me was for my last dose of methadone. Methadone had helped me kick my dependence on heroin. But I'd now tapered down my usage to such an extent that it was time to stop taking it for good.

When I next came to the DDU in a couple of days' time I would be given my first dose of a much milder medication, Subutex, which would ease me out of drug dependency completely. The counsellor described the process as like landing an aeroplane, which I thought was a good analogy. In the following months he would slowly cut back my dosage until it was almost non-existent. As he did so, he said I would slowly drop back down to earth, landing – hopefully – with a very gentle bump.

As I waited for the prescription to be made up today, I didn't really dwell on the significance of it. My head was too busy with thoughts about what lay ahead during the next forty-eight hours.

The counsellor had explained the risk to me in graphic detail. Coming off methadone wasn't easy. In fact, it was really hard. I'd experience 'clucking' or 'cold turkey', a series of unpleasant physical and mental withdrawal symptoms. I had to wait for those symptoms to become quite severe before I could go back to the clinic to get my first dose of Subutex. If I didn't I risked having what's known as a precipitated withdrawal. This was basically a much worse withdrawal. It didn't bear thinking about.

I was confident at this point that I could do it. But at the same time I had an awful niggling feeling that I could fail and find myself wanting to score something that would make me feel better. But I just kept telling myself that I had to do this, I had to get over this last hurdle. Otherwise it was going to be the same the next day and the next day and the day after that. Nothing was going to change.

This was the reality that had finally dawned on me. I'd been living this way for ten years. A lot of my life had just slipped away. I'd wasted so much time, sitting around watching the days vanish. When you are dependent on drugs, minutes become hours, hours become days. It all just slips by; time becomes inconsequential, you only start worrying about it when you need your next fix. You don't even care until then.

But that's when it becomes so awful. Then all you can think about is making money to get some more. I'd made huge progress since I'd been in the depths of my heroin addiction years earlier. The DDU had really put me back on track. But I was just sick of the whole thing now. Having to go to a chemist every day, having to visit the DDU every fortnight. Having to prove that I hadn't been using. I had had enough. I now felt like I had something to do with my life.

In a way I'd made it harder on myself by insisting on doing it alone. I had been offered the chance several times to join Narcotics Anonymous but I just didn't like the whole twelve-step programme. I couldn't do that kind of quasi-religious thing. It's almost like you have to give yourself up to a higher power. It just wasn't me.

I realised that I was making life even more difficult for myself by taking that route. The difference was I didn't think I was on my own now. I had Bob.

As usual, I didn't take him with me to the DDU clinic. I didn't like exposing him to the place. It was a part of my life I wasn't proud about, even though I did feel I'd achieved a lot since I'd first visited.

When I got home he was pleased to see me, especially as I'd stopped off at the supermarket on the way home and had a bag full of goodies intended to get us through the next two days. Anyone who is trying to get rid of an addictive habit knows what it is like. Whether it's trying to give up cigarettes or alcohol, the first forty-eight hours are the hardest. You are so used to getting your 'fix' that you can't think of anything else. The trick is to think of something else, obviously. And that's what I hoped to do. And I was just really grateful that I had Bob to help me achieve it.

That lunchtime we sat down in front of the television, had a snack together – and waited.

The methadone generally lasted for around twenty hours so the first part of the day passed easily enough. Bob and I played around a lot and went out for a short walk so that he could do his business. I played a really old version of the original *Halo 2* game on my knackered old Xbox. At that point it all seemed to be plain sailing. I knew it couldn't stay that way for much longer.

Probably the most famous recreation of someone 'clucking' is in the film *Trainspotting* in which Ewan McGregor's character, Renton, decides to rid himself of his heroin addiction. He is locked in a room with a few days of food and drink and left to get on with it. He goes through the most horrendous physical and mental experience you can imagine, getting the shakes, having hallucinations, being sick. All that stuff. Everyone remembers the bit where he imagines he is climbing inside the toilet bowl.

What I went through over the next forty-eight hours felt ten times worse than that.

The withdrawal symptoms began to kick in just after twenty-four hours after I'd had my dose of methadone. Within eight hours of that I was sweating profusely and feeling very twitchy. By now it was the middle of the night and I should have been asleep. I did nod off but I felt like I was pretty much conscious all the time. It was a strange kind of sleep, full of dreams or, more accurately, hallucinations.

It's hard to recollect exactly, but I do remember having these lucid dreams about scoring heroin. There were a lot of these dreams and they always went the same way: I would either score and spill it, score and not be able to get a needle into my vein or score but then get arrested by the police before I could use it. It was weird. It was obviously my body's way of registering the fact that it was being denied this substance that it had once been used to being fed every twelve hours or so. But it was also my subconscious trying to persuade me that maybe it was a good idea to start using it again. Deep in my brain there was obviously this huge battle of wills going on. It was almost as if I was a bystander, watching it all happen to someone else.

It was strange. Coming off heroin years ago wasn't as bad. The transition to methadone had been reasonably straightforward. This was a different experience altogether.

Time ceased to have any real meaning, but by the following morning I was beginning to experience really bad headaches, almost migraine-level pains. As a result I found it hard to cope with any light or noise. I'd try and sit in the dark, but then I'd start dreaming or hallucinating and want to snap myself out of it. It was a vicious circle.

What I needed more than anything was something to take my mind off it all, which was where Bob proved my salvation.

There were times when I wondered whether Bob and I had some kind of telepathic understanding. He could definitely read my mind sometimes, and seemed to be doing so now. He knew that I needed him so he was a constant presence, hanging around me, snuggling up close when I invited him but keeping his distance when I was having a bad time.

It was as if he knew what I was feeling. Sometimes I'd be nodding off and he would come up to me and place his face close to me, as if to say: 'You all right, mate? I'm here if you need me.' At other times he would just sit with me, purring away, rubbing his tail on me and licking my face every now and again. As I slipped in and out of a weird, hallucinatory universe, he was my sheet anchor to reality.

He was a godsend in other ways too. For a start, he gave me something to do. I still had to feed him, which I did regularly. The process of going into the kitchen, opening up a sachet of food and mixing it in the bowl was just the sort of thing I needed to get my mind off what I was going through. I didn't feel up to going downstairs to help him do his business, but when I let him out he dashed off and was back upstairs again in what seemed like a few minutes. He didn't seem to want to leave my side.

I'd have periods where I didn't feel so bad. During the morning of the second day, for instance, I had a couple of hours where I felt much better. Bob and I just played around a lot. I did a bit of reading. It was hard but it was a way to keep my mind occupied. I read a really good non-fiction book about a Marine saving dogs in Afghanistan. It was good to think about what was going on in someone else's life.

By the afternoon and early evening of the second day, however, the withdrawal symptoms were really ramping up. The worst thing was the physical stuff. I had been warned that when you go through 'clucking' you get what's called restless legs syndrome. In effect, you have incredibly uncomfortable, nervous pulses that run through your body, making it impossible for you to sit still. I started doing this. My legs would suddenly and involuntarily start kicking – it's not called kicking the habit for nothing. I think this freaked Bob out a bit. He gave me a couple of odd, sideways looks. But he didn't desert me, he stayed there, at my side.

That night was the worst of all. I couldn't watch television because the light and noise hurt my head. When I went into the dark, I just found my mind racing, filling up with all kinds of crazy, sometimes scary stuff. All the time my legs were kicking and I was feeling extremes of hot and cold. One minute I was so hot I felt like I was inside a furnace. The next I'd feel ice cold. The sweat that had built up all over me would suddenly start to freeze and suddenly I'd be shivering. So then I'd have to cover up and would start burning up again. It was a horrible cycle.

Every now and again, I'd have moments of lucidity and clarity. At one point I remember thinking that I really understood why so many people find it so hard to kick their drug habits. It's a physical thing as well as a mental thing. That battle of wills that's going on in your brain is very one-sided. The addictive forces are definitely stronger than those that are trying to wean you off the drugs.

At another point, I was able to see the last decade and what my addiction had done to me. I saw – and sometimes smelled – the alleys and underpasses where I'd slept rough, the hostels where I'd feared for my life, the terrible things I'd done and considered doing just to score enough to get me through the next twelve hours. I saw with unbelievable clarity just how seriously addiction screws up your life.

I had some weird, almost surreal thoughts as well. For instance, at one point it occurred to me that if I was to wake up with amnesia I'd get through the withdrawal, because I wouldn't know what was wrong with me. A lot of my problems stemmed from the fact my body knew exactly what was wrong with me and what I could do to fix it. I won't deny that there were moments of weakness when it crossed my mind, when I imagined scoring. But I was able to fend those thoughts off pretty easily. This was my chance to kick it, maybe my last chance. I had to stay strong, I had to take it: the diarrhoea, the cramps, the vomiting, the headaches, the wildly fluctuating temperatures – all of it.

That second night seemed to last forever. I'd look up at the clock and it seemed at times as if it was moving backwards. Outside it seemed as if the darkness was getting deeper and blacker rather than brightening up for morning. It was horrible.

But I had my secret weapon. Bob did annoy me at certain points. At one stage I was lying as still and quiet as possible, just trying to shut out the world. All of a sudden, I felt Bob clawing at my leg, digging into my skin quite painfully.

'Bob, what the hell are you doing?' I shouted at him a bit too aggressively, making him jump. Immediately I felt guilty.

I suspect he was worried that I was a little too still and quiet and was checking up to make sure I was alive. He was worried about me.

Eventually, a thin, soupy grey light began to seep through the window, signalling that morning had arrived at last. I hauled myself out of bed and looked at the clock. It was almost eight o'clock. I knew the clinic would be open by nine. I couldn't wait any longer.

I splashed some cold water on my face. It felt absolutely awful on my clammy skin. In the mirror I could see that I looked drawn and my hair was a sweaty mess. But I wasn't going to worry about that at this point. Instead I threw on some clothes and headed straight for the bus stop.

Getting to Camden from Tottenham at that time of the day was always a trial. Today it seemed much worse.

Every traffic light was on red, every road seemed to have a long tailback of traffic. It really was the journey from hell.

As I sat on the bus, I was still having those huge temperature swings, sweating one moment, shivering the next, my limbs were still twitching every now and again, although not as badly as during the middle of the night. People were looking at me as if I was some kind of nutcase. I probably looked unbelievably bad. At that point I didn't care. I just wanted to get to the DDU.

I arrived just after nine and found the waiting room half full already. One or two people looked as rough as I felt. I wondered whether they'd been through forty-eight hours as hellish as those I'd just been through.

'Hi, James, how are you feeling,' the counsellor said as he came into the treatment room. He only needed to look at me to know the answer, of course, but I appreciated his concern.

'Not great,' I said.

'Well, you've done well do get through the last two days. That's a huge step you've taken,' he smiled.

He checked me over and got me to give a urine sample. He then gave me a tablet of Subutex and scribbled out a new prescription.

'That should make you feel a lot better,' he said. 'Now let's start easing you off this – and out of this place completely.'

I stayed there for a while to make sure the new medication didn't have any odd side effects. It didn't. Quite the opposite in fact, it made me feel a thousand times better.

By the time I had got back to Tottenham I felt completely transformed. It was a different feeling from what I'd experienced on methadone. The world seemed more vivid. I felt like I could see, hear and smell more clearly. Colours were brighter. Sounds were crisper. It was weird. It may sound strange, but I felt more alive again.

I stopped on the way and bought Bob a couple of new flavoured Sheba pouches that had come on to the market. I also bought him a little toy, a squeezy mouse.

Back at the flat I made a huge fuss of him.

'We did it mate,' I said. 'We did it.'

The sense of achievement was incredible. Over the next few days, the transformation in my health and life in general was huge. It was as if someone had drawn back the curtains and shed some sunlight into my life.

Of course, in a way, someone had.

Chapter 18

Homeward Bound

I didn't think Bob and I could have become closer, but the experience we'd just been through together tightened our bond even more. In the days that followed, he stuck to me like a limpet, almost watching over me in case I had some kind of relapse.

There was no danger of that, however. I felt better than I had done in years. The thought of returning to the dark dependencies of the past made me shiver. I had come too far now to turn back.

I decided to celebrate my breakthrough by doing up the flat a little bit. So Bob and I put in a few extra hours each day outside the tube station and then used the proceeds to buy some paint, a few cushions and a couple of prints to put on the wall.

I then went along to a good second-hand furniture

shop in Tottenham and bought a nice new sofa. It was a burgundy red, heavy-duty fabric, with a bit of luck the sort of material that would be able to resist Bob's claws. The old one was knackered, partly down to natural wear and tear, but also because of Bob's habit of scratching at its legs and base. Bob was banned from scratching the new one.

As the weeks passed and the nights turned even darker and colder, we spent more and more time curled up on the new sofa. I was already looking forward to a nice Christmas for me and Bob, although, as it turned out, that was a little premature.

It wasn't often that I got post apart from bills, so when I saw a letter in my mailbox in the hallway of the flats one morning in early November 2008, I immediately noticed it. It was an airmail envelope and had a postmark – Tasmania, Australia.

It was from my mother.

We'd not been in proper contact for years. However, despite the distance that had formed between us, the letter was very chatty and warm. She explained that she had moved to a new house in Tasmania. She seemed to be very happy there.

The main point of her letter, however, was to offer me an invitation. 'If I was to pay your air fares to Australia and back, would you come and see me?' she asked. She explained that I could come over the Christmas holidays. She suggested I could also take in a trip to Melbourne to see my godparents, to whom I'd once been very close.

'Let me know,' she said, signing off. 'Love, Mum.'

There would have been a time when I'd have thrown the letter straight into the dustbin. I'd have been defiant and stubborn and too proud to take a handout from my family.

But I'd changed, my head was in a different place now. I had started to see life a lot more clearly and I could almost feel some of the anger and paranoia that I'd felt in the past falling away. So I decided to give it some thought.

It wasn't a straightforward decision, far from it. There were lots of pros and cons to take into consideration.

The biggest pro, obviously, was that I'd get to see my mother again. No matter what ups and downs we'd had over the years, she was my mother and I missed her.

We'd been in contact a couple of times since I'd fallen through the cracks and ended up on the streets but I'd never been honest with her about what had really happened. We'd met once in the past ten years, when she'd come to England briefly. I'd gone to meet her in a pub near Epping Forest. I'd taken the District Line up there and spent three or four hours with her. When I'd not returned as expected after six months, I'd spun her a story about having formed a band in London and said

I wasn't going to come back to Australia while we were 'trying to make it big'.

I stuck to that story when I met her in the pub.

I hadn't felt great about telling her a pack of lies, but I didn't have the courage or the strength to tell her that I was sleeping rough, hooked on heroin and basically wasting my life away.

I had no idea whether she believed me or not. At that point in my life, I really didn't care.

We'd talked occasionally after that, but frequently I would go for months on end without making contact, which had obviously caused her a lot of grief.

She'd gone to amazing lengths to get hold of me at times. I hadn't thought to ring her when the 7/7 bombings happened in London in July 2005, I was – thankfully – nowhere near the blasts, but – stuck on the other side of the world – my mother had no idea that I was all right. Nick, whom she was still with, was serving in the police force in Tasmania at the time. Somehow he managed to persuade a member of the Met to do him and my mum a favour. They looked me up on their records and sent a couple of cops round to my B&B in Dalston one morning.

They scared the living daylights out of me when they arrived banging on the doors.

'Don't worry mate, you haven't done anything wrong,' one of them said when I opened the door, looking petrified probably. 'There are just a couple of people on the other side of the world who want to know you are alive.'

I had been tempted to make a joke and say that they'd almost given me a heart attack but I decided against it. They didn't look like they were that pleased to have been given the job of checking up on me.

I contacted Mum and reassured her that I was OK. Again, I hadn't even considered that somebody else might have been concerned about me. I didn't think that way at that time. I was on my own and concerned only with my own survival. But now I'd changed.

After all the years of neglect and deception, it would be a chance to make it up to her and to put the record straight. I felt like I needed to do that.

The other obvious positive was that I'd get to have a decent holiday in the sun, something that I had been deprived of for years living in London and working mostly in the evenings. I still felt drained by the experience of switching to my new medication and knew that a few weeks in a nice environment would do me the power of good. My mother told me she was living on a little farm way out in the middle of nowhere, near a river. It sounded idyllic. Australia, or more specifically, the Australian landscape, had always occupied a special place in my heart. Reconnecting with it would be good for my soul.

The list of pros were long. The list of cons, however, was even longer. And at the top of the list was my biggest concern of all: Bob. Who would look after him? How could I be sure he'd be there waiting for me when I got back? Did I actually want to be separated from my soulmate for weeks on end?

The answer to the first question presented itself almost immediately.

The moment I mentioned it Belle volunteered to look after him at her flat. I knew she was totally trustworthy and would take care of him. But I still wondered what the effect would be on him.

The other big concern was money. My mother might have been offering to pay for my fare, but I still wouldn't be allowed into Australia without any money. I did some digging around and found that I'd need at least £500 in cash to gain admittance.

I spent a few days weighing up both sides of the argument but eventually decided I'd go. Why not? A change of scenery and some sunshine would do me good.

I had a lot to do. For a start I had to get a new passport, which wasn't easy given the way my life had disintegrated in recent years. A social worker gave me a hand and helped me organise the necessary paperwork, including a birth certificate.

I then had to sort out the flights. The best deal by far was to fly with Air China to Beijing and then down to Melbourne. It was a much longer journey and involved a lengthy stop-off in Beijing. But it was way cheaper than anything else on the market. My mother had given me an email address by now. I sent her an email with all the details, including my new passport number. A few days later I got a confirmation email from the website through which my mother had booked the tickets. I was on my way.

All I had to do now was raise £500. Easy.

The flight I'd found was heading to Australia in the first week of December. So for the next few weeks, I worked every hour of the day in all weather. Bob came with me most days, although I left him at home when it was raining heavily. I knew he didn't like it and I didn't want to risk him catching a chill or getting ill before I went away. There was no way I'd be able to go to Australia knowing he was ill again.

I was soon saving up a bit of cash, which I kept in a little tea caddy I'd found. Slowly but surely it began to fill up. As my departure date loomed into view, I had enough to make the trip.

I headed to Heathrow with a heavy heart. I'd said goodbye to Bob at Belle's flat. He'd not looked too concerned, but then he had no idea I was going to be away for the best part of six weeks. I knew he'd be safe with Belle but it still didn't stop me fretting. I really had become a paranoid parent.

If I'd imagined the trip to Australia was going to be a nice, relaxing adventure I was sorely mistaken. The thirty-six hours or so it took me was an absolute nightmare.

It started quietly enough. The Air China flight to Beijing took eleven hours and was uneventful. I watched the in-flight movie and had a meal but I found it hard to sleep because I wasn't feeling fantastic. It was partly because of my medication but partly also because of the damp London weather. Maybe I'd spent too many hours selling the *Big Issue* in the pouring rain. I had a horrendous cold and kept sneezing all the way through the flight. I got a few funny looks from the air steward-esses and some of my fellow passengers when I had a bad attack, but thought nothing of it until we landed in Beijing.

As we taxied towards the terminal, there was an announcement from the captain over the tannoy. It was in Chinese first but there was then an English transla-tion. It basically said that we should stay in our seats until we were asked to leave the plane.

'Odd,' I thought.

The next thing I saw was two uniformed Chinese officials wearing facemasks. They were walking down the aisle – straight towards me. When they got to me, one of them produced a thermometer.

An air stewardess was standing there to translate. 'These men are from the Chinese government. They need to take your temperature,' she said.

'OK,' I said, sensing this wasn't the time to argue.

I opened wide and sat there while one of the offi-cials kept looking at his watch. After they'd muttered something in Chinese the air hostess said: 'You need to go with these men to undergo some routine medical checks.'

It was 2008 and we were at the height of the swine flu scare. China, in particular, was being incredibly nervous about it. I'd watched a report on the news a few days earlier in which they'd talked about the way people were being turned away from China if there was the slightest hint of them being infected. A lot of people were being placed in quarantine and held there for days.

So I was a bit apprehensive as I walked off with them. I had visions of me being holed up in some Chinese isolation ward for a month.

They ran all sorts of tests on me, from blood tests to swabs. They probably found all sorts of interesting things – but they found no trace of swine flu, SARS or anything else contagious. After a couple of hours, a mildly apologetic official told me that I was free to go.

The only problem was that I now had to make my way back to my connecting flight and I was lost inside the humongous, hangar-like space that is Beijing airport.

I had about three hours to find my luggage and my connecting flight. It had been years since I'd spent any time in an airport terminal. I'd forgotten how big and soulless they were, and this one was especially so. I had to take a train from one part of Terminal 3 to another part.

After a few wrong turns I found my connecting flight less than an hour before it was due to take off.

I breathed a huge sigh of relief when I sank into my seat on the plane and slept like a log on the flight to

Melbourne, mainly through exhaustion. But then at Melbourne I hit another snag.

As I made my way through the customs area I was suddenly aware of a Labrador dog sniffing animatedly at my luggage.

'Excuse me, sir, would you mind coming this way with us,' a customs guard said.

'Oh God,' I thought. 'I'm never going to get to meet my mother.'

I was taken to an inspection room where they started going through my stuff. They then ran an electric drug detector over my bag. I could tell there was a problem from the expressions on their faces.

'I'm afraid your luggage has tested positive for cocaine,' the guard said.

I was gobsmacked. I had no idea how that was possible. I didn't take cocaine and didn't really know anyone who did. None of my friends could afford it.

As it turned out, they said that it wasn't illegal for me to have traces of it for private use.

'If you are a casual user and it's for private consumption all you have to do is tell us and you can be on your way,' the guard said.

I explained my situation. 'I'm on a drug recovery programme so I don't take anything casually,' I said. I then showed them a letter I had from my doctor explaining why I was on Subutex.

Eventually they had to relent. They gave me a final pat down and released me. By the time I emerged from the customs area, almost an hour had passed. I had to get another flight down to Tasmania, which took another few hours. By the time I got there, it was early evening and I was utterly exhausted.

Seeing my mother was wonderful. She was waiting at the airport in Tasmania and gave me a couple of really long hugs. She was crying. She was pleased to see me alive, I think.

I was really happy to see her too although I didn't cry.

The cottage was every bit as lovely as she'd described it in her letter. It was a big, airy bungalow with huge garden space at the back. It was surrounded by farm-land with a river running by the bottom of her land. It was a very peaceful, picturesque place. Over the next month I just hung out there, relaxing, recovering and rebooting myself.

Within a couple of weeks I felt like a different person. The anxieties of London were – literally – thousands of miles away, just over ten thousand, to be precise. My mum's maternal instincts kicked in and she made sure I was fed well. I could feel my strength returning. I could also sense me and my mother were repairing our relationship.

At first we didn't talk in great depth about things, but in time I began to open up. Then one night as we sat on the veranda, watching the sun go down, I had a couple of drinks and suddenly it all came out. It wasn't a big confession, there was no Hollywood drama. I just talked . . . and talked.

The emotional floodgates had been waiting to burst open for a while now. For years I had used drugs to escape from my emotions, in fact to make sure I didn't have any. Slowly but surely I'd changed that. And now my emotions were coming back.

As I explained some of the lows I'd been through over the last ten years, my mother looked horrified, as any parent would have done.

'I guessed you weren't doing so great when I saw you, but I never guessed it was that bad,' she said, close to tears.

At times she just sat there with her head in her hands muttering the word 'why' every now and again.

'Why didn't you tell me you'd lost your passport?'

'Why didn't you call me and ask for help?'

'Why didn't you contact your father?'

Inevitably, she blamed herself for it. She said she felt like she'd let me down, but I told her I didn't blame her. The reality was that I had left myself down. Ultimately, there was no one else to blame.

'You didn't decide to sleep in cardboard boxes and get off your face on smack every night. I did,' I said at one point. That set her off crying as well.

Once we'd broken the ice, so to speak, we talked much more easily. We talked a little about the past and my childhood in Australia and England. I felt comfortable being honest with her. I said that I'd felt she'd been a distant figure when I'd been younger and that being raised by nannies and moving around a lot had had an impact on me.

Naturally that upset her, but she argued that she'd been trying to provide an income for us, to keep a roof over our heads. I took her point, but I still wished she'd been there more for me.

We laughed a lot too; it wasn't all dark conversation. We admitted how similar we were and chuckled at some of the arguments we used to have when I was a teenager.

She admitted that there had been a big conflict of personality there.

'I'm a strong personality and so are you. That's where you get it from,' she said.

But we spent most of the time talking about the present rather than the past. She asked me all sorts of questions about the rehab process I'd been through and what I was hoping to achieve now that I was almost clean. I explained that it was still a case of taking one step at a time, but that, with luck, I'd be totally clean within a year or so. Sometimes she just simply listened, which was something she hadn't always done. And so did I. I think we both learned a lot more about each other, not least the fact that deep down we were very similar, which is why we clashed so much when I was younger.

During those long chats, I often talked about Bob. I'd brought a photo of him with me, which I showed everyone and anyone who took an interest.

'He looks a smart cookie,' my mother smiled when she saw it.

'Oh, he is,' I said, beaming with pride. 'I don't know where I'd been now if it wasn't for Bob.'

Spending time in Australia was great. It allowed me to clear my mind. It also allowed me to take stock of where I was – and where I wanted to go from here.

There was a part of me that hankered to move back. I had family here. There was more of a support network than I had in London, certainly. But I kept thinking about Bob and the fact that he'd be as lost without me as I'd be without him. I didn't take the idea seriously for very long. By the time I'd started my sixth week in Australia, I was mentally already on the plane back to England.

I said goodbye to my mother properly this time. She came to the airport with me and waved me off on my way to Melbourne, where I was going to spend some time with my godparents. They had been quite signifi- cant figures in my youth. They had owned what was then the biggest private telecom company in Australia and were the first to form a radio pager company in the country so had a lot of money at one point. As a boy, naturally, I used to love spending time at the mansion they'd built in Melbourne. I even lived with them for a while when me and my mother weren't getting on very well.

Their reaction to my story was the same as my mother's – they were shocked.

They offered to help me out financially and even to find me work in Australia. But again I had to explain that I had responsibilities back in London.

The journey back was much less eventful than the outward trip. I felt much better, fitter and healthier and probably looked it so I didn't attract so much attention at customs or immigration control. I was so rested and revived by my time in Australia that I slept for most of the trip.

I was dying to see Bob again, although a part of me was concerned that he might have changed or even forgotten me. I needn't have had any concerns.

The minute I walked into Belle's flat his tail popped up and he bounced off her sofa and ran up to me. I'd brought him back a few little presents, a couple of stuffed kangaroo toys. He was soon clawing away at one of them. As we headed home that evening, he immediately scampered up my arm and on to my shoulders as usual. In an instant the emotional and physical journey I'd made to the other side of the world was forgotten. It was me and Bob against the world once more. It was as if I'd never been away.

Chapter 19

The Stationmaster

Australia had been great, it had given me a boost both physically and emotionally. Back in London, I felt stronger and more sure of myself than I'd felt in years. Being reunited with Bob had lifted my spirits even more. Without him, a little part of me had been missing down in Tasmania. Now I felt whole again.

We were soon back into the old routine, sharing every aspect of our day-to-day life. Even now, after almost two years together, he remained a constant source of surprise to me.

I'd talked endlessly about Bob while I was away, telling everyone how smart he was. There had been times, I'm sure, when people looked at me as if I was crazy. 'A cat can't be that smart,' I'm sure they were thinking.

A couple of weeks after I got back, however, I realised that I'd been underselling him.

Doing his business had always been a bit of a chore for Bob. He'd never taken to the litter trays that I'd bought him. I still had a few packs of them in the cupboard gathering dust. They'd been there since day one.

It was a real palaver having to go all the way down five flights of stairs and out into the grounds to do his business every single time he needed to go to the loo. I'd noticed in the past few months, before I'd gone to Australia and again now that I was back, that he wasn't going to the toilet downstairs so often any more.

For a while I'd wondered whether it might be a medical problem and I'd taken him to the Blue Cross truck on Islington Green to have him checked out. The vets found nothing untoward and suggested that it might just be a change in his metabolism as he got older.

The explanation was actually far less scientific – and a lot more funny – than that. One morning, soon after I'd got back from Australia, I woke up really early, around 6.30a.m. My body clock was still all over the place. I hauled myself out of bed and stepped, bleary-eyed towards the toilet. The door was half open and I could hear a light, tinkling sort of noise. *Weird*, I thought. I half expected to find someone had sneaked into the flat to use the toilet, but when I gently nudged open the door I was greeted by a sight that left me totally speechless: Bob was squatting on the toilet seat.

It was just like that scene in the movie *Meet the Parents* when Robert De Niro's cat, Mr Jinxie, does the same thing. Except in this case, it was absolutely real. Bob had obviously decided that going to the toilet downstairs was too much of a hassle. So, having seen me go to the toilet a few times in the past three years, he'd worked out what he needed to do and simply mimicked me.

When he saw me staring at him, Bob just fired me one of his withering looks, as if to say: 'What are you looking at? I'm only going to the loo, what could be more normal than that?' He was right of course. Why was I surprised at anything Bob did? He was capable of anything, surely I knew that already.

Our absence for a few weeks had definitely been noticed by a lot of the locals at the Angel. During our first week back on the pitch a succession of people came up to us with big smiles. They'd say things like: 'Ah, you're back' or 'I thought you'd won the lottery.' They were almost all genuine, warm-hearted welcomes.

One lady dropped off a card with 'We Missed You' written on it. It felt great to be 'home'.

As ever, of course, there were also one or two who weren't so pleased to see us.

One evening I found myself getting into a very heated argument with a Chinese lady. I'd noticed her before, looking rather disapprovingly at me and Bob. This time she approached me, waving her finger at me as she did so.

'This not right, this not right,' she said angrily.

'Sorry, what's not right?' I said, genuinely baffled.

'This not normal for cat to be like this,' she went on. 'Him too quiet, you drug him. You drug cat.'

That was the point at which I had to take issue with her.

It was far from the first time that someone had insinuated this. Back in Covent Garden when we'd been busking, a very snotty, professorial guy had stopped one day and told me in no uncertain terms that he was 'on to me'.

'I know what you're doing. And I think I know what you're giving him to stay so docile and obedient,' he said, a bit too pleased with himself.

'And what would that be then, sir?' I said.

'Ah, that would give you the advantage and you would be able to change to something else,' he said, a bit taken aback that I was challenging him.

'No, come on, you've made an accusation, now back it up,' I said stepping up my defence.

He had disappeared into thin air fairly quickly, probably quite wisely because I think I might have planted one on him if he'd carried on like that.

The Chinese woman was basically making the same accusation. So I gave her the same defence.

'What do you think I am giving him that makes him like that?' I said.

'I don't know,' she said. 'But you giving him something.'

'Well, if I was drugging him, why would he hang around with me every day? Why wouldn't he try and make a run for it when he got the chance? I can't drug him in front of everyone.'

'Psssh,' she said, waving her arms at me dismissively and turning on her heels. 'It not right, it not right,' she said once more as she melted into the crowd.

This was a reality that I'd accepted a long time ago. I knew there were always going to be some people who were suspicious that I was mistreating Bob, didn't like cats or simply didn't like the fact a *Big Issue* seller had a cat rather than a dog, which was far more common. A couple of weeks after the row with the Chinese lady, I had another confrontation, a very different one this time.

Since the early days in Covent Garden, I'd regularly been offered money for Bob. Every now and again someone would come up to me and ask 'How much for your cat?' I'd usually tell them to go forth and multiply.

Up here at the Angel I'd heard it again, from one lady in particular. She had been to see me several times, each time chatting away before getting to the point of her visit.

'Look, James,' she would say. 'I don't think Bob should be out on the streets, I think he should be in a nice, warm home living a better life.'

Each time she'd end the conversation with a question along the lines of: 'So how much do you want for him?'

I'd rebuff her each time, at which point she'd start throwing figures at me. She'd started at one hundred pounds, then gone up to five hundred.

Most recently she'd come up to me one evening and said: 'I'll give you a thousand pounds for him.'

I'd just looked at her and said: 'Do you have children?'

'Erm, yes, as a matter of fact I do,' she spluttered, a bit thrown.

'You do, OK. How much for your youngest child?'

'What are you talking about?'

'How much for your youngest child?'

'I hardly think that's got anything to do—'

I cut her off. 'Actually, I think it does have a lot to do with it. As far as I'm concerned Bob is my child, he's my baby. And for you to ask me whether I'd sell him is *exactly* the same as me asking you how much you want for your youngest child.'

She'd just stormed off. I never saw her again.

The attitude of the tube station staff was the complete polar opposite of this. One day I was talking to one of the ticket inspectors, Davika. She loved Bob and was chuckling at the way countless people were stopping and talking to him and taking his picture.

'He's putting Angel tube station on the map, isn't he?' she laughed.

'He is, you should put him on the staff, like that cat in Japan who is a stationmaster. He even wears a hat,' I said.

'I'm not sure we've got any vacancies,' she giggled.

'Well, you should at least give him an ID card or something,' I joked.

She looked at me with a thoughtful look on her face and went away. I thought nothing more about it.

A couple of weeks later Bob and I were sitting outside the station one evening when Davika appeared again. She had a big grin on her face. I was immediately suspicious.

'What's up?' I said.

'Nothing, I just wanted to give Bob this,' she smiled. She then produced a laminated travel card with Bob's photograph on it.

'That's fantastic,' I said.

'I got the picture off the Internet,' she said to my slight amazement. What the hell was Bob doing on the Internet?

'So what does it actually mean?' I said.

'It means that he can travel as a passenger for free on the underground,' she laughed.

'I thought that cats went free anyway?' I smiled.

'Well, it actually means we are all very fond of him. We think of him as part of the family.'

It took a lot of willpower to stop myself from bursting into tears.

Chapter 20
The Longest Night

The spring of 2009 should have been on its way, but the evenings remained dark and dismal. By the time I finished selling the *Big Issue* at Angel around seven o'clock most evenings, dusk was already descending and the street-lights were blazing into life, as were the pavements.

After being quiet during the early months of the year when there were fewer tourists around, the Angel had suddenly come alive. The early evening rush hour was as busy as I'd ever seen it with what seemed like hundreds of thousands of people pouring in and out of the tube station.

Maybe it was the well-heeled crowds. The change had attracted other people to the area as well – unfortunately.

Living on the streets of London gives you really well-developed radar when it comes to sussing out people whom you want to avoid at all costs. It was around 6.30 or 7p.m., during the busiest part of the day for me, when a guy who had set off that radar a few times loomed into view.

I'd seen him once or twice before, luckily from a distance. He was a really rough-looking character. I know I wasn't exactly the most well-groomed guy on the streets of London, but this guy was really scraggy. He looked like he was sleeping rough. His skin was all red and blotchy and his clothes were smeared in dirt. What really stuck out about him, however, was his dog, a giant Rottweiler. It was black with brown markings and from the moment I first saw it I could tell immediately that it was aggressive. The sight of them walking around together reminded me of an old drawing of Bill Sikes and his dog Bull's Eye in *Oliver Twist*. You could tell they were never far away from trouble.

The dog was with him this evening as he arrived near the tube station entrance and sat down to talk to some other shifty-looking characters, who had been sitting there drinking lager for an hour or more. I didn't like the look of them at all.

Almost immediately I could see that the Rottweiler had spotted Bob and was straining at the lead, dying to come and have a go at him. The guy seemed to have the big dog under control, but it was by no means certain that it would stay that way. He seemed more interested in talking to these other guys – and getting stuck into their lager.

As it happened, I was in the process of packing up for the evening in any case. The gang's arrival only cemented that decision in my mind. I had a bad feeling about them – and the dog. I wanted to get myself and Bob as far away from them as possible.

I began gathering up my *Big Issue*s and placing my other bits and pieces in my rucksack. All of a sudden I heard this really loud, piercing bark. What happened next seemed like it was in slow motion, a bad action scene from a bad action movie.

I turned round to see a flash of black and brown heading towards me and Bob. The guy had obviously not tethered the lead correctly. The Rottweiler was on the loose. My first instinctive reaction was to protect Bob, so I just jumped in front of the dog. Before I knew it he'd run into me, bowling me over. As I fell I managed to wrap my arms around the dog and we ended up on the floor, wrestling. I was shouting and swearing, trying to get a good grip on its head so that it couldn't bite me, but the dog was simply too strong.

Rottweilers are powerful dogs and I have no doubt that if the fight had gone on a few seconds longer, I'd have come off second best. God only knows what sorts of wounds it would have inflicted. Fortunately I was suddenly aware of another voice shouting and I felt the power of the dog waning as it was pulled in another direction.

'Come here, you f*****,' the owner was shouting, pulling as hard as he could on the lead. He then walloped the dog across the head with something blunt. I don't know what it was but the sound was sickening. In different circumstances I'd have been worried for the dog's welfare, but my main priority was Bob. He must have been terrified by what had just happened. I turned to check on him but found the spot where he'd been sitting empty. I spun around 360 degrees to see if someone had perhaps picked him up to protect him but there was no sign of him. He'd disappeared.

Suddenly, I realised what I'd done. I had a pile of *Big Issues* a short distance away from our pitch, under a bench. Bob's lead didn't extend that far, so, in my anxiety to get away from the Rottweiler and his owner, I had unclipped the lead from my belt. It had only been for a second or two while I gathered everything together, but that had been long enough. That was my big mistake. The Rottweiler must have been watching it all, and Bob, and must have spotted this. That's why he'd broken free and charged at us at that precise moment.

I was immediately thrown into a blind panic.

A few people had gathered around to ask me if I was OK.

'I'm fine. Anyone seen Bob?' I said, even though I wasn't actually fine. I'd hurt myself when the Rottweiler had knocked me over and I had cuts to my hands where he'd bitten me. At that moment a regular customer of mine appeared, a middle-aged lady who often gave Bob treats. She had clearly seen the commotion and came over.

'I just saw Bob, running off in the direction of Camden Passage,' she said. 'I tried to grab his lead but he was too quick.'

'Thanks,' I said, as I just grabbed my rucksack and ran, my chest pounding.

My mind immediately flashed back to the time he'd run off in Piccadilly Circus. For some reason though, this felt like a more serious situation. Back then he had basically been spooked by a man in a funny outfit. This time he'd been in real physical danger. If I hadn't intervened the Rottweiler would almost certainly have attacked him. Who knows what impact the sight of the charging dog had had on him? Perhaps it was a reminder of something he'd seen in his past? I had no idea what he must be feeling, although I guessed he was as frightened and distressed as me.

I ran straight towards Camden Passage, dodging the early evening crowds milling around the pubs, bars and restaurants.

'Bob, Bob,' I kept calling, drawing looks from passers-by. 'Anyone seen a ginger tom running this way with his lead trailing after him?' I asked a group of people standing outside the main pub in the passage.

They all just shrugged their shoulders.

I had hoped that, just as he had done that time back in Piccadilly Circus, Bob would find refuge in a shop. But by now most of them were shuttered up for the evening. It was only the bars, restaurants and cafés that were open. As I made my way down the narrow lane and asked around, I was greeted by nothing but shakes of the head. If he'd gone beyond Camden Passage heading north, then he would have ended up on Essex Road, the main road leading to Dalston and beyond. He'd walked part of that route before but never at night or on his own.

I was beginning to despair when I met a woman towards the end of the Passage, a short distance before it opens out opposite Islington Green. She pointed down the road.

'I saw a cat running down the road that way,' she said. 'It was going like a rocket, it didn't look like it was going to stop. It was veering towards the main road, it looked like it was thinking about crossing.'

At the end of the passage, I emerged out on to the open street and scanned the area. Bob was fond of Islington Green and often stopped to do his business there. It was also where the Blue Cross vans would park. It was worth a look. I quickly crossed the road and ran into the small, enclosed grassy area. There were some bushes there where he often rummaged around. I knelt down and looked inside. Even though the light had gone and I was barely able to see my hand in front of me, I hoped against hope that I might see a pair of bright eyes staring back at me.

'Bob, Bob, are you here mate?' But there was nothing.

I walked down to the other corner of the enclosed Green and shouted a couple more times. But, apart from groans from a couple of drunks who were sitting on one of the benches, all I could hear was the insistent droning of the traffic.

I left the Green and found myself facing the big Waterstone's bookshop. Bob and I often popped in there and the staff there always made a fuss of him. I knew I really was clutching at straws now, but maybe he had headed there for refuge.

It was quiet inside the store and some of the staff were getting ready to shut up for the evening. There were just a few people browsing the shelves.

I recognised one of the ladies behind the till. By now I was sweating, breathing heavily and must obviously have looked agitated.

'Are you all right?' she asked.

'I've lost Bob. A dog attacked us and Bob ran off. He didn't come in here did he?'

'Oh, no,' she said, looking genuinely concerned. 'I've been here and I've not seen him. But let me ask upstairs.'

She picked up the phone and dialled to the other department.

'You haven't seen a cat up there have you?' she said. The slow, shake of her head that followed told me all I needed to know. 'I'm really sorry,' she said. 'But if we do see him we'll make sure to keep him.'

'Thanks,' I said.

It was only then, as I wandered back out of Waterstone's and into the now dark evening, that it hit me. I've lost him.

I was in bits. For the next few minutes I was in a daze. I carried on walking down Essex Road, but by now I had given up on asking in the cafés, restaurants and pubs.

This was the route we came in every day – and went home again every night. When I saw a bus bound for Tottenham, another thought formed in my frazzled mind. He couldn't have? Could he?

There was an inspector standing at one of the bus stops and I asked him whether he'd seen a cat getting on a bus. I knew Bob, he was smart enough to do it. But the guy just looked at me like I'd asked him whether he'd seen aliens getting on the number 73. He just shook his head and turned away from me.

I knew cats had a great sense of direction and have been known to make long journeys. But there was no way he was going to find his way all the way back to Tottenham. It was a good three and a half miles, through some pretty rough parts of London. We'd never walked that way, we'd only ever done it on the bus. I quickly decided that was simply a non-starter.

The next half hour or so was a rollercoaster of conflicting emotions. One minute I'd convince myself that he couldn't stray far without being found and identified. Loads of people locally knew who he was. And even if he was found by someone who didn't know him, if they were sensible they would see that he was microchipped and would know that all his data was at the national microchip centre.

No sooner had I reassured myself of that, than a stream of very different consciousness began washing over me as, all of a sudden, a nightmare series of thoughts started pinging away in my head.

This might have been what happened three years ago. This might have been how he'd come to end up in my block of flats that spring evening. This might have been the trigger for him to decide it was time to move on again. Inside I was utterly torn. The logical, sensible side of me was saying, 'He will be OK, you'll get him back.' But the wilder, more irrational side of me was saying something much bleaker. It was saying: 'He's gone, you won't see him again.' I wandered up and down Essex Road for the best part of an hour. It was now pitch dark, and the traffic was snarled up virtually all the way back to the end of Islington High Street. I was all at sea. I really didn't know what to do. Without really thinking, I just started walking down Essex Road towards Dalston. My friend Belle lived in a flat about a mile away. I'd head there.

I was walking past an alleyway when I saw a flash of a tail. It was black and thin, very different to Bob's, but I was in such a state my mind was playing tricks and I convinced myself it must be him.

'Bob,' I shouted, diving into the dark space, but there was nothing there.

Somewhere in the dark I heard a meowing sound. It didn't sound like him. After a couple of minutes, I moved on.

By now the traffic had eased off. The night suddenly fell ominously quiet. For the first time I noticed that the stars were out. It wasn't quite the Australian night sky but it was still impressive. A few weeks ago I'd been staring at the stars in Tasmania. I'd told everyone in Australia that I was coming back to care for Bob. *A fine job I've done of that*, I said, inwardly cursing myself.

For a moment or two I wondered whether my extended stay in Australia had actually been a factor in all this. Had that time apart loosened the ties between me and Bob? Had the fact that I'd been absent for six weeks made him question my commitment to him? When the Rottweiler had attacked, had he decided that he could no longer rely on me to protect him? The thought made me want to scream.

As Belle's road loomed into view I was still feeling close to tears. What was I going to do without him? I'd never find a companion like Bob again. It was then that it happened. For the first time in years I experienced an overwhelming need for a fix.

I tried to bat it away immediately, but once more my subconscious started fighting a battle of wills. Somewhere inside my head I could feel myself thinking that if I really had lost Bob, I wouldn't be able to cope, I'd have to anaesthetise myself from the grief I was already feeling.

Belle had, like me, been fighting for years. But I knew her flatmate still dabbled. The closer I got to her street, the more terrifying the thoughts in my head were becoming.

By the time I reached Belle's house, it was approaching ten o'clock. I had been wandering the streets for a couple of hours. In the distance, the sirens were wailing once more, the cops were on their way to another stabbing or punch-up in a pub. I couldn't have cared less.

As I walked up the path to the dimly lit front entrance I spotted a shape sitting quietly in the shadows to the side of the building. It was unmistakably the silhouette of a cat, but I'd given up hope by now and just assumed it was another stray, sheltering from the cold. But then I saw his face, that unmistakeable face.

'Bob.'

He let out a plaintive meow, just like the one in the hallway on the night we first met, as if to say: 'Where have you been? I've been waiting here for ages.'

I scooped him up and held him close.

'You are going to be the death of me if you keep running away like that,' I said, my mind scrambling to work out how he'd got here.

It wasn't long before it all fell into place. I felt a fool for not thinking of it sooner. He had been to Belle's flat with me several times, and spent six weeks there when I was away. It made sense that he would have come here. But how on earth had he got here? It must be a mile and a half from our pitch at the Angel. Had he walked all the way? If so, how long had he been here?

None of that mattered now. As I carried on making a fuss of him, he licked my hand, his tongue was as rough as sandpaper. He rubbed his face against mine and curled his tail.

I ran up to Belle's flat and she invited me in. My mood had been transformed from despair to delirium. I was on top of the world

Belle's flatmate was also there and said, 'Want something to celebrate?' smiling, knowingly.

'No, I'm fine thanks,' I said, tugging on Bob as he scratched playfully at my hand, and looking over at Belle. 'Just a beer would be great.'

Bob didn't need drugs to get through the night. He just needed his companion: me. And at that moment I decided that was all I needed too. All I needed was Bob. Not just tonight, but for as long as I had the privilege of having him in my life.

Chapter 21
Bob, The *Big Issue* Cat

As the March sun disappeared and dusk descended over the Angel, London was winding itself up for the evening once more. The traffic was already thick on Islington High Street and the honking of horns was building into a cacophony of noise. The pavements were busy too, with a stream of people flowing in and out of the station concourse. The rush hour was under way and living up to its name as usual. Everyone was in a rush to get somewhere it seemed. Well, not quite everyone.

I was checking that I had enough papers left to cope with the surge of activity I knew was about to arrive when I saw out of the corner of my eye that a group of kids had gathered around us. They were teenagers I guessed, three boys and a couple of girls. They looked South American or maybe Spanish or Portuguese.

There was nothing unusual about this. It wasn't quite Covent Garden, Leicester Square or Piccadilly Circus, but Islington had its fair share of tourists and Bob was a magnet for them. Barely a day went by without him being surrounded by an excitable group of youths like this.

What was different this evening, however, was the way they were animatedly pointing and talking about him.

'Ah, *si* Bob,' said one teenage girl, talking what I guessed was Spanish.

'*Si, si.* Bob the Beeg Issew Cat,' said another.

Weird, I thought to myself when I realised what she'd said. *How do they know his name is Bob? He doesn't wear a name tag. And what do they mean by the* Big Issue *Cat?*

My curiosity soon got the better of me.

'Sorry, I hope you don't mind me asking, but how do you know Bob?' I said, in the hope that one of them spoke decent English. My Spanish was almost non-existent.

Fortunately one of them, a young boy, replied. 'Oh, we see him on YouTube,' he smiled. 'Bob is very popular, yes?'

'Is he?' I said. 'Someone told me he was on YouTube, but I've got no idea how many people watch it.'

'Many people, I think,' he smiled.

'Where are you from?'

'*España*, Spain.'

'So Bob's popular in Spain?'

'*Si, si,*' another one of the boys said when the boy translated back our conversation. '*Bob es una estrella en España.*'

'Sorry, what did he say?' I asked the boy.

'He says that Bob is a star in Spain.'

I was shocked.

I knew that lots of people had taken photographs of Bob over the years, both while I was busking and now that I was selling the *Big Issue*. I'd jokingly wondered once whether he should be put forward for the *Guinness Book of Records*: the world's most photographed cat.

A couple of people had filmed him too, some with their phones, others with proper video cameras. I started casting my mind back over those that had shot footage of him in recent months. Who could have shot a film that was now on YouTube? There were a couple of obvious candidates, but I made a note to check it out at the first opportunity.

The following morning I headed down to the local library with Bob and booked myself online.

I punched in the search terms: Bob Big Issue Cat. Sure enough, there was a link to YouTube, which I clicked on. To my surprise there was not one, but two films there.

'Hey Bob, look, he was right. You are a star on YouTube.'

He hadn't been terribly interested until that point. It wasn't Channel Four racing, after all. But when I clicked on the first video and saw and heard myself talking he jumped on to the keyboard and popped his face right up against the screen.

As I watched the first film, which was called 'Bobcat and I', the memory came back to me. I'd been approached by a film student. He'd followed me around for a while back during the days when we were selling the *Big Issue* around Neal Street. There was nice footage of us there and of us getting on the bus and walking the streets. Watching the film it gave a pretty good summary of the day-to-day life of a *Big Issue* seller. There were clips of people fussing over Bob, but also a sequence where I was confronted by some guys who didn't believe he was a 'tame' cat. They belonged to the same group of people who thought I was drugging him.

The other video had been filmed more recently around the Angel by a Russian guy. I clicked on the link for that and saw that he'd called his film 'Bob The *Big Issue* Cat'. This must have been the one that the Spanish students had seen. I could see that it had had tens of thousands of hits. I was gobsmacked.

The feeling that Bob was becoming some kind of celebrity had been building for a while. Every now and again someone would say: 'Ah, is that Bob? I've heard about him.' Or 'Is this the famous Bobcat?' I'd always assumed it was through word of mouth. Then, a few weeks before meeting the Spanish teenagers, we had featured in a local newspaper, the *Islington Tribune*. I'd even been approached by an American lady, an agent, who asked me whether I'd thought about writing a book about me and Bob. As if!

The Spanish teenagers made me realise that it had begun to morph into something much more than local celebrity. Bob was becoming a feline star.

As I headed towards the bus stop and absorbed what I had just discovered, I couldn't help smiling. On one of the films I had said that Bob had saved my life. When I first heard it I thought it sounded a bit crass, a bit of an exaggeration too. But as I walked along the road and put it all into perspective it began to sink in: it was true, he really had.

In the two years since I'd found him sitting in that half-lit hallway, he had transformed my world. Back then I'd been a recovering heroin addict living a hand-to-mouth existence. I was in my late twenties and yet I had no real direction or purpose in life beyond survival. I'd lost contact with my family and barely had a friend in the world. Not to put too fine a point on it, my life was a total mess. All that had changed.

My trip to Australia hadn't made up for the difficulties of the past, but it had brought me and my mother back together again. The wounds were being healed. I had the feeling we were going to become close again. My battle with drugs was finally drawing to a close, or at least, I hoped it was. The amount of Subutex I had to take was diminishing steadily. The day when I wouldn't have to take it all was looming into view on the horizon. I could finally see an end to my addiction. There had been times when I'd never imagined that was possible.

Most of all, I'd finally laid down some roots. It might not have seemed much to most people, but my little flat in Tottenham had given me the kind of security and stability that I'd always secretly craved. I'd never lived for so long in the same place. There was no doubt in my mind that would not have happened if it hadn't been for Bob.

I was raised as a churchgoer but I wasn't a practising Christian. I wasn't an agnostic or atheist either. My view is that we should all take a bit from every religion and philosophy. I'm not a Buddhist but I like Buddhist philosophies, in particular. They give you a very good structure that you can build your life around. For instance, I definitely believe in karma, the idea that what goes around, comes around. I wondered whether Bob was my reward for having done something good, somewhere in my troubled life.

I also wondered sometimes whether Bob and I had known each other in a previous life. The way we bonded together, the instant connection that we made, that was very unusual. Someone said to me once that we were the reincarnation of Dick Whittington and his cat. Except the roles had been reversed this time around, Dick Whittington had come back as Bob – and I was

his companion. I didn't have a problem wit
happy to think of him in that way. Bob is
and the one who has guided me towards
and a better – way of life. He doesn't dem
complicated or unrealistic in return. He
to take care of him. And that's what I do.

I knew the road ahead wouldn't be sm
sure to face our problems here and the
working on the streets of London, after a
going to be easy. But as long as we were
a feeling it was going to be fine.

Everybody needs a break, everybod
second chance. Bob and I had taken o

Acknowledgements

Writing this book has been an amazing collaborative experience, one in which so many people have played their part.

First and foremost I'd like to thank my family, and my mum and dad in particular, for giving me the sheer bloody-minded determination that has kept me going through some dark times in my life. I'd also like to thank my godparents, Terry and Merilyn Winters, for being such great friends to me.

On the streets of London, so many people have shown kindness to me over the years, but I'd like to single out Sam, Tom, Lee and Rita, the *Big Issue* co-ordinators who have been so generous to me. I'd also like to thank outreach workers Kevin and Chris for their compassion and understanding. Thanks also the Blue Cross and

RSPCA for their valuable advice and Davika, Leanne and the rest of the staff at Angel tube station who have been so supportive of me and Bob.

I'd also like to thank Food For Thought and Pix in Neal Street who have always offered me and Bob a warm cup of tea and a saucer of milk, as well as Daryl at Diamond Jacks in Soho and Paul and Den the cobblers who have always been my good friends. I'd like also to mention Pete Watkins at Corrupt Drive Records, DJ Cavey Nik at Mosaic Homes and Ron Richardson.

This book would never have happened if it hadn't been for my agent Mary Pachnos. It was she who first approached me with the idea. It sounded pretty crazy at the time, and I'd never have been able to get it all down and turned into a coherent story without the help of her and the writer Garry Jenkins. So a heart-felt thanks to both Mary and Garry. At my publishers, Hodder & Stoughton, I'd like to thank Rowena Webb, Ciara Foley, Emma Knight and the rest of the brilliant team there. Thanks also to Alan and the staff at Waterstone's in Islington who even let me and Garry work on the book in the quiet upstairs. And a big thank you to Kitty, who without her constant support we'd both be lost.

Finally I'd like to thank Scott Hartford-Davis and the Dalai Lama who have, in recent years, given me a great philosophy by which to live my life, and Leigh Ann, who is in my thoughts.

Last, and most definitely not least, of course, I have to thank the little fellow who came into my life in 2007 and who – from the moment I befriended him – has proven to be such a positive, life-changing force in my life. Everyone deserves a friend like Bob. I have been very fortunate indeed to have found one . . .

James Bowen
London, January 2012

The World According To Bob

JAMES BOWEN

For all those who devote their lives to helping the homeless and animals in distress

Contents

There is something about the presence of a cat ...
that seems to take the bite out of being alone.

Louis Camuti

If man could be crossed with the cat, it would improve
man but deteriorate the cat.

Mark Twain

Chapter 1

The Nightwatchman

It had been one of those days, the type where anything that could go wrong had gone wrong.

It had begun when my alarm had failed to go off and I'd overslept which meant that my cat, Bob, and I were already running late when we set off to catch the bus near my flat in Tottenham, north London on our way to Islington, where I sold the homeless magazine *The Big Issue*. We were barely five minutes into our journey when things went from bad to worse.

Bob was sitting in his usual position, half-asleep on the seat next to me when he suddenly lifted his head, looking around suspiciously. In the two years since I'd met him, Bob's ability to sniff trouble had been pretty near infallible. Within moments the bus was filled with an acrid, burning smell and the panicked driver was announcing that our journey was being 'terminated' and we all had to get off. 'Immediately.'

It wasn't quite the evacuation of the *Titanic*, but the bus was three quarters full so there was a lot of chaotic pushing and jostling. Bob didn't seem in a rush so we left them to it and were among the last to get off, which, as it turned out, was a wise decision. The bus may have smelled awful, but at least it was warm.

We had come to a halt opposite a new building site from where icy winds were whipping in at a rate of knots. I was glad that, while dashing out of my flat, I'd hurriedly wrapped a particularly thick, woollen scarf around Bob's neck.

The crisis turned out to be nothing more serious than an overheated engine but the driver had to wait for a bus company mechanic to fix it. So, amid much grumbling and complaining, about two dozen of us were left standing on the freezing cold pavement for almost half an hour while we waited for a replacement bus.

The late morning traffic was terrible, so by the time Bob and I hopped off at our destination, Islington Green, we had been on the road for more than an hour and a half. We were now seriously late. I was going to miss the lunchtime rush, one of the most lucrative times for selling the magazine.

As usual, the five minute walk to our pitch at Angel tube station was a stop-start affair. It always was when I had Bob with me. Sometimes I walked with him on a leather lead, but more often than not we travelled with him perched on my shoulders, gazing curiously out at the world, like the lookout on the prow of a ship. It wasn't something people were used to seeing every day of the week, so we could never walk more than ten yards without someone wanting to say hello and stroke him, or take a photograph. That didn't bother me at all. He was a charismatic, striking-looking fellow and I knew he relished the attention, provided it was friendly. Unfortunately, that wasn't something that could be guaranteed.

The first person to stop us today was a little Russian lady who clearly knew as much about handling cats as I did about reciting Russian poetry.

'Oh, *koschka*, so pretty,' she said, collaring us in Camden Passage, the alleyway of restaurants, bars and antique shops that runs along the southern part of Islington Green. I stopped to let her say hello properly, but she immediately reached up to Bob and tried to touch him on the nose. Not a clever move.

Bob's instant reaction was to lash out, fending her off with a wild wave of his paw and a very loud and emphatic *eeeeeow*. Fortunately he didn't scratch the lady, but he did leave her a little shaken so I had to spend a few minutes making sure she was all right.

'It OK, it OK. I only want to be friend,' she said, looking as white as a sheet. She was quite elderly and I was worried that she might keel over from a heart attack. 'You should never do that to an animal, Madam,' I told her, smiling and being as polite as possible. 'How would you react if someone tried to put their hands on your face? You're lucky he didn't scratch you.'

'I no mean to upset him,' she said.

I felt a bit sorry for her.

'Come on you two, let's be friends,' I said, trying to act as the peacemaker.

Bob was reluctant at first. He'd made his mind up. But he eventually relented, allowing her to run her hand, very gently, along the back of his neck. The lady was very apologetic – and very hard to shake off.

'I very sorry, very sorry,' she kept saying.

'No problem,' I said, by now desperate to get going.

When we finally extricated ourselves and got to the tube station I put my rucksack on the pavement so that Bob could spread out on it – our regular routine – then started laying out the stack of magazines I'd bought from the local *The Big Issue* co-ordinator on Islington Green the previous day. I'd set myself a target of selling at least a couple of dozen today because, as usual, I needed the money.

I was soon being frustrated again.

Ominous, steely clouds had been hovering above London since mid-morning and before I'd managed to sell a single magazine the heavens opened, forcing Bob and me to take shelter a few yards away from our pitch, in an underpass near a bank and some office buildings.

Bob is a resilient creature, but he really hates the rain, especially when it was of the freezing cold variety like today. He almost seemed to shrink in it. His bright marmalade coloured coat also seemed to turn a little bit greyer and less noticeable. Unsurprisingly, fewer people than usual stopped to make a fuss over him so I sold fewer magazines than usual too.

With the rain showing no sign of relenting, Bob was soon making it clear that he didn't want to hang around. He kept shooting me withering looks and, like some kind of ginger hedgehog, scrunched himself up into a ball. I got the message, but knew the reality. The weekend was approaching and I needed to make enough money to keep us both going. But my stack of magazines was still as thick as when I'd arrived.

As if the day wasn't going badly enough, midway through the afternoon a young, uniformed police officer started giving me grief. It wasn't the first time and I knew it wouldn't be the last, but I really didn't need the hassle today. I knew the law; I was perfectly entitled to sell magazines here. I had my registered vendor ID and unless I was causing a public nuisance, I could sell magazines at this spot from dawn 'til dusk. Sadly, he didn't seem to have anything better to do with his day and insisted on searching me. I had no idea what he was frisking me for, presumably drugs or a dangerous weapon, but he found neither.

He wasn't too pleased about that so he resorted to asking questions about Bob. I explained that he was legally registered to me and was micro-chipped. That seemed to worsen his mood even more and he walked off with a look almost as grim as the weather.

I'd persevered for a few more hours but by early evening, when the office workers had gone home and the streets were beginning to fill with drinkers and kids looking for trouble, I decided to call it quits.

I felt deflated; I'd barely sold ten magazines and collected only a fraction of what I'd normally expect to make. I'd spent long enough living off tins of reduced price beans and even cheaper loaves of bread to know that I wouldn't starve. I had enough money to top up the gas and electric meters and buy a meal or two for Bob as well. But it meant I'd probably need to head out to work again over the weekend, something I really hadn't wanted to do, mainly because there was more rain forecast and I'd been feeling under the weather myself.

As I sat on the bus home, I could feel the first signs of flu seeping into my bones. I was aching and having hot flushes. *Great, that's all I need*, I thought, easing myself deep into my bus seat and settling down to a nap.

By now the sky had turned an inky black and the streetlights were on full blaze. There was something about London at night that fascinated Bob. As I drifted in and out of sleep, he sat there staring out of the window, lost in his own world.

The traffic back to Tottenham was just as bad as it had been in the morning and the bus could only crawl along at a snail's pace. Somewhere past Newington Green, I must have dropped off to sleep completely.

I was woken by the sensation of something lightly tapping me on the leg and the feeling of whiskers brushing against my cheek. I opened my eyes to see Bob with his face close to mine, patting me on the knee with his paw.

'What is it?', I said, slightly grumpily.

He just tilted his head as if pointing towards the front of the bus. He then started making a move off the seat towards the aisle, throwing me slightly concerned glances as he did so.

'Where are you off to?', I was about to ask, but

then I looked out on to the street and realised where we were.

'Oh, sh*t,' I said, jumping up out of my seat immediately.

I grabbed my rucksack and hit the stop button just in the nick of time. Thirty seconds later and it would have been too late. If it hadn't been for my little nightwatchman, we'd have flown past our bus stop.

On the way home I popped into the convenience store on the corner of our road and bought myself some cheap flu remedy tablets. I also got Bob some nibbles and a pouch of his favourite chicken dinner – it was the least I could do, after all. It had been a miserable day and it would have been easy to feel sorry for myself. But, back in the warmth of my little, one-bedroomed flat, watching Bob wolfing down his food, I realised that, actually, I had no real cause to complain. If I'd stayed asleep on the bus much longer I could easily have ended up miles away. Looking out the window, I could see that the weather was, if anything, getting worse. If I'd been out in this rain I could easily have developed something a lot worse than mild flu. I'd had a fortunate escape.

I knew I was lucky in a more profound way, as well. There's an old saying that a wise man is some-one who doesn't grieve for the things which he doesn't have but is grateful for the good things that he does have.

After dinner, I sat on the sofa, wrapped in a blanket sipping a hot toddy of honey, lemon and hot water topped up with a tiny shot of whisky from an old miniature I had lying around. I looked at Bob snoozing contentedly in his favourite spot near the radiator, the troubles of earlier in the day long forgotten. In that moment he couldn't have been happier. I told myself that I should view the world the same way. At this moment in my life, there were so many good things for which I had to be grateful.

It was now a little over two years since I had found Bob, lying injured on the ground floor of this same block of flats. When I'd spotted him in the dingy light of the hallway, he'd looked like he'd been attacked by another animal. He had wounds on the back of his legs and on his body.

At first I'd imagined he belonged to someone else, but – after seeing him in the same place for a few days – I'd taken him up to my flat and nursed him back to health. I'd had to fork out almost every penny I had to buy him medication, but it had been worth it. I'd really enjoyed his company and we'd formed an instant bond.

I'd assumed that it would be a short-lived relationship. He appeared to be a stray so I just naturally assumed that he'd return to the streets. But he'd refused to leave my side. Each day I'd put him outside and try to send him on his way and each day he'd follow me down the road or pop up in the hallway in the evening, inviting himself in for the night. They say that cats choose you, not the other way around. I realised he'd chosen me when he followed me to the bus stop a mile or so away on Tottenham High Road one day. We were far from home so when I'd shooed him away and watched him disappear into the busy crowds, I'd imagined that was the last I'd see of him. But as the bus was pulling away he appeared out of nowhere, leaping on board in a blur of ginger, plonking himself down on the seat next to me. And that had been that.

Ever since then we'd been inseparable, a pair of lost souls eking out an existence on the streets of London.

I suspected that we were actually kindred spirits, each of us helping the other to heal the wounds of our troubled pasts. I had given Bob companionship, food and somewhere warm to lay his head at night and in return he'd given me a new hope and purpose in life. He'd blessed my life with loyalty, love and humour as well as a sense of responsibility I'd never felt before. He'd also given me some goals and helped me see the world more clearly than I had done for a long, long time.

For more than a decade I'd been a drug addict, sleeping rough in doorways and homeless shelters or in basic accommodation around London. For large chunks of those lost years I was oblivious to the world, out of it on heroin, anaesthetised from the loneliness and pain of my everyday life.

As a homeless person I'd become invisible as far as most people were concerned. So as a result, I'd forgotten how to function in the real world and how to interact with people in a lot of situations. In a way I'd been dehumanised. I'd been dead to the world. With Bob's help, I was slowly coming back to life. I'd made huge strides in kicking my drug habit, weaning myself off heroin and then methadone. I was still on medication but could see the light at the end of the tunnel and hoped to be completely clean soon.

It wasn't plain sailing, far from it. It never is for a recovering addict. I still had a habit of taking two steps forward and one step back, and working on the streets didn't help in that respect. It wasn't an environment that was exactly overflowing with the milk of human kindness. Trouble was always around the corner, or it seemed to be for me, at least. I had a knack for attracting it. I always had done.

The truth was that I desperately longed to get off those streets and put that life behind me. I had no idea when or how that was going to be possible, but I was determined to try.

For now, the important thing was to appreciate what I had. By most people's standards, it didn't seem like much. I never had a lot of money and I didn't live in a flashy apartment or have a car. But my life was in a much better place than it had been in the recent past. I had my flat and my job selling *The Big Issue*. For the first time in years I was heading in the right direction – and I had Bob to offer me friendship and to guide me on my way.

As I picked myself up and headed to bed for an early night, I leaned over and gave him a gentle ruffle on the back of his neck.

'Where the hell would I be without you little fella?'

Chapter 2

New Tricks

We are all creatures of habit, and Bob and I are no different to anyone else. Our days together begin with a familiar routine. Some people start their mornings listening to the radio, others with their exercises or a cup of tea or coffee. Bob and I start ours by playing games together.

The moment I wake and sit up, he shuffles out of his bed in the corner of the bedroom, walks over to my side of the bed and starts staring at me inquisitively. Soon after that he starts making a chirruping noise, a bit like a phone. *Brrrr, brrrr.*

If that doesn't gain my full attention he starts making another noise, a slightly more plaintive and pleading noise, a kind of *waaaah*. Sometimes he places his paws on the side of the mattress and hauls himself up so that he is almost at eye-level with me.

He then dabs a paw in my direction, almost as if to nudge me into recognising his message: 'don't

13

ignore me! I've been awake for ages and I'm hungry, so where's my breakfast?' If my response is too slow, he sometimes steps up the charm offensive and does what I call a 'Puss in Boots'. Like the character in the *Shrek* movies, he stands there on the mattress staring at me wide-eyed with his piercing green eyes. It is heartbreakingly cute – and totally irresistible. It always makes me smile. And it always works.

I always keep a packet of his favourite snacks in a drawer by the side of the bed. Depending on how I am feeling, I might let him come up on the bed for a cuddle and a couple of treats or, if I am in a more playful mood, I'll throw them on to the carpet for him to chase around. I often spend the first few minutes of the day lobbing mini treats around, watching him hunt them down. Cats are amazingly agile creatures and Bob often intercepts them in mid-flight, like a cricketer or baseball player fielding a ball in the outfield. He leaps up and catches them in his paws. He has even caught them in his mouth a couple of times. It is quite a spectacle.

On other occasions, if I am tired or not in the mood for playing, he'll entertain himself.

One summer's morning, for instance, I was lying on my bed watching breakfast television. It was shaping up to be a really warm day and it was especially hot up on the fifth floor of our tower block.

Bob was curled up in a shady spot in the bedroom, seemingly fast asleep. Or so I'd assumed.

Suddenly he sat up, jumped on the bed and, almost using it as a trampoline, threw himself at the wall behind me, hitting it quite hard with his paws.

'Bob, what the hell?' I said, gobsmacked. I looked at the duvet and saw a little millipede lying there. Bob was eyeing it and was clearly ready to crunch it in his mouth.

'Oh, no you don't mate,' I said, knowing that insects can be poisonous to cats. 'You don't know where that's been.'

He shot me a look as if to say 'spoilsport'.

I have always been amazed at Bob's speed, strength and athleticism. Someone suggested to me once that he must be related to a Maine Coon or a lynx or some kind of wild cat. It is entirely possible. Bob's past is a complete mystery to me. I don't know how old he is and know nothing about the life he led before I found him. Unless I did a DNA test on him, I'll never know where he comes from or who his parents were. To be honest though, I don't really care. Bob is Bob. And that is all I need to know.

I wasn't the only one who had learned to love Bob for being his colourful, unpredictable self.

It was the spring of 2009 and by now Bob and I had been selling *The Big Issue* for a year or so. Initially we'd had a pitch outside Covent Garden tube station in central London. But we'd moved to Angel, Islington where we'd carved out a little niche for ourselves and Bob had built up a small, but dedicated band of admirers.

As far as I was aware, we were the only human/feline team selling *The Big Issue* in London. And even if there was another one, I suspected the feline part of the partnership wasn't much competition for Bob when it came to drawing – and pleasing – a crowd.

During our early days together, when I had been a busker playing the guitar and singing, he had sat there, Buddha-like, watching the world going about its business. People were fascinated – and I think a bit mesmerised – by him and would stop, stroke and talk to him. Often they'd ask our story and I'd tell them all about how we'd met and formed our partnership. But that was about the extent of it.

Since we'd been selling *The Big Issue*, however, he'd become a lot more active. I often sat down on the pavement to play with him and we'd developed a few tricks.

It had begun with Bob entertaining people on

his own. He loved to play, so I'd bring along little toys that he would toss around and chase. His favourite was a little grey mouse that had once been filled with catnip.

The mouse had ceased to have any trace of catnip a long time ago and was now a battered, bedraggled and rather pathetic looking thing. Its stitching had begun to come apart and, although it had always been grey, it had now become a really dirty shade of grey. He had loads of other toys, some of which had been given to him by admirers. But 'scraggedy mouse', as I called it, was still his number one toy.

As we sat outside Angel tube he would hold it in his mouth, flicking it from side to side. Sometimes he'd whirl it around by its tail and release it so that it flew a couple of feet away and then pounce on it and start the whole process all over again. Bob loved hunting real life mice, so he was obviously mimicking that. It always stopped people in their tracks and I'd known some commuters to spend ten minutes standing there, as if hypnotised by Bob and his game.

Out of boredom more than anything else, I had started playing with him on the pavement. To begin with we just played at shaking hands. I'd stretch out my hand and Bob would extend his paw to hold it. We were only replicating what we did at home in my flat, but people seemed to find it sweet.

They were constantly stopping to watch us, often taking pictures. If I'd had a pound for every time someone – usually a lady – had stopped and said something like 'aah, how sweet' or 'that's adorable' I'd have been rich enough to, well, not have to sit on the pavement any more.

Freezing your backside off on the streets isn't exactly the most fun you can have, so my playtimes with Bob became more than simple entertainment for the passing crowds. It helped me to pass the time and to enjoy my days a little more too. I couldn't deny it: it also helped encourage people to buy copies of the magazine. It was another one of the blessings that Bob had bestowed on me.

We'd spent so many hours outside Angel by now that we'd begun to develop our act a little further.

Bob loved his little treats, and I learned that he'd go to extraordinary lengths to get hold of them. So, for instance, if I held a little biscuit three feet or so above him, he'd stand on his hind legs in an effort to snaffle the snack from my hands. He would wrap his paws around my wrist to steady himself, then let go with one paw and try to grab it.

Predictably, this had gone down a storm. By now there must have been hundreds of people walking the streets of London with images of Bob reaching for the sky on their telephones and cameras.

Recently, we'd developed this trick even more. The grip he exerted when he grabbed my arms to reach the treat was as strong as a vice. So every now and again I would slowly and very gently raise him in the air so that he was dangling a few inches above the ground.

He would hang there for a few seconds, until he let go and dropped down or I eased him back to earth. I always made sure he had a soft landing of course and usually put my rucksack under him.

The more of a 'show' we put on, the more people seemed to respond to us, and the more generous they became, not just in buying *The Big Issue*.

Since our early days at Angel, people had been incredibly kind, dropping off snacks and nibbles not just for Bob, but for me as well. But they had also started giving us items of clothing, often hand-knitted or sewn by them.

Bob now had a collection of scarves in all sorts of colours. So many, in fact, that I was running out of space to keep them all. He must have had two dozen or more! He was fast becoming to scarves what Imelda Marcos had been to shoes.

It was a little overwhelming at times to know that we were on the receiving end of such warmth, support and love. But I never for a moment kidded

myself that there weren't those who felt very differently about us. They were never very far away . . .

It was approaching the busiest time of the week,
the Friday evening rush hour, and the crowds passing in and out of Angel tube were growing thicker
by the minute. While I wheeled around the street
trying to sell my stack of magazines, Bob was
totally oblivious to the commotion, flapping his tail
absent-mindedly from side to side as he lay on my
rucksack on the pavement.

It was only when things had died down, around
7pm, that I noticed a lady standing a few feet
away from us. I had no idea how long she had
been there, but she was staring intently, almost
obsessively at Bob.

From the way she was muttering to herself and
shaking her head from side to side occasionally, I
sensed she disapproved of us somehow. I had no
intention of engaging her in conversation, not least
because I was too busy trying to sell the last few
copies of the magazine before the weekend.

Unfortunately, she had other ideas.

'Young man. Can't you see that this cat is in
distress?', she said, approaching us.

Outwardly, she looked like a school teacher, or

even a headmistress, from some upper-class public school. She was middle-aged, spoke in a clipped, cut-glass English accent and was dressed in a scruffy and un-ironed tweed skirt and jacket. Given her manner, however, I doubted very much that any school would have employed her. She was brusque, bordering on the downright aggressive.

I sensed she was trouble, so didn't respond to her. She was obviously determined to pick a fight, however.

'I have been watching you for a while and I can see that your cat is wagging its tail. Do you know what that means?' she said.

I shrugged. I knew she was going to answer her own question in any case.

'It means it's not happy. You shouldn't be exploiting it like this. I don't think you're fit to look after him.'

I'd been around this track so many times since Bob and I had started working the streets together. But I was polite, so instead of telling this lady to mind her own business, I wearily began defending myself once again.

'He's wagging his tail because he's content. If he didn't want to be there, Madam, you wouldn't see him for dust. He's a cat. They choose who they want to be with. He's free to run off whenever he wants.'

'So why is he on a lead?' she shot back, a smug look on her face.

'He's only on a lead here and when we are on the streets. He ran off once and was terrified when he couldn't find me again. I let him off when he goes to do his business. So, again, if he wasn't happy, as you claim, he'd be gone the minute I took the lead off wouldn't he?'

I'd had this conversation a hundred times before and knew that for 99 people out of that 100, this was a rational and reasonable response. But this lady was part of the 1 per cent who were never going to take my word for it. She was one of those dogmatic individuals who believed they were always right and you were always wrong – and even more wrong if you were impertinent enough not to see their point of view.

'No, no, no. It's a well-known fact that if a cat is wagging its tail it is a distress signal,' she said, more animated now. I noticed that her face was quite red. She was flapping her arms and pacing around us rather menacingly.

I could tell Bob was uncomfortable about her; he had an extremely good radar when it came to spotting trouble. He had stood up and begun backing himself towards me so that he was now standing between my legs, ready to jump up if things got out of hand.

One or two other people had stopped, curious to see what the fuss was about so I knew I had witnesses if the lady did or said anything outrageous.

We carried on arguing for a minute or two. I tried to ease her fears by telling her a little about us.

'We've been together for more than two years. He wouldn't have been with me two minutes if I was mistreating him,' I said at one point. But she was intransigent. Whatever I said, she just shook her head and tutted away. She simply wasn't willing to listen to my point of view. It was frustrating in the extreme, but there was nothing more I could do. I resigned myself to the fact that she was entitled to her opinion. 'Why don't we agree to differ?' I said at one point.

'Hffff,' she said, waving her arms at me. 'I'm not agreeing with anything you say young man.'

Eventually, to my huge relief, she started walking away, muttering and shaking her head as she shuffled off into the crowds jostling around the entrance to the tube station.

I watched her for a moment, but was soon distracted by a couple of customers. Fortunately, their attitude was the complete opposite of the one this lady had displayed. Their smiles were a welcome relief.

I was handing one of them their change when I heard a noise behind me that I recognised immediately. It was a loud, piercing *wheeeeeow*. I spun round and saw the woman in the tweed suit. Not only had she come back, she was now holding Bob in her arms.

Somehow, while I had been distracted, she had managed to scoop him up off the rucksack. She was now nursing him awkwardly, with no affection or empathy, one hand under his stomach and another on his back. It was strange, as if she'd never picked up an animal before in her life. She could have been holding a joint of meat that she'd just bought at the butcher or a large vegetable at a market.

Bob was clearly furious about being manhandled like this and was wriggling like crazy.

'What the hell do you think you are doing?' I shouted. 'Put him down, right now or I'll call the police.'

'He needs to be taken somewhere safe,' she said, a slightly crazed expression forming on her reddening face.

Oh God no, she's going to run off with him, I said to myself, preparing to drop my supply of magazines and set off in hot pursuit through the streets of Islington.

Luckily, she hadn't quite thought it through because Bob's long lead was still tethered to my rucksack. For a moment there was a kind of stand-off. But then I saw her eye moving along the lead to the rucksack.

'No you don't,' I said, stepping forward to intercept her.

My movement caught her off guard which in

turn gave Bob his chance. He let out another screeching *wheeeeow* and freed himself from the woman's grip. He didn't scratch her but he did dig his paws into her arm which forced her to panic and suddenly drop him on to the pavement.

He landed with a bit of a bump, then stood there for a second growling and hissing and baring his teeth at her. I'd never seen him quite so aggressive towards anyone or anything.

Unbelievably, she used this as an argument against me.

'Ah, look, see, he's angry,' she said, pointing at Bob and addressing the half dozen or more people who were watching events unfold.

'He's angry because you just picked him up without his permission,' I said. 'He only lets me pick him up.'

She wasn't giving up that easily. She clearly felt she had some kind of audience and was going to play to them.

'No, he's angry because of the way you are treating him,' she said. 'Everyone can see that. That's why he should be taken away from you. He doesn't want to be with you.'

Again there was a brief impasse while everyone held their breath to see what happened next. It was Bob who broke the silence.

He gave the woman a really disdainful look, then padded his way back towards me. He began rubbing his head against the outside of my leg, and purring noisily when I put my hand down to stroke him.

He then plonked his rear down on the ground and looked up at me again playfully, as if to say, 'now can we get on with some more tricks?' Recognising the look, I dipped my hand into my coat pocket and produced a treat. Almost immediately, Bob got up on his hind legs and grabbed hold of my arms. I then popped the treat into his mouth drawing a couple of audible *aaahs* from somewhere behind me.

There were times when Bob's intelligence and ability to understand the nuances of what's going on around him defied belief. This was one such moment. Bob had played to the crowd totally. It was as if he had wanted to make a statement. It was as if he was saying: 'I'm with James, and I'm really happy to be with James. And anyone who says otherwise is mistaken. End of story.' That was certainly the message that most of the onlookers got. One or two of them were familiar faces, people who had bought magazines off me in the past or stopped to say hello to Bob. They turned to the woman in the tweed suit and made their feelings plain.

'We know this guy, he's cool,' one young man in a business suit said.

'Yes, leave them alone. They're not doing anyone

any harm and he looks after his cat really well,' another middle-aged lady said. One or two other people made supportive noises. As various other voices chipped in, not one of them backed up the lady in the tweed suit.

The expression that had formed on her face by this point told its own story. She was, by now, even redder than ever, almost purple in fact. She spluttered and grumbled for a moment or two but made no real sense. Clearly the penny had dropped and she realised that she had lost this particular battle. So she turned on her heels and disappeared once more into the crowds, this time – thankfully – permanently.

'You OK, James?' one of the onlookers asked me, as I kneeled down to check on Bob. He was purring loudly but his breathing was steady and there was no sign of any injury from when he was dropped to the ground.

'I'm fine, thanks,' I said, not being entirely honest.

I hated it when people implied I was using Bob in some way. It hurt me deeply. In a way we were victims of our circumstances. Bob wanted to be with me, of that I was absolutely certain. He'd proven that time and time again. Unfortunately, at the moment, that meant that he had to spend his days with me on the streets. Those were the simple facts of my life. I didn't have a choice.

The downside was that this made us easy
targets, sitting ducks for people to judge. We were
lucky, most people judged us kindly. I had learned
to accept that there would always be those who
would not.

Chapter 3
The Bobmobile

It was a balmy, early summer afternoon and I had decided to knock off from work early. The sunny weather seemed to have put a smile on everyone's face and I'd reaped the benefits, selling out my supply of magazines in a few hours.

Since I'd started selling *The Big Issue* a couple of years earlier, I'd learned to be sensible, so I'd decided to plough some of the money back into buying some more magazines for the rest of the week. With Bob on my shoulders, I headed over to see Rita, the co-ordinator on the north side of Islington High Street on the way back to catch the bus home.

From a distance, I could see that she was having an animated conversation with a group of vendors in red bibs who were huddled around something. It turned out to be a bicycle. I got on well with Rita, so knew that I could gently take the mickey.

'What's this, Rita?' I joked. 'Riding in the Tour de France?'

'Don't think so, James,' she smiled. 'Someone just sold it to me in exchange for ten magazines. I really don't know what to do with it to be honest. Bikes aren't really my thing.'

It was obvious the bike wasn't in prime condition. There were hints of rust on the handlebars and the light at the front had cracked glass. The paintwork had a few chips and nicks and, just for good measure, one of the mudguards had been snapped in half. Mechanically, though, it looked like it was in reasonable condition.

'Is it roadworthy?' I asked Rita.

'Think so,' she shrugged. 'He muttered something about one of the sets of brakes needing a bit of attention but that's all.'

She could see my mind was working overtime.

'Why don't you give it a try, see what you think?'

'Why not?' I said. 'Can you keep an eye on Bob for a second?'

I was no Bradley Wiggins but I had ridden bikes throughout my childhood and again in London. As part of my rehabilitation a few years earlier, I had been briefly involved with a bicycle building course so I knew a bit about cycle maintenance. It felt good to know some of that training hadn't gone to waste.

Handing Bob's lead to Rita, I took the bike and flipped it upside down to inspect it properly. The tyres were inflated and the chain looked like it was well oiled and moving pretty freely. The seat was a little low for me, so I adjusted it up a little. I then took the bike down on to the road and gave it a quick workout. The gears were a tad on the sticky side and, as Rita had warned me, the front brakes weren't working properly. I had to apply maximum pressure on the handle to get any reaction and even then it wasn't enough to bring the bike to a halt. I figured there was a problem with the wire inside the cable. It was easily fixed I suspected. The rear brakes were fine, however, which was all I needed to know.

'What does that mean?' Rita said when I reported all this back to her.

'It means it's OK to ride,' I said.

By now I'd made a decision.

'Tell you what, I'll give you a tenner for it,' I said.

'Really. You sure?' Rita said, a little taken aback.

'Yes,' I replied.

'OK, deal. You'll need this as well,' she said, fishing around under her trolley and producing a rather battered, old black cycle helmet.

I'd always been a bit of a hoarder, collecting bits and pieces, and for a while my little flat had been full of all sorts of junk, from mannequins to road signs. But this was different. This was actually one of the first, sensible investments I'd made in a while. I knew the bike would be useful back up in Tottenham where I could use it for short journeys to the shops or the doctors. I'd make the £10 back in saved bus fares in no time. For the longer journey to work at Angel or into central London I'd carry on taking the bus or the tube. That journey was too treacherous to cycle because of the main roads and junctions I'd have to negotiate. Some of them were notorious cycling accident spots.

It was only then, as I mentally mapped out the journeys that I'd be able to cycle from now on, that it suddenly struck me.

'Ah, how am I going to get this home?'

Bus drivers don't let bikes on board and there was no prospect of getting it on a tube. I'd be stopped at the barriers immediately. I might get away with taking it on an overground train, but there were no lines that went anywhere near my flats.

There's only thing for it, I told myself.

'OK, Bob, looks like you and I are riding this home,' I said.

Bob had been soaking up the sunshine on the pavement near Rita but had been keeping half an eye on me throughout. When I'd climbed on the bike, he tilted his head to one side slightly, as if to say: 'what's that contraption and why are you sitting on top of it?'

He looked suspiciously at me again as I strapped on the cycle helmet, slung my rucksack on my shoulders and started wheeling the bike towards him.

'Come on, mate, climb on board,' I said, reaching down to him and letting him climb on my shoulders.

'Good luck,' Rita said.

'Thanks. I think we'll need it!' I said.

The traffic on Islington High Street was heavy and, as usual, at a virtual standstill. So I walked the bike along the pavement for a while, towards Islington Memorial Green. We passed a couple of police officers who gave me a curious look, but said nothing. There was no law against riding a bike with a cat on your shoulders. Well, as far as I was aware there wasn't. I guess if they'd wanted to pull me over they could have done. They obviously had better things to do with their afternoon, thank God.

I didn't want to cycle along the High Street so I wheeled the bike across a pedestrian crossing. We drew more than our fair share of glances; the looks on people's faces ranged from astonishment to hilarity. More than one person stopped in their tracks, pointing at us as if we were visitors from another planet.

We didn't linger and cut across the corner of the Green, past the Waterstones bookshop, and turned into the main road to north London, Essex Road.

'OK, here we go, Bob,' I said, bracing myself to enter the heavy traffic. We were soon weaving our way through the buses, vans, cars and lorries.

Bob and I soon got the hang of it. As I focussed

on staying upright, I could feel him re-adjusting himself. Rather than standing he decided, sensibly, to drape himself across my neck, with his head down low and pointing forward. He clearly wanted to settle down and enjoy the ride.

It was mid-afternoon and a lot of children were heading home from school. All along Essex Road groups of kids in uniforms would stop and wave at us. I tried waving back at one point but lost my balance a little bit, sending Bob sliding down my shoulder.

'Oops, sorry, mate. Won't do that again,' I said, as we both regained our equilibrium.

Progress was steady but a little slow at times. If we had to stop because of traffic we were instantly shouted at by someone asking for a photo. At one point, two teenage schoolgirls jumped out into the road to snap themselves with us.

'Oh my God, this is so cute,' one of them said, leaning into us so heavily as she posed for her photo that she almost knocked us over.

I hadn't ridden a bicycle for a few years and I wasn't exactly in prime physical condition. So I took a little breather every now and again, attracting a posse of onlookers each time I did so. Most smiled their approval but a couple shook their heads disapprovingly.

'Stupid idiot,' I heard one middle-aged guy in a suit say as he strode past us.

It didn't feel stupid at all. In fact, it felt rather fun. And I could tell Bob was having a good time too. His head was right next to mine and I could feel him purring contentedly in my ear.

We travelled all the way down to Newington Green and from there towards Kingsland Road where the road headed down towards Seven Sisters. I had been looking forward to this section. For most of the journey, apart from a couple of little inclines here and there, the road had been fairly flat. At that point, however, I knew that it dropped downhill for a mile or so. I'd be able to freewheel down it quite easily.

To my delight, I saw there was a dedicated bike lane, which was completely empty. Bob and I were soon flying down the hill, the warm summer air blowing through our hair. 'Woohoo. Isn't this great Bob?,' I said at one point. I felt a bit like Elliott in E.T. – not that I expected us to take off and fly our way back across the north London rooftops at any point, obviously, but we must have been clocking close to 20 miles per hour at one point.

The traffic in the main lane to our right was grid-locked, and people were winding down their windows to let in some air. Some of the expressions on their faces as we whizzed past them were priceless.

A couple of children stuck their heads out of the sun roofs of their cars and shouted at us. A few people just looked on in utter disbelief. It was understandable, I supposed. You don't see a ginger cat whizzing down a hill on a bike very often.

It only took me about half an hour to get home, which was pretty impressive considering we'd had so many unplanned stops.

As we pulled up in the communal area outside the flats, Bob just hopped off my shoulders as if he was disembarking the bus. This was typical of his laid-back attitude to life. He had taken it all in his stride; just another routine day in London.

Back in the flat, I spent the rest of the afternoon and evening tinkering with the bike. I'd soon fixed the front brakes and given it a general tuning up.

'There you go,' I said to Bob, as I stood back to admire my handiwork. 'I think we've got ourselves a Bobmobile.'

I couldn't be sure, but I was pretty sure that the look he gave me signalled his approval.

People often ask me how Bob and I communicate with each other so well.

'It's simple,' I usually answer. 'He has his own language, and I've learned to understand it.'

It might sound far-fetched, but it's true.

His main means of communication is body

language. He has a range of signals that tell me exactly what he is feeling, and more to the point, what he wants at any particular moment. For instance, if he wants to go to the toilet, when we are walking around the streets, he starts grumbling and growling a little bit. He then starts fidgeting on my shoulder. I don't need to look at him to know what he is up to; he's scouting around for a spot with some soft dirt where he can do his business.

If, on the other hand, he is walking on his lead and gets tired he lets out a light, low-pitched grumble or moan-cum-growl. He also refuses to walk an inch. He just looks at me as if to say 'come on mate, pick me up I'm worn out'.

If he ever gets scared he backs up on my shoulder, or if he is standing on the floor, he performs a reverse manoeuvre so that he is standing between my legs in position in case I need to pick him up. To his credit, it is rare that anything frightens him. The sound of an ambulance or a police car going by with their sirens blaring barely bothers him at all. He is very used to it, living and working in central London. The only thing that freaks him a little is the pressurised air brakes on big lorries and buses. Whenever he hears that loud, hissing sound he recoils and looks scared. On bonfire nights, he also gets a little nervous about the loud bangs and explosions, but he generally enjoys watching the bright, sparkling lights in the sky from the window of my flat.

There are other signals too. For instance, I can tell a lot about his mood from the way he moves his tail. If he is snoozing or asleep his tail is still and quiet, of course. But at other times he wags it around, using different movements. The most common wag is a gentle side-to-side movement, rather like a wind-screen wiper on its slowest setting. This is his contentment wag. I've spent endless hours sitting around London with him and have seen him doing it when he is being entertained or intrigued by some-thing. The lady who'd tried to steal him at Angel hadn't been the first to misread this movement. Others had made the same mistake and miscon-strued it as a sign of anger. Bob does get angry, but he signals that with a very different tail movement in which he flicks it around, a bit like a fly swatter.

There are subtler messages too. If, for instance, he is worried about me, he comes up really close as if to examine me. If I am feeling under the weather, he often sidles up and listens to my chest. He does a lot of loving things like that. He has this habit of coming up and rubbing against me, purring. He also rubs his face on my hand tilting his head so that I can scratch behind his ear. Animal behav-iourists and zoologists are entitled to their opin-ions, but to me this is Bob's way of telling me that he loves me.

Of course, the most frequent message he wants to get across relates to food. If he wants me to come to the kitchen to feed him, for instance, he goes around banging on the doors. He is so clever, he could easily unpick one of the child locks I've had to fit specifically to keep him out, so I always have to go and check. By the time I get there, he has always removed himself to a spot by the radiator in the corner where he'll be wearing his most innocent look. But that doesn't last for long and he'll soon be pleading for a snack.

Bob is nothing if not persistent and won't leave me alone until he gets what he wants. He can get quite frustrated if I choose to ignore him and tries all sorts of tricks from tapping me on the knee to giving me the 'Puss in Boots' look. There is no end to his creativity when it comes to filling a gap in his tummy.

For a while, his biggest challenge was distracting me while I played computer games on the second-hand Xbox I'd picked up in a charity shop. Most of the time Bob was quite happy to watch me playing. He was fascinated by certain games, especially motor racing ones. He would stand beside me experiencing each bend and manoeuvre. On one occasion, I could have sworn I saw his body swaying as we took a particularly sharp hairpin bend together. He drew the line at action games with a lot of shooting, however. If I was playing one of these he would carry himself off to another corner of the room. If the game – or I – ever got too loud he'd lift up his head and look across. The message was simple: 'turn it down please, can't you see I'm trying to snooze'.

I could get really wrapped up in a game. It wasn't unheard of for me to start a game at 9pm and not finish until the wee small hours. But Bob didn't appreciate this and would do his damnedest to get my attention, especially when he was hungry.

There were times, however, when I was immune to his charms so he took more drastic measures.

I was playing a game with Belle one night when Bob appeared. He'd had dinner a couple of hours earlier and had decided that he needed a snack. He went through his usual attention-seeking routine, making a selection of noises, draping himself across my feet and rubbing himself against my legs. But we were both so heavily involved in reaching the next level of this game that we didn't respond at all.

He sloped off for a moment, circling the area where the TV and Xbox were plugged in. After a moment, he moved in towards the control console and pressed his head against the big, touch sensitive button in the middle.

'Bob, what are you up to?' I asked innocently, still too engrossed in the game to twig what he was doing.

A moment later, the screen went black and the

Xbox started powering down. He had applied enough pressure to the button that he'd switched it off. We had been halfway through a really tricky level of the game, so should have been furious with him. But we both sat there with the same expression of disbelief on our faces.

'Did he just do what I think he did?' Belle asked me.

'Well, I saw it too, so he must have. But I don't believe it.'

Bob stood there looking triumphant. His expression said it all: 'So how are you going to ignore me now?'

We don't always rely on signals and body language. There are times when we have a strange kind of telepathy, as if we both know what the other one is thinking, or doing. We've also learned to alert each other to danger.

A few days after I'd acquired the bike, I decided to take Bob to a local park that had just been given a bit of a makeover. By now he was completely comfortable riding around on my shoulders and had become more and more confident, leaning in and out of the corners like a motorbike pillion rider.

The park turned out to be a bit of a disappointment. Apart from a few new benches and shrubs and a decent playground for young children, it seemed nothing much had changed. Bob was keen to explore, nevertheless. If I felt it was safe, I occasionally let him off his lead so that he could enjoy himself scrabbling around in the overgrowth while he did his business. I had just done so today and was sitting, reading a comic and soaking up a few rays of sunshine, when, in the distance, I heard the barking of a dog.

Uh oh, I thought.

At first, I guessed it was a couple of streets away. But as the barking grew louder I realised it was a lot closer than that. In the distance I saw a very large, and very menacing looking, German Shepherd running towards the entrance to the park. The dog was no more than 150 yards away and was off its leash. I could tell it was looking for trouble.

'Bob,' I shouted at the overgrowth where, I knew, he was busy conducting his call of nature. 'Bob, come here.'

For a moment, I was panic stricken. But, as so often in the past, we were on the same wavelength and his head soon popped up in the bushes. I was waving my arms at him, encouraging him to join me without making too much fuss. I didn't want the dog to spot me. Bob understood what was happening immediately and bolted out of the bushes. He wasn't afraid of dogs, but he picked his battles wisely. Judging by the noise the German Shepherd was making, this wasn't a dog with which we wanted to pick a fight.

Bob's bright ginger coat wasn't exactly hard to spot amidst the greenery, though, and the dog soon began accelerating towards us, barking even more fiercely. For a moment I had a terrible feeling that Bob had left it too late so I grabbed the bike and got ready to ride it into the firing line if necessary. I knew if the German Shepherd intercepted him, Bob could be in serious trouble.

As so often in the past, however, I'd underestimated him.

He sprinted across the grass and arrived as I crouched down on one knee. In one seamless move, I flipped him on to my shoulder, jumped straight on to the bike, and – with Bob standing on my shoulders – hit the pedals and began cycling out of the park.

The frustrated German Shepherd pursued us for a short time, at one point running alongside as we sped down the street. I could hear Bob hissing at him. I couldn't see his face, but it wouldn't have surprised me at all if he was taunting him.

'What are you going to do about it now, tough guy?' he was probably saying.

As I hit the main road back towards our block of flats, I looked round to see our nemesis receding into the distance where he had been joined by his owner, a big, burly guy in a black jacket and jeans. He was struggling to get the dog back on its lead, but that was his problem, not mine.

'That was a close one, Bob,' I said. 'Thank goodness for the Bobmobile.'

Chapter 4
The Odd Couple

It was rare I got visitors at the flat. I didn't have
many friends locally and kept to myself within the
building. I would pass the time of day with neighbours but I could count the number of times any of
them had popped round for a chat on the fingers of
one hand. So I was always wary whenever someone knocked on the door or pressed the building's
intercom at the entrance downstairs. I automati-
cally assumed the worst, expecting to find myself
confronted by a bailiff or a debt collector chasing
me for money that I didn't have.

That was my immediate reaction when the intercom buzzer went just after 9am one weekday
morning as Bob and I got ready for work.

'Who the heck is that?' I said, instinctively
twitching at the curtains even though I had no view
of the entrance from up on the fifth floor.

'James, it's Titch. Can I come up with Princess?'
a familiar voice said over the speaker.

'Ah. Titch. Sure, head on up, I'll put the kettle on,' I said, breathing a sigh of relief.

Titch was, as his name suggested, a tiny little bloke. He was wiry and had short, thinning hair. Like me, he was a recovering addict who had started selling *The Big Issue*. He had been having a hard time and had crashed out at my place a couple of times in recent months. He'd got into trouble with work after becoming a co-ordinator in Islington. He had been 'de-badged' and given a six month suspension. He was still waiting for his ban to be lifted and had been really struggling to make ends meet.

I felt like I'd been given a second chance in life since I'd met Bob so had given Titch another opportunity as well. I also quite liked him. Deep down, I knew, he had a good heart.

Another reason that Titch and I got on was that we both worked on the street with our pet as our companion. In Titch's case it was his faithful black Labrador-Staffordshire Bull Terrier-cross, Princess. She was a lovely, sweet-natured dog. When he'd stayed with me previously, he'd left Princess somewhere else. He knew that I had Bob and that having a dog in the house might cause problems for me. But, for some reason, that wasn't the case today. I braced myself for what might happen when the pair of them arrived at the front door.

Bob's ears pricked up at the sound of knocking. When he saw Titch and Princess walking in, his first reaction was to arch his back and hiss. Cats arch their backs to make themselves look bigger in a fight, apparently. This is why they also get their hair to stand on end. In this particular case, however, Bob needn't have bothered. Princess was a really easy-going and affectionate dog. She could also be a little nervous. So the moment she saw Bob in full, confrontational mode she just froze to the spot. It was a complete reversal of the normal roles, where the physically bigger dog intimidates the smaller cat.

'It's all right, Princess,' I said. 'He won't hurt you.'

I then led her into my bedroom and shut the door so that she felt safe.

'James, mate. Is there any way you can look after Princess for the day?' Titch said, cutting straight to the chase when I handed him a mug of tea. 'I've got to go and sort out my social security situation.'

'Sure,' I said, knowing how long those sorts of things could take. 'Shouldn't be a problem. Should it Bob?'

He gave me an enigmatic look.

'We are working at Angel today. She'll be all right with us there won't she?' I said.

'Yeah, no problem,' Titch said. 'So how about if I pick her up there this evening at about 6pm?'

'OK,' I said.

'Right, better dash. Got to be in the front of the queue if I want to be seen this side of Christmas,' Titch said, popping his head into my bedroom.

'Be a good girl, Princess,' he said, before heading off.

As he'd demonstrated again already this morning, Bob didn't have a major problem with dogs unless they were aggressive towards him. Even then, he could handle himself pretty well and had seen off a few scary looking mongrels with a growl and a loud hiss. Back during our early days busking around Covent Garden, I'd even seen him give one over-aggressive dog a bop on the nose with his paw.

Bob wasn't just territorial with dogs. He wasn't a huge fan of other cats, either. There were times when I wondered whether he didn't actually know he was a cat. He seemed to look at them as if they were inferior beings, unfit to breathe the same air as him. Our route to and from work had become more complicated in recent months thanks to the cancellation of a bus service that used to take us straight from Tottenham High Road to Angel. So we'd started taking different buses, one of which required us to change in Newington Green, a mile or so from Angel. When money was tight, we'd walk to Angel. As we did so, Bob would sniff and stare whenever we went past what was clearly a cat house.

If he ever saw another cat out and about he would let them know in no uncertain terms that this was his turf.

Once when he saw a tabby cat, skulking around on Islington Green Bob had been transformed. He had been straining so hard to get at this upstart invading his territory, it had been as if I'd had a particularly aggressive dog on the end of the lead. He'd had to stamp his authority on the situation. Obviously, he'd already felt the need to do the same with Princess.

If I had any reservations, they were that Princess might be a bit of an inconvenience. Dogs were so much more hard work than cats. For a start, you couldn't put them on your shoulders as you walked down the street, a design flaw that, I soon discovered, slowed you down considerably.

Walking to the bus stop Princess was a right royal pain. She pulled on the lead, stopped to sniff random patches of grass and veered off to squat down and go to the toilet no less than three times in the space of a couple of hundred yards.

'Come on Princess, or we'll never get there,' I said, already regretting my decision. Suddenly I remembered why I had never wanted to adopt a dog as a pet.

If I was struggling to establish some kind of control over her, however, Bob had no such trouble. On the bus, he took up his normal position on the seat next to the window, from where he kept a watchful eye on Princess, who was tucked under my feet. Bob's face had always been expressive. The looks he gave Princess whenever she encroached on his territory during the journey were hilarious. The area under the seat wasn't exactly spacious and Princess would occasionally wiggle to improve her position. Each time she did so Bob would give her a look that simply said: 'why don't you sit still you stupid dog?'.

Outside the weather was atrocious, with rain hammering down. Arriving in Islington, I took Bob to the little park at Islington Green to quickly do his business and decided to let Princess do the same. Big mistake. She took forever to find a suitable spot. I then realised I'd forgotten to bring any plastic bags with me so had to fish around in a rubbish bin to find something with which to scoop up her droppings. I really wasn't enjoying my day as a dogsitter, I decided.

With the rain getting heavier by the minute, I took shelter under the canopy of a café. When a waitress appeared I decided I might as well ask her for a cup of tea, a saucer of milk for Bob and some water for Princess. I then popped inside to use the toilet, leaving my two companions tied to the table with their leads.

I only left them for a couple of minutes, but when I got back it was clear that some kind of jostling for position had been going on. I'd left them with Bob sitting on a chair and Princess standing under the table. But when I came back Bob was sitting on the table, lapping at a saucer of milk, while Princess was sitting under the table looking far from happy with her bowl of water. I had no idea what had gone on, but Bob had clearly established himself as the senior partner once again.

As always, Bob was also attracting attention from passers-by. Despite the weather, a couple of ladies stopped to stroke him and say hello. But poor Princess was hardly even acknowledged. It was as if she wasn't even there. In a funny way, I knew how she felt. I live in Bob's shadow sometimes.

The rain eventually eased off and we headed towards Angel and our pitch. While Bob and I took up our usual positions, Princess lay down a few feet away with her head deliberately placed so that she could take in most of the scene around us. Part of me had thought she'd be a burden but it turned out to be quite the opposite: she proved to be rather a useful asset.

As I paced around trying to persuade passers-by to fork out a couple of quid for a magazine, Princess sat there attentively, her head on the pavement and her eyes swivelling around like surveillance cameras, carefully weighing up everyone who approached us. If they got her seal of approval, she remained rooted to the spot, but if she had any suspicions she would suddenly sit upright ready to intervene. If she didn't like the cut of someone's jib she would let out a little growl or even a bark. It was usually enough to get the message across.

An hour or so after we'd settled down, a drunk carrying a can of extra strength lager came weaving his way towards us. They could be the bane of my existence at Angel. Almost every day I'd be asked for a quid for a beer by someone off his face on Special Brew. Princess spotted him, stood up and barked a quick warning as if to say 'steer clear'. She wasn't the world's biggest dog, but she looked intimidating enough. She was more Staffie than Lab in that respect. He had soon veered off on another course, heading off to bother someone other poor soul instead.

Princess was at her most alert whenever anyone knelt down to stroke and say hello to Bob. She would take a step towards them, jutting her head forward so that she could make sure that they were treating the smallest member of our trio with the proper respect. Again, if she disapproved of anyone she made her feelings clear and they would stand back.

She actually made my job a little easier. It could often be a challenge to keep an eye on Bob while trying to sell the magazine at the same time, especially when the street was busy. The incident with the lady in the tweed suit had made me especially wary.

'Thank you, Princess,' I began saying on a regular basis, handing her a little treat from my rucksack.

Even Bob shot her a couple of approving looks. Somewhere, deep inside his feline mind I felt sure he was revising his opinion of our unexpected new recruit. *'Maybe she's not so bad after all,'* he may have been thinking.

The weather remained miserable all afternoon, so when the clock started edging towards six, I started looking out for Titch. I'd done pretty well selling magazines and wanted to start heading homewards. It was no night to be out late. But there was no sign of him. Six pm came and went and still there was nothing. I saw one of the *The Big Issue* co-ordinators heading home from work. Everyone knew Titch, so I asked if she'd seen him.

'No, haven't seen him for weeks actually,' she said. 'Not since all that trouble, you know?'

'Yeah,' I said.

By 6.30pm I'd become thoroughly disillusioned. I knew street people weren't the world's greatest timekeepers, but this was getting ridiculous.

'Come on you two, let's head for home. He can come and collect you there, Princess,' I said, gathering all my stuff together. I was cheesed off with Titch, but I was also a little worried. Bob had tolerated Princess being in the flat for a few minutes earlier but having her for a 'sleepover' was another matter altogether. I could foresee lots of barking from Princess, complaints from the neighbours and a sleepless night for me.

I stopped at the convenience store to grab some food for Princess. I had no idea what she liked to eat, so gambled on a tin of standard fare dog food and some doggie biscuits.

Back in the kitchen as we all settled down to dinner, Bob once more ensured that the pecking order was clear. When Princess made a move towards the bowl of water I'd laid out for her, Bob hissed and snarled loudly, forcing the interloper to back off. He had to lap up his own bowl of milk first.

It didn't take them long to reach an accommodation though. In fact, Bob was so content with his new companion that he allowed her to clear out the remains of his dinner bowl.

I've seen it all now, I thought to myself. Actually, I hadn't.

I was shattered by 10pm and fell asleep in front of the television. When I woke up I saw something that made me wish I owned a video camera. I would have made a small fortune on those television shows that feature cute animal clips.

Bob and Princess were both splayed out on the carpet, snoozing quietly. When I'd left them they were at opposite ends of the room, with Bob near his favourite spot by the radiator and Princess near the door. While I'd been sleeping, Princess had clearly sought out the warmth of the radiator and slid alongside Bob. Her head was now barely a foot from Bob's nose. If I hadn't known any better, I'd have guessed that they were lifelong pals. I locked the front door, switched off the lights and headed off to bed leaving them there. I didn't hear a peep from either of them until the following morning when I was woken up by the sound of barking.

It took me a moment to remember that I had a dog in the house.

'What's wrong, Princess?' I said, still half asleep.

They say that some animals can sense their owners are nearby. My best friend Belle sometimes stayed at the flat with us and she had told me that Bob often sensed when I was coming home. Several times he had jumped up on the window sill in the kitchen looking anxiously down to the street below minutes before I arrived at the front door. Princess clearly had the same gift because a couple of moments later I heard the buzzer. It was Titch.

From the look of his unshaven and rather bleary face, he had slept rough, which, knowing Titch, was quite possible.

'Really sorry to leave you in the lurch last night but something came up,' he said, apologetically. I didn't bother asking what it was. I'd had nights like that myself, far too many of them.

I made another cup of tea and stuck some bread in the toaster. He looked like he could do with something warm inside him.

Bob was lying next to the radiator, with Princess curled up a couple of feet away, his eyes once more fixed on his new friend. The expression on Titch's face was priceless. He was dumbstruck.

'Look at those two, they get on like a house on fire now,' I smiled.

'I can see it, but I can't quite believe it,' he said, grinning widely.

Titch wasn't a man to miss an opportunity.

'So would you mind looking after her again if I'm in the lurch?' he asked, munching on his toast.

'Why not?' I said.

Chapter 5

The Ghost on the Stairs

The rain had been relentless for days, transforming the streets of London into miniature paddling pools. Bob and I were regularly returning home soaked to the skin, so today I'd given up and headed home early.

I arrived back at the flats around mid-afternoon desperate to get out of my wet clothes and let Bob warm himself by the radiator.

The lift in my building was erratic at the best of times. After a few minutes repeatedly pressing the button for it to come down from the fifth floor, I realised it was out of order once more.

'Brilliant,' I muttered to myself. 'It's the long walk up again I'm afraid Bob.'

He looked at me forlornly.

'Come on then,' I said, dipping my shoulder down so that he could climb on board.

We were just beginning the final couple of flights of stairs, from the fourth to the fifth floor, when I noticed a figure in the shadows on the landing above us.

'Hold on here for a second, Bob,' I said, placing him down on the steps and heading up on my own.

Moving in closer I could see that it was a man and he was leaning against the wall. He was hunched over with his trousers partially dropped down and there was something metallic in his hand. I knew instantly what he was doing.

In the past, the flats had been notorious as a haunt for drug users and dealers. Addicts would find their way in and use the staircase and hallways to smoke crack and marijuana or inject themselves with heroin like this guy was doing. In the years since I'd moved in, the police had improved the situation dramatically, but we'd still occasionally see young kids dealing in the stairwell on the ground floor. It was nowhere near as bad as a previous sheltered housing project I'd lived in, over in Dalston, which was over-run with crack addicts. But it was still distressing, especially for the families who lived in the flats. No one wants their children arriving home from school to find a junkie shooting up on the staircase outside their home.

For me, of course, it was a reminder of the past I was desperate to put behind me. I continued to struggle with my addiction; I always would. That, unfortunately, was the nature of the beast. But, since teaming up with Bob, I'd made the break-through and was on the way to complete recovery. After weaning myself off heroin and then methadone, I'd been prescribed a drug called subutex, a milder medication that was slowly but surely reducing my drug dependency. The counsellor at my drug dependency unit had likened this final part of my recovery to landing an aeroplane: I would slowly drop back down to earth. I'd been on subutex for several months now. The landing gear was down and I could see the lights of the runway in front of me. The descent was going according to plan, I was almost back on solid ground.

I could do without seeing this, I said to myself.

I saw that the guy was in his mid-forties with a short, crew-cut hairstyle. He was wearing a black coat, t-shirt and jeans and a pair of scruffy trainers. Fortunately he wasn't aggressive. In fact he was quite the opposite. He was really apologetic, which was pretty unusual. Selflessness isn't really a strong suit in heroin addicts.

'Sorry, mate, I'll get out of your way,' he said in a thick East End accent, taking his 'works' out of his leg and pulling up his trousers. I could tell that he'd finished injecting. His eyes had that tell-tale glazed look.

I decided to let him go first. I knew better than to

completely trust an addict. I wanted to keep him ahead of me where I could see him.

He was pretty unsteady on his feet and stumbled up the short flight of stairs to the landing on the fifth floor, through the doors and into the hallway heading for the lift.

Bob had trotted up the final flight of stairs behind me on the end of his lead. I just wanted to get him inside to safety so headed for the door of our flat. I had just put the key in the door and let Bob in when I heard a loud groan. I turned round and saw the guy collapse. He just suddenly went down like a sack of potatoes, hitting the ground with a smack.

'Mate, are you all right?' I said, running over to him. He clearly wasn't.

I could see immediately that he was in a really bad way. He didn't seem to be breathing.

'Oh God, he's OD'd!' I said to myself, recognising the symptoms of an overdose.

Fortunately, I had my cheap Nokia mobile on me. I called 999 and asked for an emergency ambulance. The lady on the other end of the line took my address but then told me it was going to take at least ten minutes.

'Can you describe his condition to me?' she asked, her voice calm and professional.

'He's unconscious and he's not breathing,' I said. 'And his skin is changing colour.'

'OK, sounds like his heart has stopped. I'm going to ask you to give him CPR. Do you know what that is?' the lady said.

'Yes, I do. But you will have to talk me through it really carefully.'

She got me to turn the guy on his side and to check that his airwaves were clear. I then had to turn him on to his back so that I could apply compression to his chest to try to jump start his heart. Then I had to breathe into his mouth to try to get him to respond.

Within moments I was pressing down on his chest with both hands, counting as I did so. When I got to thirty I stopped to see if there was any change in his condition.

The lady from the emergency services was still on the line.

'Any response?' she asked.

'No. Nothing. He's not breathing,' I said. 'I'll try again.'

I carried on like this for what must have been several minutes, pressing his chest furiously in short bursts then breathing into his mouth. Looking back on it later, I was surprised at how calm I felt. I realise now that it was one of those situations where the brain goes into a different mode. The emotional reality of what was happening wasn't registering in my mind at all. Instead, I was just focussing on the physical side of things, trying to get this guy to breathe again. Despite my best efforts, however, his condition remained the same.

At one point he started making a gurgling, snoring sound. I'd heard about the 'death rattle' a person makes as they draw their last breath. I didn't want to think it, but I feared that's what I was hearing here.

After what seemed like an age, I heard the buzzer of my door going so ran over to my flat.

'Ambulance service,' a voice said. I hit the buzzer and told them to come up. Thankfully our flaky lift was now working again, so they arrived on the fifth floor within seconds. They threw down their bags and immediately produced a CPR kit with paddles to conduct electric shocks. They then cut open his t-shirt.

'Stand back, Sir,' one of them said. 'We can take it from here.'

For the next five or so minutes they kept working feverishly to get him moving. But his body was lying there, limp and lifeless. By now the shock was kicking in and I was standing by the doorway, shaking.

Eventually, one of the ambulance men slumped over and turned to the other one: 'No. He's gone,' he said. Slowly and really reluctantly they draped a silver blanket over him and put away their gear.

It was as if I had been struck by a lightning bolt. I was absolutely pole-axed. The ambulance guys asked me if I was all right.

'Just need to go inside and sit down for a second I think,' I told them.

Bob had been inside the flat throughout the drama but had now appeared in the doorway, perhaps sensing that I was upset.

'Come on, mate, let's get you inside,' I said, picking him up. For some reason I didn't want him to see the body lying there. He'd seen similar scenes on the streets of central London, but I just felt protective of him.

A few minutes later I got a knock on the door. The police and some paramedics had arrived in the hallway and a young constable was standing in my doorway.

'I gather you were the person who found him and called 999,' he said.

'Yeah,' I said. I'd gathered myself together a little bit by now, but I was still feeling shaken.

'You did the right thing. I don't think there was much more you could have done for him,' the PC said, reassuringly.

I described how I'd found him on the staircase and seen him go down.

'It seemed to affect him really quickly,' I said.

I told them that I was a recovering addict which, I think, allayed any suspicions they might have had about me somehow being involved with this guy. They knew what addicts were like, as indeed did I. At the end of the day all they care about is themselves. They are so selfish would literally sell their own grandmother or watch their girlfriend die. If an addict had discovered another addict who had overdosed in this way they would have done two things; empty the poor sod's pockets of cash, relieve him of any jewellery and then run away – fast. They might call an ambulance but they wouldn't have wanted to get involved.

The policemen also seemed to know about the flats and its dodgy past. They were pretty understanding.

'OK, Mr Bowen, that's all I need for now, it's unlikely we will need a further statement for the inquest, but we will keep your details on file in case we need to speak to you again,' the PC told me.

We chatted for another moment or two. He told me that they had found some ID on the guy and also some medication which had his name and address on it. It turned out he was on day release from a psychiatric ward.

By the time I saw the officer back out into the hallway, the scene had been completely cleared. It was as if nothing had happened. It was as quiet as a grave in the flats. No one else seemed to be around at this time of the day.

In the quiet I suddenly felt myself being

overwhelmed by what I'd just seen. I couldn't hold back my emotions any longer. Back inside the flat, I just burst into floods of tears. I called Belle on my mobile and asked her to come over that night. I needed to talk to someone.

We sat up until well past midnight and drank a few too many beers. I couldn't get the image of the guy collapsing out of my head.

I was in a state of mild shock for days. On one level, I was shaken by the fact that this poor guy had died in that way. He'd spent his final moments on the floor of an anonymous block of flats, in the company of a complete stranger. That wasn't the way life should work. He was someone's son, maybe someone's brother or even someone's father. He should have been with them or his friends. Where were they? Why weren't they looking after him? I also wondered why on earth he had been allowed out of his psychiatric ward for the day if he was that vulnerable?

But, if I was honest, the thing that hit me hardest was the realisation that this could so easily have been me. It might sound silly now, but I remember thinking that it felt a little bit like Scrooge being visited by the ghost of his not-so-distant past.

For the best part of a decade, I had lived like that. I too had been a phantom figure, hiding away in stairwells and alleyways, lost in my heroin addiction. I had no real memory of the details, of course. Large chunks of my life back then were a complete blur. But it was safe to guess that there were probably dozens – maybe hundreds – of occasions when I could have died alone in some anonymous corner of London, far from the parents, relatives and friends from whom I'd cut myself off.

Thinking about it in the wake of this man's death, part of me couldn't actually believe that I'd lived that way. Had I really been reduced to that? Had I really done those things to myself? A part of me couldn't imagine how on earth I'd been able to insert a needle into my flesh, some-times four times a day. It seemed unreal, except I knew it was reality. I still bore the scars, liter-ally. I only had to look at my arms and legs to see them.

They reminded me of how fragile my situation remained still. An addict is always living on a knife edge. I would always have an addictive personality and some mental health issues that I knew made me prone to destructive behaviour. All it needed was one moment of weakness and I could be on the way down again. It scared me. But it also stiffened my determination to continue that slow descent to earth that my counsellors had talked about. I didn't want to be that anonymous man on the stairs again. I had to keep moving on.

Chapter 6

The Garbage Inspector

We all have our obsessions in life. For Bob, it's packaging.

The assorted collection of boxes, cartons, wrapping papers and plastic bottles which we use during our day-to-day life around the flat, absolutely fascinate him. And some materials fixate him more than others.

Bubble wrap, naturally, is a source of endless entertainment. What child doesn't love popping the bubbles? Bob goes absolutely crazy with excitement whenever I let him play with a sheet of it. I always keep a watchful eye on him. Each time he pops a cell with his paw or mouth, he turns and gives me a look as if to say 'did you hear that?'

Wrapping paper is another fascination. Whenever I unwrap a present for him, he shows more interest in playing with the fancy paper than with the actual toy itself. He is also endlessly obsessed by the crispy, crunchy cellophane used inside cereal packets and by supermarkets to wrap bread. It never ceases to amaze me, but he can spend half an hour rustling a ball of cellophane. Balls of scrunched up aluminium kitchen foil have the same effect.

There is, however, no question about his absolute favourite type of packaging: cardboard boxes. He basically sees every box he comes across as a toy, an object designed to provide him with hours of fun. If I ever walk past Bob with a cardboard box in my hand he lunges at me as if to grab it. It doesn't matter whether it is a cereal box, a milk carton or a bigger box, he bounds up, paddling his paws quickly as if to say 'give me that, I want to play with it NOW'.

He also loves hiding away in the bigger boxes, a habit that has given me a case of the heebeegeebees on at least one occasion.

I don't let Bob wander out of our flat on his own and the windows are always closed to avoid him climbing out. (I knew cats had the ability to 'self-right' themselves in the air and we were 'only' five floors up, but I didn't want to test his flying abilities!) So when, one summer evening, I couldn't find him in any of his usual spots I panicked slightly.

'Bob, Bob, where are you mate?' I said.

I looked high and low, a process that didn't take too long given the smallness of my flat. But there was no sign of him in my bedroom or in the kitchen or bathroom. I was beginning to genuinely worry about his welfare when it suddenly struck me that I'd put a box containing some hand-me-down clothes I'd been given by a charity worker in the airing cupboard. Sure enough, I opened the cupboard to see a distinctive ginger shape submerged in the middle of the box.

He'd done the same thing again not long afterwards, with almost disastrous consequences.

Belle had come around to help me tidy the place up a bit. It wasn't the most organised and orderly of homes, at the best of times. It didn't help that, for years I had been a bit of a magpie. I don't know whether I subconsciously harboured dreams of opening a junk shop or whether I was just fascinated by old stuff, but somehow I'd collected all sorts of bits and bobs, everything from old books and maps, to broken radios and toasters.

Belle had persuaded me to chuck out some of this old tat and we'd organised a few cardboard boxes full of them. We were going to throw some in the rubbish but take others to charity shops or the local recycling place. Belle was taking one box down to the rubbish area outside the flats and was waiting for the lift to arrive when she felt her box jiggling around. It freaked her out a bit and I heard her scream from inside my flat. By the time I opened the door to see what the trouble was she'd dropped the box to the floor and discovered Bob inside. He was extricating himself from a collection of old books and magazines where he'd curled up for a nap.

Soon after that I'd actually made him a bed out of a cardboard box. I'd figured that if he slept in one he might be less obsessed with them at other times. I'd taken one side off a box then lined it with a little blanket. He was as snug as a bug in there. He loved it.

It didn't entirely get rid of his obsession, however. He remained deeply interested in the rubbish bin in the kitchen. Whenever I put something into the bin he would get up on his hind legs and stick his nose in. If I ever challenged him he would throw me a look as if to say 'hey, what are you throwing in there? I haven't decided if I want to play with that or not.' For a while, I started jokingly calling him the garbage inspector. It wasn't always a laughing matter, however.

I was just emerging from the bath one morning when I heard weird noises coming from the kitchen. I could make out a thin, metallic, scraping sound, as if something was being dragged around. It was accompanied by a kind of low moaning sound.

'Bob, what are you up to now?' I said, grabbing a towel to dry my hair as I went to investigate.

I couldn't help giggling at the sight that greeted me.

Bob was standing in the middle of the kitchen floor with an empty tin of cat food wedged on the top of his head. The tin was sitting at a jaunty angle on his head right over his eyeline. He looked like a cross between the Black Knight from the movie *Monty Python and the Holy Grail* and a Welsh guard outside Buckingham Palace with his bearskin hat hanging over his eyes.

It was obvious that he couldn't see much because he was walking backwards across the kitchen floor, dragging the tin with him in an attempt to reverse himself out of it. He was being very deliberate, padding backwards one careful step at a time, occasionally wiggling the tin or raising it a little before giving it a tap against the floor in the hope the impact would dislodge it. His plan wasn't working. It was comical to watch.

It didn't take Hercule Poirot or Columbo to work out what had happened. In the corner of the room I could see the black bin liner containing the rubbish I was going to put in the wheelie bins downstairs this morning. I normally emptied the bin and put the sack out at night, specifically to stop Bob playing with it. But for some reason today I'd forgotten and left it on the kitchen floor. Big mistake.

Bob had clearly taken advantage of my absence and ripped and chewed at the bottom of the bag so that he could try his luck rummaging in the waste. He'd drawn a blank on the cardboard front, but he had found the old tin. Unfortunately for him, in his enthusiasm to explore its contents, he'd got his head stuck in there. It was the kind of thing you saw on YouTube or video clip programmes like *You've Been Framed* all the time. He'd got himself in a terrible mess and was letting out this rather sad and pathetic little moaning sound. It wasn't the first time he'd done something like this. One day I'd been sitting in the living room when I heard another odd sound coming from the kitchen, a kind of tapping sound. *Pat . . . pat . . . pat* followed by a faster *pat, pat, pat, pat.*

I'd found Bob walking around with a miniature container of butter attached to one of his paws. He loved butter so had obviously found this and been dipping his paw in so that he could lick it clean. He'd somehow wedged the paw inside the container and was now walking around with it attached. Every now and again, he'd raise his paw and tap it against a cupboard door in an effort to dislodge it. Eventually I'd had to help him remove it. I could see I would have to do the same thing here.

He was clearly feeling a little bit sorry for himself and knew he'd done something stupid.

'Bob, you silly boy. What have you done to

yourself?' I said, leaning down to help him. Thank goodness he hadn't shoved his head all the way inside the tin, I thought. It had a serrated edge where it had been opened so I was careful in removing it from his head. I smelled inside the tin. It wasn't the most pleasant odour I'd ever encountered, that was for sure.

The instant I extricated the top of his head from the tin, Bob scooted off into the corner. There were bits of food stuck to his ear and the back of his head so he began licking and washing himself frantically. As he did so he kept shooting me rather sheepish looks, as if to say: 'yes, I know it was a dumb thing to do. Don't tell me you've never done anything stupid yourself.'

As we headed off into work an hour or so later, he was still wearing the same, rather embarrassed expression and I was still smiling to myself about it.

The first sign that something was amiss came a few days later when he began eating more than usual. Bob's daily diet had been a well-established routine for a long time now. Even though money was tight, I always tried to feed him decent 'Scientific Formula' food from the most popular cat food brands. I'd ration it carefully, following the recommended portions. So in the morning he had a flat tea cup full of high-nutrition biscuits and at the end of the day, about an hour before his bed time, he'd then have a further half a tea cup of biscuits along with half a pouch of meat as his evening meal.

These two meals would be supplemented by the little snacks he had while we were out working. It was always more than sufficient to keep him happy and healthy. In fact, he normally left a quarter or so of his morning biscuits because it was too much for him. Sometimes he'd leave it there, at other times he'd eat it just before we headed out to work, as a mid-morning snack.

A few days after he'd got his head caught in the tin can, however, I noticed that he was wolfing down all his breakfast in double-quick time. He was even licking the bowl clean.

He was also more demanding. I had always decided when to give him a reward for his tricks. But now he began to ask for snacks himself. There was something different about the way he pleaded for these snacks as well. It wasn't the usual plaintive, 'Puss in Boots' look. It was as if he was really desperate for food. And it was the same when we got home. Ordinarily, he was pretty laid back about getting his dinner, but he began to hassle me as soon as we were in the door. He would be quite agitated until I filled his bowl up. Again, he'd shovel everything down him as fast as possible and give me a look straight out of *Oliver Twist*. 'Please, dad, can I have some more?'

The alarming thing, however, was that after a week or so of this behaviour he wasn't gaining any weight.

That's odd, I said to myself one evening when he'd finished his dinner and still looked like he could have eaten more.

Adding to my suspicions that something was wrong was the fact that he was going to the toilet more often. Bob was, like most cats, a creature of habit when it came to toilet time. Over the years he'd overcome his dislike of going in the litter tray at home and did his business there in the mornings. He'd then go again when we were out in London. Suddenly, however, this habit had changed and he had started going three times or more each day. He might have been going more than that, as far as I knew. I'd caught him using the toilet in the flat once. I hadn't seen him use it again since then, for some reason. Maybe he didn't like me watching him? But as I began to worry more and more about this change in his habits I noticed the water in the toilet bowl was a little off colour sometimes.

He had also started demanding to be taken to the toilet more often at Angel. It was always a real palaver, packing up and heading over to the Green so that he could get on with things, but it had to be done.

'What is wrong with you, Bob?' I said, losing patience with him after a few days of this. He just gave me an aloof look, as if to tell me to mind my own business.

The moment I knew I had a real problem, however, was when I found him dragging his bottom along the floor. The first time I noticed it was one morning soon after I'd woken up. I saw him deep in concentration, scooting his undercarriage on the carpet in the living room.

I wasn't best pleased.

'Bob, that's disgusting, what do you think you're doing?' I scalded him.

But I soon realised that it must mean that he had a problem. As usual, I was short of money and didn't want to splash out on a visit to the vet and the inevitable medicine expenses that would follow. So the next morning on the way into work I decided to drop into the local library and have a little root around on the internet. I had my suspicions but had to be sure. My hunch was that he had some kind of stomach infection involving a parasite. It didn't necessarily explain the eating, but it was consistent with going to the toilet more often and scooting his bottom on the floor.

My greatest fear was that it was a parasite infection. I cast my mind back to my childhood in Australia when I'd seen a couple of cats develop worms. It wasn't pleasant, and was also contagious. A lot of children in Australia used to contract worms from their cats. It was quite gross actually.

Of course, researching illness on the internet is always the biggest mistake you can make. I'd done it before, but hadn't heeded the lesson. Sure enough, within about half an hour I'd convinced myself that Bob's symptoms were consistent with a really serious kind of worm, a hookworm or a tapeworm. Neither is usually a fatal illness, but they can be really nasty, causing severe loss of weight and a deterioration in the coat if untreated.

I knew I had no option but to check his poo the next time he went to the toilet. I didn't have to wait long. Within about an hour of us settling down at Angel, he started making his tell-tale noises and gestures and I had to take him off to the Green. I braced myself to sneak a quick look before he covered up his business in the soft earth. He didn't take kindly to my intrusion.

'Sorry, Bob, but I've got to take a peek,' I said, inspecting his droppings with a twig.

It may sound bizarre, but I was delighted when I saw some tiny, white wiggly creatures in there. It was worms, but only tiny little ones.

'At least it's not tapeworm or hookworm,' I consoled myself for the rest of that day.

Heading home that night I felt a strange, slightly confusing mix of emotions. The responsible cat owner in me was really miffed. I was so careful about his diet, avoiding raw meats and other things that are known to be risky when it comes to worms.

I had also been diligent in making sure he was regularly checked for fleas, which can act as hosts for worms. He was also a really clean and healthy cat, and I made sure the flat was in a decent condition for him to live. I felt like it reflected badly on me. I felt like I'd let him down a little bit. On the other hand, however, I was relieved that I now knew what I needed to do.

As luck would have it, I knew the Blue Cross drop-in van was going to be at Islington Green the following day. So I made sure that we headed off early to beat the lengthy queues that always built up before the clinic began.

The staff there knew Bob and I well; we'd been regular visitors over the years. Bob had been micro-chipped there and I'd spent the best part of a year dropping in to slowly pay off the fees I'd incurred for that and other treatments. I'd also had him checked out frequently, including for fleas, ironically.

The vet who was on duty that morning asked me to describe the problem, then took a quick look at Bob and a sample of poo that I'd put in a plastic, pill container I had lying around the house before coming to a predictable conclusion.

'Yes, he's got worms I'm afraid, James,' he said. 'What's he been eating lately? Anything out of the ordinary? Been rummaging in the bins or anything like that?'

It was as if a light had gone on in my head. I felt so stupid.

'Oh, God, yes.'

I'd completely forgotten about the tin can incident. He must have found a piece of old chicken or other meat in there. How could I have failed to see that?

The vet gave me a course of medication and a syringe with which to apply it.

'How long will it take to clear things up?' I asked.

'Should be on the mend within a few days, James,' he said. 'Let me know if the symptoms persist.'

Years earlier, when I'd first taken Bob in and had to administer antibiotics to him I'd had to do it by hand, inserting tablets in his mouth and then rubbing his throat to help them on their way down into his stomach. The syringe would, in theory, make that process simpler. But he still had to trust me to insert the contraption down his throat.

Back at the flat that evening, I could tell that he didn't like the look of it. But it was a measure of how much he trusted me that he immediately let me place the plastic inside his mouth and release the tablet before rubbing his throat. I figured that he must know I wouldn't do anything to him that wasn't absolutely necessary.

As the vet had predicted, Bob was back to his normal self within a couple of days. His appetite waned and he was soon eating and going to the toilet normally again.

As I thought about what had happened, I gave myself a ticking off. The responsibility of looking after Bob had been such a positive force in my life. But I needed to live up to that responsibility a little better. He wasn't a part time job that I could clock into whenever the mood took me.

I felt particularly negligent because it wasn't the first time Bob had suffered because of his habit of rummaging in bins. A year or so earlier, he'd got quite sick after investigating the inside of the wheelie bins outside the block of flats.

I told myself that I could never let a bin bag lie around like that again. It was stupid of me to have done so in the first place. Even if everything was sealed, Bob was such a resourceful and inquisitive character, he'd find a way in.

Most of all though, I breathed a sigh of relief. It wasn't often that he was off colour or ill, but whenever he was, the pessimist in me always jumped to the worst possible conclusions. As daft and over-dramatic as it was, over the past days I'd found myself imagining him dying and me having to carry on life without him. It was a prospect that was too scary to contemplate.

I always said that we were partners, that we needed each other equally. Deep down I believed that wasn't really true. I felt like I needed him more.

Chapter 7

Cat on a Hoxton Roof

Bob and I have always been a fairly distinctive pair. There aren't many six foot tall blokes walking around the streets of London with a ginger cat sitting on his shoulders, after all. We certainly turn heads.

For a few months during the summer and autumn of 2009 we made an even more eye-catching sight. Unfortunately, I was in too much pain to enjoy the attention.

The problems had begun the previous year when I'd travelled to Australia to see my mother. My mum and I had always had a difficult relationship and we'd become estranged for the best part of a decade. Apart from a brief visit to London, the last time I'd seen her was when she'd seen me off at the airport as an 18-year-old heading from Australia to 'make it' as a musician in London. In the lost decade that followed, we'd barely talked. Time had healed the wounds a little, so, when she offered to pay for me to visit her in Tasmania, it seemed right that I should go.

With Bob's help I'd just managed to make a massive breakthrough and wean myself off methadone. It had left me feeling weak so I needed the break. Bob had stayed with my friend Belle, at her flat near Hoxton in north London, not too far from Angel.

The long flights to and from Australia had taken their toll on me physically, however. I had known about the risks of spending hours immobile on long haul flights, especially when you are tall, like me, and had done my best to avoid sitting for too long in a cramped seating position. But despite doing my best to walk around the plane as often as possible, I'd come home with a nagging pain in my upper thigh.

At first it had been manageable and I'd dealt with it by taking ordinary, over-the-counter pain killers. Slowly but surely, however, it had grown worse. I had begun experiencing an incredible cramping feeling, as if my blood had stopped flowing and my muscles were seizing up. I know no human feels rigor mortis, but I had a suspicion if we did, this was the sensation. It was as if I had the leg of a zombie.

The pain had soon become so bad that I couldn't sit or lie down with my leg in anything resembling a normal position. If I did I would be in constant muscular pain. So whenever I was watching television or eating a meal at home in the flat I had to sit with my leg on a cushion or another chair. When it came to bedtime I had to sleep with my foot elevated over the end of the bed head.

I'd been to see the doctor a couple of times, but they had only prescribed stronger pain killers. During the dark days of my heroin addiction, I had injected myself everywhere in my body, including in my groin. I'm sure they felt that my condition, whatever it was, was just some kind of hangover from my abusive past. I hadn't pushed it, part of me was used to being fobbed off still. It reinforced that old feeling I'd had as a homeless person that I was somehow invisible, that society didn't regard me as its concern.

The real problem for me was that I still needed to earn a crust. So that meant that, regardless of how much discomfort I was in, I still had to haul myself out of bed and head to Angel on a daily basis.

It wasn't easy. The moment I put my foot on the floor, the pain shot up through my leg like an electric shock. I could only walk three or four steps at a time. So the walk to the bus stop became a marathon, often taking me twice or three times as long as it would normally.

Bob didn't know what to make of this at first. He kept giving me quizzical looks, as if to say: 'what are you doing, mate?' But he was a smart boy and had soon worked out there was something wrong and started changing his behaviour accordingly. In the morning, for instance, rather than greeting me with his usual repertoire of sounds, nudges and pleading looks, he had started looking at me with an inquisitive and slightly pitying expression. It was as if he was saying 'feeling any better today?'

It was the same story as we headed to work. Often Bob would walk alongside me rather than taking up his usual position on my shoulders. He obviously preferred travelling on the upper deck, as I put it, but he would trot along beside me as much as he possibly could. I think he could see I was in pain.

When he felt that I had been soldiering on for too long he would actually try to make me stop and sit down. He would cut across my path, trying to steer me in the direction of a bench or wall where I could take a break. I took the view that it was better to finish my journey rather than stopping every few steps so, for a while, it developed into a bit of a battle of wills.

It must have been quite entertaining when locals in Tottenham saw us picking our way down the road near my flats. Whenever he heard me complain about the pain Bob would stop and give me a look that suggested I should take a breather or sit down. I'd look back at him and say, 'No, Bob, I need to keep moving.' If I hadn't been in so much agony, I'd probably have found it quite amusing myself. We probably resembled a bickering old married couple.

After a while, however, it became pretty clear that I couldn't carry on like this. Often I'd arrive home from work exhausted, only to discover that the lift was out of order again. The walk to the fifth floor was absolutely excruciating and could take an eternity. So I had begun staying with Belle.

There were all sorts of advantages to this. To begin with her flat was on the first floor rather than the fifth floor which saved me a lot of aggravation. Getting to work from there was also a less painful process with a bus stop only yards away.

It helped a little, but the pain continued to grow gradually worse. My dread of putting my foot on the floor had now become so great that one morning I decided to make myself a crutch. With Bob in tow, I'd headed into the pretty little park near Belle's flat and found a branch from a fallen tree that fitted perfectly under my arm, allowing me to keep the weight off my painful leg when I walked. It only took me a day or so to get the hang of it.

I got a lot of very strange looks, understandably. With my long hair and shaggy beard, I must have looked like some kind of modern-day Merlin or Gandalf from *The Lord of the Rings*. As if that wasn't odd enough, the sight of a ginger cat sitting on my shoulder must have conjured up images of wizards walking around with their 'familiars'. The truth was that I didn't really care what it looked like at that point. Anything that eased the pain was a Godsend.

Getting anywhere on foot had become a real ordeal. I was taking a few steps and then keeling over and sitting on the nearest brick wall. I'd tried using the bike to get around but that was an utter impossibility. The moment I applied any pressure to the pedal with my right leg I was in agony. The Bobmobile was in the hallway back in Tottenham, gathering dust.

There was no question that Bob understood that there was something seriously wrong with me and at times I felt like he was losing patience. Some mornings, as he watched me struggling to get my trousers on ready to go to work, he would give me a withering look as if to say: 'why are you doing this to yourself? Why don't you stay in bed?' The answer to that, of course, was that I had no option. We were skint, as usual.

My daily routine became a real chore. We'd get off the bus at Islington Green and head to the little park there so that Bob could do his business. From there, I'd hobble over to the *The Big Issue* co-ordinator's spot, which was just outside Starbucks coffee shop. I'd then cross the main road and head to the tube station, and our pitch.

Having to stand there for five or six hours a day wasn't feasible. I would have passed out. Fortunately, one of the florists outside the tube station saw the state I was in one day and came over to me holding a couple of buckets that he used to hold flowers.

'There you go, sit on that. And get Bob to sit on the other one,' he had said, giving me an encouraging pat on the back.

I really appreciated it. There was no way I was going to be able to stand for more than a few minutes at a time.

At first, I'd been worried that sitting on the bucket would be a disaster for my business. (People always laughed when I called selling *The Big Issue* a business, but that's actually what it was. You had to buy magazines in order to sell them so, as a vendor, you had to make fine judgements about stock and budgeting week in, week out. The principle was actually no different from running a giant corporation and the stakes were just as high, if not higher. Succeed and you survived, fail and you could starve to death.) Ordinarily, I paced around the area outside the station coaxing and cajoling people into parting with their hard-earned cash. When I started sitting on the bucket, I was terrified that people simply wouldn't see me sitting there. I should have known better. Bob took care of it.

Maybe it was because I was sitting down with him more of the time, but during this period he became a real little showman. In the past, it had usually been me who had instigated the playful routines. But now he began taking the initiative himself. He would rub up against me and give me a look as if to say, 'come on mate, get the snacks out, let's do a few tricks and earn ourselves a few quid'. There were times when I was convinced he knew precisely what was happening. I was certain he'd worked out that the sooner we earned a decent amount of money, the sooner we could get home and rest my leg. It was eerie how he understood so much.

I wished I could see life so clearly sometimes.

Living at Belle's with Bob had its pros and cons. I was still desperately trying to work out what was wrong with my leg, but just hoped that by resting it the problem would somehow go away. While I spent as much time as I could off my feet, Belle looked after me, cooking me nice meals and doing my laundry, and Bob got on well with her. During the time he'd spent with her while I was in Australia, they had clearly formed a strong bond. She was the only other person whom he would ever consider allowing to pick him up, for instance.

There was no doubt that he regarded her home as a safe haven as well. The previous year, when he'd run away from Angel one evening after being attacked by a dog, he'd headed for Belle's flat, even though it had been a long walk away. It had taken me hours to work out that he'd taken refuge there. It had been the longest night of my life.

The closeness of their relationship certainly made life easier for me. But it also gave Bob licence to be mischievous.

One morning I got up and headed into the kitchen to make myself a cup of coffee, expecting to find Bob settled there. Just like at home, he tended to hang around in the kitchen early in the day, mainly in the hope of picking up any spare bits of food that might be going. There were times when he could be a real gannet.

Today, however, there was no sign of him. There was no sign of Belle either.

It had been raining heavily that morning but the weather had already cleared. It was now a really bright sunny morning and the temperature was already rising. The forecast was predicting sweltering heat later in the day. I noticed that Belle had already opened the window in the kitchen to let the fresh air into the flat.

'Bob, where are you mate?' I said, heading off in search of him, still wearing just my boxer shorts and a t-shirt.

There was no sign of him in the sitting room or the hallway, so I headed to the back bedroom where Belle slept. When I saw the window there was also ajar I got an instant sinking feeling.

Belle's flat was on the first floor and the back bedroom window overlooked the roof of the extension on the ground floor flat below us. That roof overlooked a yard and, beyond it, the car park for the building. From there it was a short walk to the main road, one of the busiest in that part of north London.

'Oh, no, Bob, you haven't gone out there have you?'

I managed to squeeze my head through the gap in the window and scanned the rooftops below. There were extension roofs protruding all the way along the building. Sure enough, five flats along from Belle's, there was Bob sitting, sunning himself on the roof.

When I shouted his name he slowly turned his head in my direction and gave me a confused look. It was as if he was saying: 'what's wrong?'

I had no problem with him sunbathing. I was more concerned with the fact that he could slide off the slippery roof, or that he might go down into the yard and from there out through the car park on to the main road.

I panicked and began taking the security screws off the window so that I could open it fully and climb out on to the roof. After a couple of minutes I was able to squeeze myself through the gap. I still hadn't managed to put on any clothes.

The slate tiles were slippery from the rain earlier in the morning, so keeping a grip wasn't easy, especially given the fact I was in agony with my leg. Somehow, however, I managed to scamper across the rooftops to where Bob was sitting. I was within a few feet of him when I realised that I was on a wasted mission.

Bob suddenly picked himself up and scuttled his way back across the rooftops, nonchalantly passing me. When I tried to grab at him, he just growled at me and made a sudden spurt towards Belle's open window. Again, he shot me a disdainful look. He was soon disappearing back indoors.

I, of course, had a long way to go. It took me a few minutes to scramble back across the slippery slates. To my complete embarrassment, a couple of faces appeared in the windows. The looks on their faces spoke volumes. They were a mix of shock, mild pity and hilarity.

Moments after I got back into the safety of the flat, I heard the front door closing and saw Belle standing in the hallway with a small bag of groceries.

She burst out laughing.

'Where the hell have you been?' she said.

'On the bloody roof trying to rescue Bob,' I said.

'Oh he goes out there all the time,' she said with a dismissive wave of a hand. 'He even goes down into the yard sometimes. He always comes back up.'

'I really wish you'd told me that sooner,' I said, shuffling off to my temporary bedroom to finally put on some clothes.

It wasn't long before he'd turned the tables, however. Soon after that, it was Belle who was cursing his playful ways.

As I'd discovered the hard way, Bob loved exploring the back of Belle's block of flats and took full advantage of the fact that he was on the first rather than the fifth floor.

In some ways it was a healthy thing. Bob loved going out there to do his business in the mornings and evenings. But, of course, this also allowed him to exercise his other natural instincts.

I knew that it was part of his DNA to hunt. No matter how much people might think they are cute little fluffballs, cats are also predators – seriously effective predators at that. As we settled into life at Belle's flat, he began to bring us presents. One day we were sitting in the front room when he arrived with a small mouse dangling from his mouth. He'd placed it carefully at my feet, as if he was offering me a gift.

I'd chastised him about it.

'Bob, you will make yourself sick again if you eat that,' I said.

Realistically I knew there was nothing I could do, apart from keeping him under house arrest, which I didn't want to do. And I wasn't going to resort to putting a bell on him, at this stage, at least.

Predictably, this meant that he became a little bolder in his behaviour.

One morning, I was lying on my bed, reading, when I heard the most almighty scream. It was Belle.

'Oh, my God, oh my God.'

I jumped up and ran into the living room where she was doing some ironing. There, sitting on top of a pile of freshly-pressed shirts and bed sheets, was a little brown frog.

'James, James, pick it up, get rid of it. Please,' she said, calming down slightly.

I noticed Bob standing in the doorway taking all this in. There was a strange expression on his face, what I could only call mischievousness. It was as if he knew exactly what had happened.

I got hold of the little frog and cupped it in my hands. I then walked the long way round via the front door to the area at the back of the building with Bob following me every step of the way.

I went back inside, started to read my book and forgot all about it. But then, about an hour or so later, I heard another scream, accompanied by the sound of something hitting a wall. This time it was coming from the hallway.

'What is it now?' I said, heading towards the kerfuffle.

Belle was standing at one end of the corridor with her hands on her head and a horrified expression on her face. She pointed down the corridor at a pair of slippers that she'd clearly thrown down the hallway.

'It's inside my slipper now,' she said.

'What's inside your slipper?' I said, puzzled.

'The frog.'

I had to suppress a laugh. But, again, I retrieved the frog and took it out to the garden. Again Bob marched behind me, trying to look like it was a pure coincidence that this frog had now appeared inside the flat twice in the space of an hour or so.

'Stay there, mate,' I said, sensing that I had to make sure I disposed of the frog properly this time.

He looked at me disapprovingly then turned and slinked off back into the house as if to say, 'you're really no fun at all!'

As comfortable as we were at Belle's, after a while I began to realise that it wasn't ideal, in particular for my relationship with Bob.

The pain in my leg had made me short-tempered and generally less fun to be around than usual. So, perhaps inevitably, as time wore on, Bob and I had started spending less and less time together. Sensing that I was sleeping longer and wasn't in the best of moods when I woke up, he wouldn't always come into the bedroom for an early morning play. Often Belle would rustle up a breakfast for him instead. He would also head off out of the window to explore the back of the flats on a regular basis and would sometimes be gone for long stretches. I imagined he must be having a great time out there.

I also had a very strong suspicion that he was eating elsewhere too. He had begun arriving home from his sessions out on the roof and in the yard around supper time. But when Belle or I put down a bowl for him, he did little more than play with his food. At first my heart sank a little. *He's eating in the bins again*, I said to myself. But Belle and I checked the garbage area at the back of the building and came to the conclusion there was no way he could get into the giant, locked receptacles. The explanation must lay elsewhere.

One day, when we were heading out to work, I saw an elderly gentleman downstairs, collecting his mail. Bob saw him and fixed him with a knowing stare.

'Hello young fellow,' the man said. 'Nice to see you again.'

Suddenly it made sense. I remembered that children's book *Six Dinner Sid* by Inga Moore, about a cat that charms its way into the affections of everyone on his street, earning himself a dinner in every house each night. Bob had pulled the same stunt. He had become Six Dinner Bob.

In a way it was a sign of how comfortable and happy he was making himself there. But it was also a sign that he was getting used to life without me at the centre of his world. Lying there at night, trying to think about anything and everything but the throbbing pain in my leg, I began to ask myself something I'd not asked in all the time we'd been together. Would he be better off without me?

It was a fair question. Who needed to be hanging around with a crippled, ex-junkie with no money and no job prospects? Who needed to be out on the streets in all kinds of weather being poked and prodded by passers-by? Especially when there were friendlier, less complicated souls around to give you a square meal every day.

I'd always felt that I could give Bob as good a life as anyone else, if not a better one. We were soul mates, two chips off the same block, I told myself. For the first time since we'd got together, I wasn't so sure about that any more.

Chapter 8

None So Blind

It's incredible what pain does to the human mind. At night in particular, you lie there, unable to sleep, hallucinating, thinking the most insane things. At one point, for instance, I began to fantasise about having my leg amputated. I imagined having a prosthetic limb instead of the throbbing, bloated one I now had – and was actually comforted by the thought.

Another time, I was limping through the car park in a local supermarket when I saw a wheelchair, sitting there unoccupied. A man was lowering a hydraulic ramp on the back of a small van, from where, I assumed, the chair's owner would soon be helped out. The thought of being able to travel around without having to put any weight on my foot was really tempting. For a split second, I thought about stealing it. I was ashamed of myself the moment the idea entered my head.

As I lay there in a kind of fever some nights, I

also found myself thinking more and more about Bob, or more specifically, losing Bob. The worse my leg became, the more I became convinced that he was ready to leave. I imagined him in the company of the old man next door, being pampered and fussed over. I pictured him lying on the sunny roof at Belle's without a worry in the world while I hobbled off to sell *The Big Issue* on my own.

It wasn't such a leap of the imagination. Back at Belle's I was spending more and more time on my own, lying in my room asleep. As a result, I had less patience for Bob than usual. He'd sidle up to me on the bed, waiting to play catch with some treats, but I'd fail to respond. Sometimes he would try to drape himself around my leg, which I found unbearable. By now my leg was a violent, red colour and the pain was relentless.

'Go away and play somewhere else, Bob,' I'd say, brushing him to one side. He'd reluctantly slide off me and head out of the bedroom door, throwing me a disappointed look as he went. It was hardly a surprise that he was starting to look elsewhere for affection, I told myself afterwards.

I'm not much of a friend to him at the moment.

I knew it wasn't helping anyone, least of all myself, but I didn't know what to do to dig myself out of the black hole that had been slowly consuming me these past few weeks. One morning, however, I woke up and decided that enough was enough. I simply had to do something about it. I didn't care what the doctors thought about me and my past: I wanted some answers, I wanted this problem to go away. I got dressed, grabbed my crutch and headed for the local surgery, determined to have a proper examination.

'That's an interesting crutch you have there, Mr Bowen,' the doctor said when I turned up in the consulting room.

'Necessity is the mother of invention,' I said, sticking the weather-beaten pole in the corner and climbing on to the examination table where he began casting an eye over my thigh and leg.

'This doesn't look too good. You need to keep pressure off that leg for a week or so. Can you take time off work?' he asked me.

'No, not really. I sell *The Big Issue*,' I told him.

'OK, well you need to see what you can do to keep your foot elevated at all times,' he said. 'I also need you to have what's known as a D-Dimer blood test which looks for clotting in the blood cells. I suspect that's where your problems lie.'

'OK,' I said.

'Now, what are we going to do about this crutch

of yours? I think we can do better than a tree branch,' he said.

'No chance of a wheelchair?' I said, suddenly remembering the one I'd seen in the car park.

'Afraid not. But I could offer you a decent set of crutches while we try to get this swelling and inflammation down.'

By the end of the morning I was the proud owner of a pair of proper metallic crutches, complete with rubber grips, arm holders and shock absorbers. I was soon clunking my way around with my legs flailing in front of me. I was acutely conscious of the way it must have looked. I felt silly, even sillier than I'd looked with a pole under my arm. I could feel what people were thinking about me. It was depressing.

The time for feeling sorry for myself was over, however. I didn't waste any time and went to have the blood test done the following day. It wasn't that straightforward, of course. Taking a blood sample from a recovering heroin addict is easier said than done.

The practice nurse at the clinic asked me to roll up my sleeve but when she tried to find a vein she failed miserably.

'Hmmm, let's try this other arm instead,' she said. But it was the same again.

We exchanged a look that spoke volumes. I didn't need to spell it out.

'Maybe I should do it,' I said.

She gave me a sympathetic look and handed me the needle. Once I'd found a vein in my leg, I let her extract the sample. The humiliations of being a recovering addict were endless, but I wasn't going to let that deter me.

A couple of days later when I rang the clinic the female doctor confirmed my worst suspicions. She told me that I had developed a deep vein thrombosis, or DVT.

'You have a blood clot which I'd like to have further investigated. So I need you to go to University College Hospital for an ultrasound test,' she told me.

In a way it was a relief. I'd always suspected I'd caused myself a problem on those long flights to and from Australia. Looking back on it I could see that I'd suppressed the thought for all sorts of silly reasons, partly because I hadn't wanted to sound paranoid but partly also because I hadn't wanted to have my suspicions confirmed. I knew that DVTs could cause all sorts of problems, particularly coronary ones, strokes in particular.

Given all this, I was on edge over the next week or so while I waited for the ultrasound appointment. Bob and I carried on going to work but I was only going through the motions. I was terrified to do something that might trigger a stroke or heart attack. I even stopped interacting with him when we sat on the buckets together. He'd look at me every now and again, expecting me to produce a treat so that we could start performing for the commuters. But more often than not my heart wasn't in it and I'd turn away. Looking back, I was too wrapped up in myself. If I'd looked I'm sure I'd have seen the disappointment written all over his face.

When the appointment day came I dragged myself to UCH on the Euston Road and passed through a room of expectant mothers waiting in the ultra-sound department. I seemed to be the only person who wasn't excited to be there.

I was led off by a specialist who slapped loads of jelly on my leg so that he could run the camera around, the same as they did for the mums-to-be. It turned out that I had a massive, six-inch-long blood clot. The specialist sat me down and told me that he suspected it had started as a small clot but had thickened and clotted further along the edge of the vein.

'It was probably hot weather that set it off and then you've exacerbated it by walking around on it,' he said. 'We will prescribe you a blood thinning medicine and that should sort it out.'

I was relieved. Unfortunately, I wasn't quite in the clear.

I was prescribed an anti-coagulant that is used a lot to thin the blood of potential stroke victims. But I didn't pay any attention to the leaflet that came with it. It didn't occur to me that there might be side effects.

A few nights after I started taking the tablets, I got up at around 5am to go to the toilet. Outside it was pitch black, but there was just about enough light in the flat for me to find my way to the bathroom and back. As I walked down the corridor I could feel something trickling down my thigh. I turned on a light and was horrified to see that my leg was covered in blood. When I got back into my room and switched on the lights, I saw that the sheets of my bed were soaked red as well.

Bob had been fast asleep in the corner, but woke up. He could tell there was something wrong and shot up to stand at my side.

I had no idea what was happening. But I did know that I had to get myself to a hospital – and fast. I threw on a pair of jeans and a jumper and ran out of the flat, heading towards Tottenham High Road where I figured I had a chance of catching a bus.

When I got to UCH, they admitted me immediately. I was told that the anti-coagulant had thinned my blood to such an extent that it had started bleeding from the pores of the weakened skin where I used to inject myself.

I was kept in for two days while they sorted out my medication. They eventually settled on another drug, which wouldn't have the same effect. That was the good news. The bad news was that I'd have to inject it into my stomach myself for a period of up to six months.

Having to inject myself was awful, for all sorts of reasons. To begin with it was painful, injecting directly into my stomach muscles. I could feel the contents of the syringe entering the tissue. Secondly, it was another reminder of my past. I hated the prospect of having a syringe and a needle as part of my daily life once more.

Worst of all, however, it didn't work.

Even after I'd been injecting myself with the new drug for a couple of weeks, my leg was no better. I couldn't walk more than two paces, even with the crutches. I was now beginning to despair. Once again, I began to imagine losing my leg altogether. I went back to UCH and explained the situation to one of the doctors I'd seen previously.

'We'd better have you back in for a week. I'll check to see what the bed situation is right now,' he said, picking up the phone.

I wasn't best pleased about it. It meant I'd not be able to work and I'd already lost two days in hospital. But I knew that I simply couldn't carry on in this condition. I was told that they had a bed the following day. So I went home that night and explained the situation to Belle. She agreed to look after Bob, which was a huge comfort for me. I knew he was happy there. The following morning I got up and packed a small bag of stuff to take to hospital.

I'm not the greatest hospital patient. The clue is in the word *patient*. That's not something I've ever been accused of being. I get easily distracted.

During the first few days, I didn't sleep very well at all, even when they gave me medication to help me nod off. Inevitably, I started taking stock of my life and lay there worrying about everything – my leg, my long term health, my pitch at Angel and, as always, the lack of money. I also lay there and fretted about Bob.

The idea that we should go our separate ways had refused to go away. We'd been together for more than two and a half years now and he had been the most loyal friend imaginable. But all friendships go through phases, and some come to an end. I could see that I'd not been the most brilliant company in recent weeks. Should I ask Belle if she wanted to keep him? Maybe I should ask the nice bloke next door with whom he'd already struck up a bond, it seemed? I would, of course, be devastated to lose him. He was my best friend, my rock. I didn't have anyone else in my life. Deep down I needed him to keep me on the straight and narrow, to maintain my sanity sometimes. But at the same time, I had to make the right choice. I really didn't know what to do. But then it struck me. It wasn't my decision.

As the old saying went, cats choose you, not the other way around. That's what had happened with Bob and me years earlier. For whatever reason, he'd seen something in me that made him want to stick around. I'd always believed in karma, the notion that you get back in life what you put out into the world. Maybe I'd been gifted his company in reward for something good I'd done earlier in life? Not that I could remember doing that much good. Now I had to wait to see if he'd choose me again. If he wanted to remain with me, then it would be his decision. And his alone.

I'd find out his answer soon enough, I felt sure.

When the results of the latest round of tests came in, I was told that the dosage of the drug that had originally been prescribed wasn't strong enough. They were going to increase it, but they also wanted to keep me in longer to make sure it actually had an impact.

'It will only be a couple more days, just to see it

works and doesn't have any side effects,' the doctor told me.

Belle popped in to see me, dropping off a couple of books and some comics. She told me Bob was fine.

'I think he's found someone else to feed him as well as that old guy,' she said, laughing. 'He really is living up to the name Six Dinner Bob.'

After a couple of days it was obvious that the new dosage was finally sorting out my DVT. When I looked at my leg the swelling was beginning to go down and the colour returning to normality. The nurses and doctors could see this as well, so they wasted no time in getting me off my back.

'It's not good for you lying there all day, Mr Bowen,' one of them kept saying to me.

So they insisted that I got out and walked up and down the corridor at least a couple of times a day. It was actually a joy to be able to pace around without wincing with pain. When I put weight on my leg, I didn't get those same excruciating shooting sensations. It still hurt, but it wasn't anywhere near as bad as previously.

True to their word, about a week after I'd been admitted, the doctors told me that I could go home. I texted Belle with the good news. She texted me back to say she'd try to come to the hospital to meet me later that afternoon.

The hospital paperwork took longer than I'd

hoped so it was approaching evening by the time I slipped out of my pyjamas, got dressed, gathered together my belongings and limped my way to the exit on Euston Road. I still had the crutches but didn't really need them. I could now put pressure on my leg without any real pain.

Belle had texted me again to say that she would meet me outside.

'Can't come into hospital. Will explain when I see you,' she'd written.

We'd agreed to meet by the infamous new modern art sculpture outside the main entrance. I'd heard people at the hospital talking about the work of art, a giant, six ton polished pebble. It had cost the hospital tens of thousands of pounds apparently and was meant to make patients and visitors 'feel better' as they arrived and departed. It didn't inspire me particularly, but I certainly felt the benefit of it when my body hit the cold evening air outside. I leaned on it for a moment or two as I tried to catch my breath after walking what seemed like miles along the corridors without the aid of crutches.

I was a couple of minutes early so there was no sign of Belle. That was no surprise at this time of the evening; I could see that the rush hour traffic was already building up. I was resigned to waiting a while, but then, to my relief, I saw her emerging from the bus stop across the road. She was carrying a large, holdall style bag which, I assumed, had some clean clothes and my jacket in it. At first I didn't spot it, but as she got closer I saw a flash of ginger fur poking out of the unzipped top of the bag.

As she reached the bottom of the steps, I saw his head poking out.

'Bob,' I said, excited.

The moment he registered my voice he began scrambling out of the bag. In an instant he had his front paws on Belle's arm and the back ones on the top of the bag, ready to spring forward.

We were still a few feet apart when Bob launched himself off the bag towards me. It was the most athletic leap I'd ever seen him make, and that was saying a lot.

'Whoaah there, fella,' I said, lurching forward to catch him then holding him close to my chest. He pinned himself to me like a limpet clinging on to a rock that was being pounded by waves. He then nuzzled his head in my neck and started rubbing me with his cheeks.

'Hope you don't mind, but that's why I couldn't come in. I had to bring him,' Belle said beaming. 'He saw me packing a few things for you and started going crazy. I think he knew I was coming to get you.'

Whatever doubts I'd had about our future together were swept away in that instant. On the way home, Bob was all over me – literally. Rather than sitting alongside me he sat on my lap, crawled on my shoulders and sat up with his paws on my chest, purring away contentedly.

It was as if he never wanted to let me go again. I felt exactly the same way.

They say that there are none so blind as those who will not see. In the days and weeks that followed, I realised that I had been unwilling, or maybe unable, to see what was glaringly obvious. Far from wanting to leave me, Bob had been desperate to help ease my pain and get me on the road to recovery. He'd given me space to recover. But he'd also been nursing me without my knowledge.

Belle told me that whenever I was asleep in my room, Bob would check up on me. He would lie on my chest and even run checks every now and again.

'He'd give you a little tap on the forehead and wait for you to react. I think he just wanted to make sure you were still with us,' she smiled.

At other times, she told me, he would wrap himself around my leg.

'It was as if he was trying to apply a tourniquet or something. It was like he wanted to take away the pain,' she said. 'You would never lie still long enough for him to stay there for long. But he knew where the pain was and was definitely trying to do something about it.'

I hadn't seen any of this. What was worse, whenever Bob had tried to help or comfort me when I was awake, I'd driven him away. I'd been selfish. Bob loved – and needed – me as much I loved and needed him. I wouldn't forget that.

Lying in bed for days on end had focussed my mind on something else as well. A few weeks after I was back on my feet, I took the most important step I'd made in years. Perhaps in my entire life.

When I'd actually heard the words at a regular appointment with my drug counsellor at the specialist dependency unit in Camden, they'd not sunk in at first.

'I think you've reached the finishing line, James,' he'd said.

'Sorry what do you mean?'

I'm going to write you your final prescription. A few more days of taking your medication and I think you'll be ready to call yourself clean.'

I'd been attending the clinic for several years now. I'd arrived there a mess, addicted to heroin and on a fast track to an early grave. Thanks to a brilliant collection of counsellors and nurses, I'd been hauling myself back from the brink ever since.

After coming off first heroin and then methadone, my new medication, subutex, had slowly but surely been helping me to wean myself off opiates completely. I'd been taking it for around six months now.

They called it a miracle drug and, as far as I was concerned, at least, that's exactly what it was. It had allowed me to reduce my craving for drugs gently and without any hiccups. I'd been reducing my dosage of subutex steadily, first from 8 milligrams to 6 then to 4 and then 2. From there I'd started taking even smaller doses, measured in 0.4 grams. It had been a pretty seamless process, much easier than I'd anticipated.

So I wasn't quite sure why I left the unit that morning feeling so apprehensive about the fact that I was about to stop taking subutex altogether.

I should have been delighted. It was time for that soft aeroplane landing that one of my counsellors had talked about. But I was curiously on edge, and remained that way for the next two days.

That first night, for instance, I started sweating and having minor palpitations. They weren't serious. They were certainly nothing compared to what I'd been through when I'd come off methadone. That had been hellish. It was almost as if I was waiting for something awful to happen, for me to have some dramatic reaction. But nothing happened. I just felt, well, absolutely fine.

Bob was attuned to my mood and sensed that I needed a little more TLC. He wasn't overt; he didn't need to perform any of his late night diagnoses or tap me on the head to check I was still breathing. He just positioned himself a few inches closer on the sofa and gave me an extra rub of his head on my neck every now and again.

I carried on with my life as normal over the next couple of days. Bob and I had headed back to the flat in Tottenham where we'd adjusted to life there again. It was such a relief to be able to walk properly and to ride my bike around with Bob on board.

In the end there was a slight sense of anti-climax. Five or six days after I had been given the final prescription, I pulled the foil container out of its packet and saw that there was just one tablet left.

I squeezed the oval shaped pill out, placed it under my tongue until it had all dissolved then downed a glass of water. I scrunched the foil up into a ball and threw it on the floor for Bob to chase.

'There you go, mate. That's the last one of those you'll get to play with.'

That night, I went to bed expecting to have a rough night. *I will never sleep*, I told myself. I felt sure that my body was going to be racked by withdrawal pangs. I expected nightmares, visions, restless twisting and turning. But there was none of that. There was nothing. Maybe I'd simply exhausted myself with anxiety, but the moment my head hit the pillow I was out like a light.

When I woke up the next morning, I gathered my senses and thought to myself: *Jeez. That's it. I'm clean*. I looked out the window at the London skyline. It wasn't a glorious blue sky, unfortunately. It wasn't quite that clichéd. But it certainly was a clear one. And, just as when I'd come off methadone, it seemed somehow brighter and more colourful.

I knew that the days, weeks, months and years stretching ahead of me weren't going to be easy. There would be times when I would feel stressed, depressed and insecure and at those times I knew that niggling temptation would return and I'd think about taking something to deaden the pain, to kill the senses.

That had been why I'd fallen for heroin in the first place. It had been loneliness and hopelessness that had driven me into its arms. But now I was determined that wasn't going to happen again. Life wasn't perfect, far from it. But it was a million times better than it had been when I'd formed my addiction. Back then I couldn't see beyond the next hit. Now I felt like I could see a way forward. I knew that I could soldier on.

From that day onwards, each time I felt myself weakening I told myself: 'hold on, no, I'm not sleeping rough, I'm not alone, it's not hopeless. I don't need it.'

I carried on seeing a counsellor for a while, but soon I didn't need that either. A month or so after I'd taken my last tablet of subutex he signed me off.

'I don't need to see you again,' he said as he ushered me out of the door. 'Stay in touch, but good luck. And well done.'

And I am happy to say I have not seen or heard from him since.

Chapter 9

Bob's Big Night Out

As we walked south across the Thames at Waterloo Bridge, the lights of the Houses of Parliament and the London Eye were blazing bright in the late November night sky and the pavement was busy with people. Most were heading in the same direction, away from the West End and the City towards the commuter trains of Waterloo station. Some were weary looking office workers, shuffling home from a late night at work, others were in a jollier mood after a night out in the West End.

It was approaching 10.30pm, the end of their day. For me and Bob, on the other hand, it was the beginning of what promised to be a very, very long night.

I'd been persuaded by *The Big Issue* to take part in a new event that they were staging. I had first read about it in the magazine a few months earlier. It was called the 'The Big Night Out' and had been planned to coincide with the 18th birthday of the magazine. With that in mind, some bright spark had decided it would be a good idea to organise an 18 mile walk through the streets of London in the middle of the night.

The idea was that ordinary people could walk through the deserted city between 10pm and 7am with a group of *The Big Issue* vendors so that they could learn a little about the reality of living rough and sleeping on the streets. The adverts in the magazine called it 'a fantastic opportunity to join other like-minded people who have a sense of adventure and a desire to help empower homeless and vulnerable people across the UK'. We hadn't even finished the walk to the start of the event, but I was already beginning to wonder whether it was an adventure too far for me and Bob, especially given the problems I'd had with my leg. It was a bitterly cold night – and getting colder by the minute.

I'd made the decision to take part for a couple of reasons. First and foremost, it was a chance to earn a few extra pounds. Every vendor that took part in the walk was eligible for 25 to 30 free copies of *The Big Issue*. That meant that I could earn about £60 potentially. Beyond that, however, I saw it as an opportunity to talk to people about the magazine and the lives of the people who sold it.

Despite the ups and downs I'd had with the company, I was still a believer in its mission. It was, without question, the salvation for many people who lived on the streets. It had certainly helped give me direction and purpose – not to mention enough money to keep the wolf from the door – along the way.

We were meeting at the IMAX cinema at the Bullring roundabout on the south side of Waterloo Bridge. It was a fitting location. Not so long ago, the roundabout – well, more specifically the labyrinth of concrete, subterranean walkways underneath it – had been home to the shanty town that Londoners knew as Cardboard City. During the 1980s and early 1990s, it had become a home for more than 200 'rough sleepers' as the social workers called us. A lot of those who hung out there were transient junkies and alcoholics but many created homes for themselves from wooden pallets and cardboard boxes. Some even had living rooms and bedrooms with mattresses. It had been a haven, but not necessarily a safe one, for 15 years. I'd stayed there briefly during its final days, at the end of 1997 and early 1998, when everyone was evicted to make way for the IMAX cinema.

My memories of the place were sketchy, but when I walked into the IMAX I saw the organisers of the walk had created a little picture exhibition on the history of Cardboard City. With Bob on my shoulder, I scanned the grainy black and white images for faces that I recognised. As it turned out, I was looking in the wrong place.

'Hello, James,' a female voice said behind me. I recognised it straight away.

'Hello, Billie,' I said.

Back around the year 2000, when my life was at its lowest ebb, Billie and I had become friendly, helping each other out and keeping each other company. We hadn't met until after the demise of Cardboard City and had huddled up against the cold together at the cold-weather shelters that charities like Centrepoint and St Mungo's used to put up during the winter months.

It turned out that Billie had turned her life around too. She'd had an epiphany one night when she was sleeping rough in central London and was disturbed from her sleep by a *Big Issue* seller. At first she'd been annoyed at being woken up by him. She hadn't even known what the magazine was. But she'd looked at it then and grasped the idea. She had then rebuilt her life and, a decade later, was now a 'poster child' for The Big Issue Foundation.

We reminisced about the bad old days over a cup of tea.

'Remember that pop-up at Admiralty Arch during that really snowy winter?' she said.

'Yeah, what year was that? 1999 or 2000 or 2001?' I said.

'Can't remember. Those days are all a blur aren't they?' she said with a resigned shrug.

'Yep. Still, we are here, which is more than can be said for some of the poor sods we were with then.'

Goodness knows how many of the people who had been on the streets with us had perished in the cold or from drugs or violence.

Billie was very committed to this walk.

'It will give people an idea what we had to go through,' she said. 'They won't be able to slip off home into a warm bed, they'll have to stay out there with us.'

I wasn't quite so sure. No one, no matter how well meaning, could really understand what it was like to live on the streets.

Billie, like me, had a companion these days. Hers was a lively Border Collie called Solo. She and Bob weighed each other up for a few minutes but then decided there was nothing to worry about.

Just before 10.30pm John Bird, the founder of *The Big Issue* arrived. I'd encountered him a few times and found him a charismatic character. As usual, he was good value, and fired everyone up with an inspiring little speech about the difference the magazine had made during its 18 years. By now 100 or more people had gathered there along with a couple of dozen vendors, co-ordinators and staff. We all filed out into the night, ready for John Bird to do the countdown.

'Three, two, one,' he shouted and then we were off.

'Here we go, Bob,' I said, making sure he was positioned comfortably on my shoulders.

For me it was a real journey into the unknown. On the one hand, I was really worried about whether my leg would stand up to 18 miles of wear and tear, but on the other I was just delighted to be off my crutches and walking normally again. It was such a relief not to be going 'clonk, clonk, clonk' down the road all the time, having to swing my legs in front of me every step of the way. So, as we set off on the first leg around the South Bank and across the Millennium Bridge, I told myself to simply enjoy it.

As usual, Bob was soon attracting a lot of attention. There was a real party atmosphere and a lot of the charity fundraisers began taking snaps of him as we walked. He wasn't in the friendliest of moods, which was understandable. It was way past his bed time and he could feel the cold coming off the Thames. But I had a generous supply of snacks as well as some water and a bowl for him. I'd also been assured there would be a bowl of milk at the stop-off points. We will give it our best shot, I said to myself.

Bob and I settled into a group in the middle of the procession as it worked its way along the riverside. They were a mix of students and charity workers, as well as a couple of middle-aged women. They were obviously genuine people who wanted to help in some way. One of the ladies started asking me questions, the usual things: 'where do you come from?', 'how did you end up on the streets?'

I'd told the story a hundred times before during the past decade. I explained how I'd come to London from Australia when I was 18. I'd been born in the UK but my parents had separated and my mum had taken me with her when she'd moved down under. We'd moved around a lot in the following years and I'd become a bit of a trouble-maker. When I came to London I had hopes of making it as a musician, but it didn't really work out. I'd been staying with my stepsister but had fallen out with her husband. I'd started sleeping on friends' sofas but had eventually run out of places to crash the night. I'd ended up on the streets and it had been downhill from there. I'd experimented with drugs before but when I became homeless it became a way of life. It was the only way to block out the fact that I was lonely and that my life was screwed up. It anaesthetised the pain.

While we were talking we passed a building near Waterloo Bridge where I remembered sleeping a few times. 'I didn't use it often,' I told the lady, pointing it out. 'One night while I was crashing out there another guy got robbed and had his throat slashed while he slept.'

She looked at me ashen-faced.

'Did he die?' she said.

'I don't know. I just ran away,' I said. 'To be honest, you just worry about making it through the night yourself. It's every man for himself. That's what life on the streets reduces you to.'

The woman stood there just looking at the door-way for a moment, as if she was saying a brief, silent prayer.

After about an hour and a half, we made it to the first stopping off point – the Hispaniola floating restaurant on the Embankment on the north side of the Thames.

I helped myself to some of the soup on offer while Bob lapped up some milk that someone had kindly sorted out for him. I was feeling pretty positive about the whole thing and was already totting up the miles that I'd done – and how many more were to come.

But then, as we were heading off the ship, we had a bit of a setback. Perhaps because he'd been refuelled or perhaps because he knew that my leg still wasn't 100 per cent, Bob had decided to walk off the boat. As he padded his way down the ramp, right to the end of his lead, he walked straight into another *The Big Issue* seller who was coming up the walkway with a dog, a Staffie. It instantly went for Bob and I had to jump in front of it with my arms and legs out to stop him lunging at Bob. To be fair to the other guy, he gave his dog a real dressing down and even gave him a slap on the nose. Staffies do get a bad reputation for being violent, but I don't think this one was. He was just being curious, not evil. Unfortunately, however, it freaked Bob out a bit. As we resumed our walk he wrapped himself around me tightly, partly through nervousness but mostly because it was his way of insulating himself against the cold. There was a bone-chilling mist rising off the Thames.

Part of me wanted to call it a night and take Bob home. But I spoke to a couple of the organisers and was persuaded to carry on. Fortunately, as we headed away from the river, the temperatures lifted a little bit. We wound our way through the West End and headed north.

I got talking to another couple, a pretty young blonde girl and her French boyfriend. They were more interested in the story of how Bob and I had got together. That suited me fine. Walking around London like this brought back so many memories, many of them too dark and distressing for words. As a heroin addict living on the streets, I was reduced to doing some hideous things just to survive. I wasn't in the mood to share those details with anyone.

For the first six miles or so, my leg had been fine. I'd been too distracted by what was going on around me to think about it. But as the night wore on, I began to feel a throbbing pain in my thigh, where the DVT had been. It was inevitable. But it was still annoying.

For the next hour or so I ignored it. But whenever we stopped for a cup of tea I could feel an acute shooting pain. Early on I had been in the middle of the procession, walking along with the largest numbers of fundraisers. But I had been falling further and further behind, eventually reaching the back of the line. A couple of fundraisers and a guy from *The Big Issue* office were bringing up the rear and I tagged along with them for a mile or so. But I'd had to take a couple of breaks to let Bob do his business and have a cigarette. Suddenly I realised that we were now cut loose from the rest.

The next official stop was up in Camden, at the Roundhouse pub, a few miles away. I really didn't think I could make it that far. So when we passed a bus stop with a night bus that headed in our direction, I made a decision.

'What do you think, Bob, shall we call it quits?'

He didn't say anything, but I could tell that he was ready for his bed. When a bus loomed into view and opened its doors, he bounded on board and on to a seat, bristling with pleasure at being in the warm.

The bus was surprisingly busy given it was well after 3am. Sitting towards the back of the bus, Bob and I were surrounded by a cluster of clubbers, still high from their night out in the West End or wherever it was they'd been. There were also a couple of lonely looking guys sitting there as if they were on the road to nowhere. I'd been there and done that, of course. I not only had the t-shirt, I had a wardrobe full of them.

But that was the past. Tonight it felt very different. Tonight I felt rather pleased with myself. I know walking a dozen or so miles might not have seemed much of an achievement to some people, but to have made it that far given the state my leg had been in weeks earlier, was – for me, at least – the equivalent of running the London Marathon.

I'd also been reunited with some familiar faces, in particular, Billie. It had been a joy to see her again and to see how well she was doing. All in all, I just felt like I'd done something positive, that I'd given something back. I'd spent so many years taking from people, mainly because I had nothing to give. Or at least, I didn't think I had anything to give. Tonight had shown me that wasn't necessarily true. Everyone has something to contribute, no matter how small. Sharing my experiences tonight, for instance, I'd felt like I'd connected with a few people and, maybe, I'd opened their eyes to the reality of life on the streets. That wasn't to be dismissed. It was worth something. And so, I began to quietly tell myself, was I.

Chapter 10

Tales of Two Cities

As I drew back the bedroom curtains and looked out across the north London rooftops, it was obvious the Wintry weather the forecasters had been predicting had finished its journey from Siberia or whichever frozen wasteland had sent it in our direction.

Thick banks of iron-grey clouds were stacked up overhead and I could hear the wind gusting and whistling outside. If ever there was a day to stay at home and wrap up warm, today was that day. Unfortunately, that wasn't a luxury I could really afford.

Things were particularly tight at the moment. Both the gas and electric meters needed topping up so the flat was icy cold. Bob had got into the habit of snuggling up close to the bed at night, hoping to soak up some of the heat that I generated under the duvet. For now, at least, the bottom line was that I had to keep selling *The Big Issue* and I couldn't afford to take many days off – even if the weather looked as unpleasant as it did today.

So as I got my rucksack sorted the only question was whether Bob was going to come with me. As always, it was going to be his decision. I knew it was a decision he generally got right.

Cats – like a lot of other animals – are very good at 'reading' the weather and other natural events. Apparently they are very skilled at predicting earthquakes and tsunamis, for instance. The most likely explanation I've heard is that they are sensitive to air pressure. So it follows that they can also detect the changes in the air that predict bad weather is coming. Bob had certainly shown an aptitude for detecting that rain was in the air. He hated getting wet and had often curled up and refused to come out when the weather had been seemingly fine outside only for the heavens to open an hour or two later when I'd taken to the streets on my own.

So when I showed him his lead and scarf and he came towards me as normal, I guessed that his weather forecasting instincts were telling him it was safe to venture out.

'You sure about this, Bob?' I said. 'I'm happy to go on my own today.'

I picked out one of his thickest and warmest scarves. I wrapped it snugly around his neck and headed out into the greyness.

The moment I set foot on the street outside the wind cut through me like a scalpel. It pinched. I felt Bob's midriff curling itself even tighter than usual around my neck.

I dreaded having to wait at the bus stop for half an hour, but fortunately our regular service appeared within a few minutes and Bob and I were soon on board. Feeling a warmth on the back of my leg from a heater lifted my spirits briefly. But things soon took a turn for the worse.

We'd barely been on the road for ten minutes when I noticed the first flakes of snow swirling around outside. At first they were few and far between, but within what seemed like a few moments, the air was thick with chunky, white flakes that I could see were already sticking to the pavement and the roofs of parked cars.

'This doesn't look good,' I said to Bob, who was transfixed by the transformation that was taking place on the streets outside.

By the time we got to Newington Green, a mile or so from Angel, the traffic had ground to an almost total standstill. I faced a real Catch 22 – I knew it was going to be tough to earn a few quid today and that conditions were going to be really challenging but at the same time, I was so short of money. I wasn't sure I had enough to get back home, let alone put a few quid in the electricity meter over the next day or so.

'Come on, Bob, if we're going to earn anything today we'd better walk the last mile,' I said, reluctantly.

We hopped out on to the pavement to discover everyone was walking at a snail's pace, looking grim-faced as they picked their way along what was becoming a really treacherous surface. For Bob, however, this was a fascinating new world, one that he was soon eager to explore. I had put him on my shoulders as usual, but I'd barely walked a few yards before he was repositioning himself ready to clamber down to earth.

It hadn't really occurred to me, but as I put him down I realised that it was the first time Bob had been out and about in snow, with me, at least. I stood there watching him dabbing a paw into the powdery whiteness then standing back to admire the print he'd left in the virgin surface. For a moment I imagined what it must be like to see the world through his eyes. It must have seemed so bizarre to see everything suddenly turned white.

'Come on, mate, we can't hang around all day,' I said after a minute or two.

By now the snow was so heavy, it was hard to see in front of us.

Bob was still having a great time lifting his feet up in and out of the ever deepening snow. Eventually, however, it got so deep that his belly was lined with white crystals.

'Come on, mate, let's get you back up here,' I said, grabbing him and sticking back on my shoulders.

The problem now was that the snow was falling so steadily and heavily that it was settling on both of us. Every few yards I had to brush an inch of fresh snow off my shoulders then do the same thing to Bob.

I had a rather knackered old umbrella which I produced from my rucksack. But it was next to useless in the strong winds so I gave up on it within minutes.

'This is no good, Bob. Think we need to find you a coat,' I said. I dived into a small convenience store, stamping my feet clean of snow in the doorway.

At first the owner, an Indian lady, looked shocked to see the pair of us standing there, which was hardly surprising really. We must have made a bizarre sight. But her mood soon thawed.

'You are brave walking about in this weather,' she smiled.

'I don't know about brave,' I said. 'Mad might be closer to the truth.'

I wasn't quite sure what I was looking for. At first I wondered about buying a new umbrella, but they were too expensive for me. I only had a small amount of change. But then I had an idea and headed for the area where the kitchen supplies were stocked. I saw a roll of small, heavy duty bin liners.

'That might do the trick, Bob,' I said quietly.

'How much for a single bag?' I asked.

'I can't sell them as singles. I have to sell you the whole roll. It's £2,' she said.

I didn't want to fork out that much. I really was broke. But then I noticed she had little black carrier bags on the counter top for customers to carry their shopping.

'Is there any chance I could take one of those?' I said.

'OK,' she said, looking sheepishly at me. 'They are 5p.'

'OK, I'll take one. Do you have any scissors?'

'Scissors?'

'Yes, I want to make a hole in it.'

This time she looked at me as if I truly was off my rocker. But, probably against her better instinct, she dipped down behind the counter and produced a small pair of sewing scissors.

'Perfect,' I said.

I grabbed the closed end of the bag and cut a small semi-circle about the size of Bob's head. I then opened the bag up and slipped Bob's head through it. The improvised poncho fitted like a glove and covered his body and legs perfectly.

'Oh, I see,' the lady said, laughing. 'Very clever. That should do the trick.'

It took us about fifteen minutes to get to Angel. One or two people shot us funny looks as we walked along, but to be honest most were more concerned with getting from A to B safely in the drifting snow.

I knew there was no way we were going to be able to survive outside the tube at our normal pitch. The pavement was thick with slushy snow. So Bob and I positioned ourselves in the nearest underpass where the bulk of commuters were taking refuge.

I really didn't want to keep Bob out in the cold for too long, so I put some extra effort into selling the magazine. Fortunately, a lot of people seemed to take pity on us and dipped into their pockets. My pile of magazines was soon dwindling.

By late afternoon, I'd accumulated enough cash to keep us going for a day or two, I reckoned. The main thing was that I had enough to keep the gas and electricity topped up until, hopefully, the weather improved.

'Now, all we've got to do is get home,' I said to Bob as we once more bent ourselves into the icy winds and headed back to the bus stop.

There have to be easier ways of earning a crust than this, I told myself in the warmth of the bus.

Making money was so hard, especially because the gap between those that had it and those that didn't was growing ever greater. Working on the streets of London really was a tale of two cities, as I was reminded again a few days later.

I was standing just outside the concourse of Angel tube station with Bob on my shoulders around lunchtime, when I noticed a bit of a commotion going on inside at the ticket gate where passengers emerged from the trains below. A group of people were having an animated conversation with the attendants. When it was over they were let through seemingly without paying and started heading in our direction.

I recognised the large, slightly scruffy, blond-haired figure at the centre of the group immedi-ately. It was the Mayor of London, Boris Johnson. He was with a young boy, his son I assumed, and a small group of smartly-dressed assistants. They were marching straight towards my exit.

I didn't really have time to think so I just reacted instinctively as he approached me.

'How about a *Big Issue*, Boris?' I said, waving a magazine in the air.

'I'm in a bit of a rush,' he said, looking flustered. 'Hold on.'

To his credit he started digging around in his pockets and produced a pile of coins which he then proceeded to drop into my hands.

'There you go. More valuable than British pounds,' he said.

I didn't understand what he meant but was grateful nevertheless.

'Thanks very much indeed for supporting Bob and me,' I said, handing him a magazine.

As he took it, he smiled and tilted his head slightly at Bob.

'That's a nice cat you've got there,' he said.

'Oh yes, he's a star, he's even got his own travelcard so he can travel around,' I said.

'Amazing. Really,' he said, before heading off in the direction of Islington Green with his entourage.

'Good luck, Boris,' I said as he disappeared from view.

I hadn't wanted to be rude and check what he'd given me a moment or two earlier, but, judging by the weight and number of the coins, it felt way more than the cover price of the magazine.

'That was generous of him wasn't it, Bob?' I said, fishing around for the coins which I'd hurriedly stuffed in my jacket pocket.

As I looked at the small pile of cash, however, my heart sank. The coins all bore the mark *Confoederatio Helvetica*.

'Oh no, Bob,' I said. 'He gave me bloody Swiss Francs.'

It was only then that the penny dropped, as it were.

'That's what he meant when he said *more valuable than British pounds*,' I muttered to myself.

Except, of course, they weren't more valuable.

It obviously hadn't occurred to him that, while foreign bank notes can be exchanged at most banks and bureaux de change, coins cannot. They were, effectively, worthless. To me, at least.

One of our friends at the tube station, Davika, passed by a moment or two later.

'Saw you with Boris, James,' she smiled. 'Did he see you all right?'

'No he didn't as a matter of fact,' I said. ' He gave me a pile of Swiss Francs.'

She shook her head.

'That's the rich for you,' she said. 'They live on a different planet from the rest of us.'

I just nodded quietly in agreement. It wasn't the first time something like this had happened to me.

A few years earlier, I'd been busking in Covent Garden. It had been approaching 7.30pm, curtain-up time at most of the theatres and opera houses in the area, and a lot of people were breaking into a panicky trot as they emerged from the tube station. Unsurprisingly, few of them had any time to notice me strumming away with Bob at my feet, but one particularly flustered looking character in a bow tie did acknowledge me.

He saw me from a few yards away and instantly dug into his pocket. He was a very grand looking character with a mane of grey hair. I could have sworn I recognised him from the television, but couldn't place him. When I saw him reach into his trouser pocket and pull out a scrunched up note, I thought my luck was in. It was red and looked all the world like a big denomination, possibly a £50 note. That was the only note I knew that had red in it.

'There you go, my man,' he said, thrusting it into my hand as he slowed down for a brief moment.

'Cheers. Thanks very much indeed,' I said.

'Have a good evening,' he said, laughing as he picked up speed again and ran towards the Piazza.

I had no idea why he was laughing. I assumed he was in a good mood.

I waited a few minutes until the crowds had died down a little before recovering the scrunched up note out of my pocket.

It didn't take me long to work out that it wasn't a £50 note. As I'd thought, it was red, but it had a picture of a bearded bloke I'd never seen before on it. It had the number 100 written on it. The writing was in some kind of Eastern European language. The only word that looked familiar was *Srbije*. I had no idea what it was or what it might be worth. It might have been more than £50 for all I knew. So I packed up my stuff and headed for a Bureau de Change the other side of the Piazza which I knew was open late for tourists.

'Hi, can you tell me what this is worth, please?' I said to the girl who was behind the window.

She looked at it and gave me a puzzled look.

'Don't recognise it, hold on, let me check with someone else,' she said.

She went into a back office where I could see an older bloke sitting.

After a short confab she came back.

'Apparently it's Serbian, it's 100 Serbian dinar,' she said.

'OK,' I said. 'Can I exchange it?'

'Let's see what it's worth,' she said tapping away at a computer and then a calculator.

'Hmmm,' she said. 'That comes out at just over 70p. So we wouldn't be able to exchange it.'

I felt disappointed. I'd secretly hoped that it might be enough money to get me and Bob through the weekend. Fat chance. There were times when I got really depressed by the predicament I found myself in. I had turned 30. The majority of guys of my age had a job or a car, a home and a pension plan, maybe even a wife and a few children. I had none of those things. Part of me didn't actually want them, truth be told. But I did yearn for the security that some of those things brought. I was fed up with living off my wits on the streets. And I was fed up with being humiliated by those who had absolutely no concept of – nor sometimes any sympathy for – the life I was having to lead. There were times when I felt like I was close to breaking point. A few days after that incident with the Mayor, I felt like I had reached it.

Bob and I finished work early and headed down to the tube, jumping on a Northern line train to Euston then switching on to the Victoria line to Victoria Station. As we weaved our way through the tunnels, Bob walked ahead of me on his lead part of the way. He knew where we were heading.

We were meeting my father, something I'd begun to do more regularly in recent months. Relations between us had been pretty fraught in the past. When my parents had separated, my mother had won custody and taken me to live on the other side of the world, in Australia, so he'd barely known me when I was growing up as a little boy. By the time I'd come to London as a teenager, I was a real handful. Within a year of getting here, I had disappeared off the face of the earth and started sleeping rough. When I'd resurfaced, he'd tried to help me get back on track, but, to be honest, I had been almost beyond salvation.

We'd become a bit closer when I'd started cleaning up my act a little and had got into the habit of meeting for a few drinks at a pub at Victoria Station. The staff there were pretty friendly and

149

would let me slip Bob in provided I kept him hidden from the other punters. I'd learned to keep him under a table where he was happy snoozing. It was a cheap and cheerful place and we'd usually have a meal as well. It was always my dad's treat. Well, I was never going to have the money to treat him, was I?

As usual, he was waiting there for me.

'So what's your news?'

'Not a lot,' I said. 'I'm getting cheesed off with selling *The Big Issue*. It's too dangerous. And London is full of people who don't give a sh*t about you.'

I then told him the story about Boris Johnson. He gave me a sympathetic look but his reply was predictable.

'You need to get yourself cleaned up and you need to get yourself a proper job, Jamie,' he said. (He was the only person who called me that.)

I resisted the temptation to roll my eyes.

'That's easier said than done, Dad,' I said.

My dad had always been a grafter, a hard worker. He was blue collar to the core. He'd graduated from being an antique dealer to having a washing machine and domestic appliance repair service to a mobility vehicle business. He'd always been his own boss. I don't think he quite grasped why I hadn't been able to do the same thing. To his credit, he had never washed his hands of me. He'd tried to help. At one

point I had been keen on getting into music production and he'd wanted to give me a helping hand to
get on a course but it hadn't panned out. The thought
was there but the motion behind it wasn't. He had
remarried since splitting with my mum and had two
children, my half siblings Caroline and Anthony, to
look after. It got complicated.

I'd never really considered working for his business and he'd never really offered. Quite rightly, he
felt that business and family didn't mix. Besides,
deep down he knew that I wasn't reliable – or
presentable – enough to interact with the public.

'What about training in computing or something
like that. There are loads of courses around,' he
said.

This was true enough but I didn't have the qualifications to get on most courses. That was partly
my own fault.

A few years back I'd had a mentor, a great guy
called Nick Ransom who worked for a charity
called Family Mosaic. He had been a really good
friend. He'd either come to my flat or I'd go into
his office in Dalston where he'd help me with
everything from paying the bills to applying for
jobs. He had tried to get me involved in a variety of
courses, from bike building to computing. But the
struggle to kick my addiction had been all consuming and I'd never knuckled down to it. Busking
had always been an easier option for me and when

Nick moved on to pastures new the chance slipped through my fingers. It wasn't the first opportunity I'd messed up, nor would it be the last.

My dad said he'd ask around to see if there was anything going. 'But things are pretty rough everywhere at the moment,' he said, holding up a copy of the evening paper. 'Every time I look at the paper it's all doom and gloom. Jobs going everywhere.'

I wasn't that disconnected from reality. I knew there were millions of people in the same situation as me, every single one of them with better qualifications. I was so far down the pecking order in the jobs market I felt that it wasn't even worth applying for jobs.

My dad wasn't a man to bare his emotions with me. I knew he was frustrated by the way I lived my life. Deep down I knew he felt I wasn't trying. I understood why he felt that way, but the truth was that I was trying. Just in my own way.

To lighten things up a little we talked a little bit about his family. I wasn't particularly close to Anthony and Caroline; we met very infrequently. He asked me what I was doing for Christmas – I'd spent a couple of Christmases with him but it hadn't really been a barrel of laughs for either of us.

'I'm just going to spend it with Bob,' I said. 'We enjoy being together.'

My dad didn't really get my relationship with Bob. Tonight, as usual, he stroked him occasionally and kept an eye on him when I popped to the toilet. He even got the waitress to bring him a saucer of milk and gave him a couple of snacks. But he wasn't a natural cat lover. And on the one or two occasions when I had talked about how much Bob helped me in sorting myself out he just looked baffled. I suppose I couldn't blame him for that.

As usual, my Dad asked after 'my health' which I always took to be code for 'are you still off the drugs?'

'I'm doing all right,' I said. 'I saw a guy drop dead from an overdose on the landing of my flats a while back. That freaked me out quite a lot.'

He looked horrified. He had no understanding of drug culture or the way it worked and, like a lot of men of his generation, was a little bit scared of it truth be told. For that reason, I don't think he'd ever really grasped how bad my situation had been when I'd been at my lowest ebb on heroin.

He'd seen me during that period, but, like all addicts, I had learned to keep that side of my life hidden when necessary. I'd met him a couple of times when I was off my face on gear. I'd just told him I had a bout of the flu and assumed he wouldn't know any different. He wasn't stupid though, he probably sensed something was wrong but wouldn't have been able to put his finger on what it was specifically. He had no concept of what it was like to do drugs. I quite envied him that.

We spent an hour and a half together, but then he had to catch a train back to south London. He gave me a few quid to tide me over and we agreed to see each other again in a few weeks' time.

'Look after yourself, Jamie,' he said.

The station was still busy. It was the back end of the rush hour. I had a few magazines left in my satchel so decided to try and shift them before heading home. I found an empty pitch outside the railway station and was soon doing pretty well.

Bob had a full stomach and was on good form. People were stopping and making a fuss. I was just weighing up whether to spend the money I was making on a takeaway curry when trouble reared its head again.

I knew the pair were trouble the moment I set eyes on them heading across the road towards the main entrance to Victoria Station. I recognised one of them from my days selling *The Big Issue* in Covent Garden. He was a wiry, grey-haired guy in his mid-forties. He was wearing the distinctive, red tabard but I knew he wasn't a legitimate seller. He had been 'de-badged' a long time ago for various misdemeanours. His mate wasn't familiar, but I didn't need to know him to be able to tell he was a rough character. He was a big brute and was built like a sack of potatoes.

I immediately worked out what they were doing.

The smaller one was waving a single copy of *The Big Issue* around, stopping people, collecting money but never handing over the magazine. They were running a scam called One Booking, in which vendors used a single, out-of-date magazine to generate a string of sales. Each time someone handed over some money, the seller would come out with some sob story about it being their last copy and being in particularly dire straits. It was begging, basically. There was no other word for it.

I was always amazed that anyone fell for it. But there were always a few gullible – or maybe gener-ous – souls around.

I was worried that they were heading in our direction. Sure enough, they were soon outside the tube station entrance, with the smaller of the pair approaching travellers on the edge of the steps. It was blindingly obvious he wasn't an official seller. The tabard was ripped to shreds and looked like it had been pulled out of a dustbin. It was also miss-ing the official badge that legitimate vendors wore on the left hand side of their vests.

As his mate went about his business, the bigger of the two made a bee-line for me. He was every bit as aggressive as he looked.

'Oi, you, get lost, or I'll kill that cat of yours,' he said, sticking his big red face close to mine. There was a trace of Irish in his accent and his breath stank of booze.

Bob, as always, had spotted the danger and was hissing at him already. I knelt down and got him to climb on my shoulders before there was any trouble.

I wasn't going to be intimidated and stuck my ground.

'I've got a right to sell here and I've just got these few magazines to sell,' I said. 'You know what you are doing is wrong. You are nothing but a leech, you are forcing him to beg for you.'

He didn't like this and warned me again.

'You've got two minutes to pack your stuff up and f*** off,' he said, temporarily distracted by his mate who was waving to him for some reason. He then pushed his way into the crowds.

People were flooding in and out of the station, so I lost them for a few minutes. I knew the score. They were both drug addicts and were only running this scam until they had enough money to head off and fix themselves up. I was hoping that his mate's signal indicated that they'd hit their target and were going to disappear. No such luck.

In hardly any time, the big guy reappeared, looking even angrier than before. He was literally frothing at the mouth and spitting out expletives. 'Didn't you hear what I told you?' he snarled.

The next thing I knew he had hit me. He just walked up to me and punched me on the nose. It happened so fast, I didn't even see him pull back his arm. He just jabbed a giant fist into my face. I didn't have a hope of deflecting the blow.

'What the hell?' I said, back-pedalling, Bob hanging on for dear life.

When I drew my hand away from my face I could see that it was covered in blood. It was gushing out and my nose felt like it had some broken cartilage in there.

I decided it wasn't a fight I could win. There was no sign of the Police so I was on my own against a pretty nasty pair of individuals.

Working on the streets was risky, I knew that. But there were times when it was downright dangerous. I'd heard stories of *Big Issue* sellers being killed. There had been a case up in Norwich where two or three guys set about a vendor there and kicked him to death. I really didn't want to add to the statistics.

'Come on, Bob, let's get out of here,' I said, grabbing my stuff and heading off.

I felt a mix of anger and despair. I was desperate for a change in my fortunes. I didn't think I could take much more of this life. But, try as I might, I couldn't see how on earth I was going to break free. Suddenly all that talk with my father of jobs and training seemed ridiculous, a complete pipe dream. Who was going to pay a recovering junkie a decent salary? Who was going to hire someone with a curriculum vitae as barren as the Australian outback where I spent part of my childhood? On that day, feeling as low as I did, the answer was as plain and bloody obvious as the nose on my face: no one.

Chapter 11

Two Cool Cats

One lunchtime in September 2010, I arrived at Angel tube to be greeted by Davika. She was a ticket attendant and had been one of our most loyal friends since Bob and I had started working in Islington. She often brought Bob a little treat or something to drink, especially during hot weather. Today, however, she simply wanted to deliver a message.

'Hi James, there was someone here looking for you and Bob,' she said. 'He was a reporter from one of the local papers. He asked me to call him back if you were willing to talk to him.'

'Really?' I said. 'I guess I don't mind. Tell him he can come and see us during our regular hours.'

It wasn't the first time someone had paid us attention. There were a couple of films on the internet about Bob and I that had been viewed by a few thousand people and a couple of London bloggers had written nice things about us, but no one from the newspapers had shown any interest. To be honest, I took it with a pinch of salt. I'd had all sorts of weird and wonderful approaches over the years, 99 per cent of which came to nought.

A couple of days later, however, I arrived at Angel to find this guy outside the tube station waiting for us.

'Hi James, my name is Peter,' he said. 'I was wondering if I could do an interview with you for the *Islington Tribune*?'

'Sure, why not?'

He proceeded to take a picture of Bob perched on my shoulder with the Angel tube station sign behind us. I felt a bit self-conscious. I hadn't exactly dressed up for the occasion and was wearing a thick, early winter's beard, but he seemed happy enough with the results.

We then had a bit of a chat about my past and how we'd met. It wasn't quite the Spanish inquisition, but it clearly gave him enough ammunition for his piece which he said would appear in the next edition of the *Tribune*. Again, I didn't really take it too seriously. I worked on the principle that I'd believe it when I saw it. It was easier that way.

It was a few days later on a Thursday morning, that Rita and Lee, the co-ordinators at *The Big Issue* stall on Islington Green called me over.

'Hey James, you and Bob are in the paper today,' Rita said, producing a copy of the *Tribune*.

'Are we?' I asked.

Sure enough there was a half-page article on us written by Peter Gruner. The headline read:

TWO COOL CATS . . .
THE BIG ISSUE SELLER
AND A STRAY CALLED BOB.

The story began:

> Not since the legendary Dick Whittington has a man and his cat become such unlikely celebrities on the streets of Islington. *The Big Issue* seller James Bowen and his docile ginger cat Bob, who go everywhere together, have been attracting comments since they first appeared outside Angel Tube station. The story of how they met – widely reported in blogs on the internet – is one of such extraordinary pathos that it seems only a matter of time before we get a Hollywood film.

I had to laugh out loud at some of the journalistic licence. Dick Whittington? Hollywood film? And I wasn't terribly pleased with the way I looked in the photo, sporting that thick beard. But it was a lovely piece, I had to admit.

I popped into the newsagent and grabbed a few copies to take home. Bob saw me looking at the piece again on the bus that evening and did a kind of double take. It didn't happen very often, but for a split second he had this slightly baffled expression on his face. It was as if he was saying: 'No, it can't be. Can it? Really?'

Plenty of people knew it was really us though. And the publicity was soon reaping dividends, if only small ones. I'd agreed to do the interview mainly because I thought it would be good for sales of my magazines. I thought that by raising my profile it might encourage a few more customers to stop and talk to me at Angel tube station. And it did. In the days that followed, more and more people started saying hello to us not only at Angel, but on the bus and on the street.

One morning I was taking Bob to do his business on Islington Green when a group of schoolchildren appeared in front of us. They could only have been about nine or ten-years-old and were in very smart, blue uniforms.

'Look, it's Bob,' one of them, a little boy, said, pointing excitedly.

It was clear the rest of the class didn't have a clue what he was talking about.

'Who's Bob?' a voice asked.

'That cat there on that man's shoulders. He's famous. My mum says he looks like Garfield,' the boy said.

I was touched that we were being recognised

by young children but I wasn't quite so sure I was happy about the comparison with the world's best-known cartoon cat. Garfield was famous for being obese, obsessed with eating, lazy and slightly obnoxious. He also hated any form of exercise or hard work. Bob had always been in fine fettle, ate pretty sensibly and had the friendliest, most laid back attitude of any cat I'd ever come across. And no one could ever call him work-shy.

There were lots of similar encounters during the days after the piece was published, but the most significant came from someone I'd spoken to once before.

I'd already been approached one evening by an American lady who said she was a literary agent. Her name was Mary. She told me she lived nearby and had noticed Bob and I outside the tube station many times.

She'd asked me if I had considered writing a book about my life with Bob. I said I would think about it, but, truth be told, I hadn't really taken her seriously. How could I? I was a recovering drug addict who was struggling to survive selling *The Big Issue*. I didn't write a diary. I didn't even write texts on my mobile phone. Yes, I loved to read and consumed all the books I could lay my hands on. But, as far as I could see, at least, writing a book was about as realistic as building myself a space rocket or running for Parliament. In other words, it was a complete and utter non-starter.

Fortunately, she'd persisted and we'd spoken again. She had anticipated my concerns and suggested that I meet a writer who was experienced at helping people tell their stories. She told me he was busy at the time, but that he would be free towards the end of the year and would come and see me. After the *Islington Tribune* piece she contacted me again to confirm that I was happy to meet him.

If he thought there was a book in Bob and me, he would spend time with me, getting me to tell my story then helping to shape it up and write it. She would then try and sell it to a publisher. Again, it sounded too far-fetched for words.

I didn't hear anything for a while, but then, towards the end of November, I got a call from this writer guy. His name was Garry.

I agreed to meet him and he took me for a coffee in the Design Centre across the road from my pitch. We had Bob with us, so we had to sit outdoors in the biting cold. Bob was a better judge of character than me, so I made a point of going to the toilet and leaving them alone a couple of times. They got on famously, which I took to be a good omen.

I could tell he was trying to work out whether my story was suitable for a book and was as open as I felt was possible.

As far as I was concerned, I really didn't want to have to go into the dark side of my life. But as we spoke, he said something that struck a chord. He could see that Bob and I were both broken souls. We'd come together when we were both at rock bottom. We'd helped mend each other's lives.

'That's the story you have to tell,' he told me.

I had never thought of it in those terms. Instinctively, I knew that Bob had been a hugely positive force in my life. I'd even seen me on a video on YouTube saying that he'd saved my life. I guessed that, to some extent, it was true. But I just couldn't imagine that being a story that would interest anyone.

Even when I had seen Garry again for another, longer chat, it all seemed a bit of a pipe dream. There were so many ifs and maybes. If Garry and Mary were willing to work with me, maybe a publisher would be interested in releasing a book. I really couldn't see all three of those things happening. The obstacles seemed too great. As the festive season and the end of the year loomed into view, I told myself there was more chance of Father Christmas being real. Bob and I had grown to love Christmas together. The first year we'd been together we'd spent it alone in the flat, sharing a couple of ready meals and watching TV. Given that I'd spent several of the past ten Christmases on my own, in a hostel or off my face on heroin, it had felt like the happiest holiday ever.

I'd missed the second one by travelling to Australia, but ever since then we'd been together.

During the run up to Christmas, we had, as usual, been given a host of presents, from scarves for Bob to gift certificates for both of us at shops like Sainsbury's, Marks and Spencer and H&M. There was no question about which was Bob's favourite: an advent calendar filled with his favourite treats. He'd fallen in love with it instantly, naturally, and had quickly learned to make a fuss first thing in the morning when it was time to produce the latest snack on the countdown to Christmas.

We also got a fantastic Santa Paws outfit. Belle had made me one for our very first Christmas together but it had somehow got lost. This one had a snug red jacket and a very striking red hat for Bob to wear during the festive season. Passers-by at Angel were besotted by it.

When it came to Christmas Day itself Bob spent more time playing with the wrapping paper than the actual present itself. He rolled around on the carpet, nibbling at it. I left him to it and spent the afternoon watching television and playing video games. Belle popped round for a few hours. It felt like a real family Christmas to me.

It was a couple of weeks into the New Year when I got a phone call from Mary telling me that a major London publisher, Hodder and Stoughton, wanted to meet me – and Bob, of course.

A few days later, I went along to their offices in a rather grand tower block near Tottenham Court Road. At first, the security people weren't going to let Bob into the building. They looked baffled when we said he was going to be the subject of a book. I could see their point. Hodder's other authors included people like John Grisham and Gordon Ramsay. What on earth would they be doing publishing a book about a scruffy-looking bloke and his ginger tom cat?

Someone from the publishers came down to sort it out, however, and after that Bob and I were both made to feel very welcome. In fact Bob was treated like visiting royalty. He was given a little goodie bag with some little snacks and catnip toys and allowed to wander around the offices exploring. Wherever he went he was greeted like some kind of celebrity. People were snapping away on their phones and cooing over him. I knew he had star quality but I didn't realise it was this potent.

I, on the other hand, had to sit in on a meeting in which a long line of people popped in to talk about their different specialities, from marketing and publicity to production and sales. There was all sorts of business talk about publishing dates and production schedules. They might as well have been talking Serbo-Croat or Mandarin. But the long and the short of it was that they had seen some of the material Garry and I had worked on and they wanted to publish a book based on it. Between them, they'd even come up with a title: *A Street Cat Named Bob*. Tennessee Williams may have been spinning in his grave, but I thought it was very clever.

Soon I was being asked to visit the literary agency where Mary worked over in Chelsea. Again, it was a very grand and slightly intimidating place. They were more used to welcoming Nobel and Booker prize winners so there were a few odd looks when people realised that a *Big Issue* seller and his cat had walked into their rarefied atmosphere. While Bob explored the offices, Mary ran me through the contract that I'd been offered by the publishers. She told me it was a good deal, especially given I was an 'unknown author'. I placed my trust in her and signed all the paperwork.

Over the course of the last ten years I'd been more used to signing drug prescriptions and police release forms. It felt weird scrawling my name, but also, I had to confess, very, very exciting.

There were times when I woke up in the morning thinking it was all a figment of my imagination. This couldn't really be happening. Not to me.

I didn't want Garry coming round to my flat at that point. So I began meeting him once or twice a week in Islington. There were pros and cons to the arrangement. On the plus side, it meant that I could top up my money and spend a few hours working afterwards. But it also meant that I had Bob with me, which meant that finding somewhere to sit and talk was a challenge, especially when the weather was bad. The local cafés wouldn't let a cat on the premises and there wasn't a library nearby. So we had to find alternatives.

The first people to invite us in from the cold, ironically, were Waterstones, the bookshop on Islington Green. They knew me in there. I'd often pop in with Bob to look through the Science Fiction section. The manager there, Alan, was on duty and we asked him if he minded us working upstairs in a quiet corner. He not only said yes, he got a member of staff to organise two chairs for us in the history section. He even brought a couple of coffees in.

When the sun was out, we used a place on the Essex Road that had tables outside. I could smoke there as well, which was a bonus for me.

Garry and I were determined that the book wouldn't just be about my life with Bob. We wanted it to offer people some insights into life on the streets. I wanted to get across to people how easy it was for people like me to fall through the cracks, to become forgotten and overlooked by society. Of course, in order to do that, I had to tell my 'back-story' as well.

I really wasn't looking forward to that part of the exercise. Talking about myself wasn't something that came easily to me, especially when it came to the darker stuff. And there was a lot of that. There were aspects of my life as an addict that I had buried away in the farthest corners of my mind. I'd made choices that I was deeply ashamed about, done things that I didn't want to share with anyone, let alone put in a book. But once we began talking, to my surprise, it was less painful than I'd feared. I couldn't afford to see a psychologist or a psycho-analyst but there were times when talking to Garry was as good as talking to a shrink. It forced me to confront some painful truths and was strangely cathartic, helping me to understand myself a little better.

I knew I wasn't the easiest person to deal with. I had a defiant, self-destructive streak that had consistently got me into trouble. It was pretty obvious that I'd had a childhood that had messed me up. My parents' divorce and my peripatetic years, flitting between the UK and Australia, hadn't exactly been stabilising forces. I'd always tried really hard to fit in and be popular as a kid, but it had never worked. I'd ended up trying too hard – and become a misfit and an outcast as a result.

By the time I was an adolescent my behavioural problems had begun. I was angry and rebellious and fell out with my mother and stepfather. For a period of around two years, between the ages of 11 and 13, I'd been constantly in and out of the Princess Margaret Hospital for Children outside Perth. At one point I'd been diagnosed as either bi-polar or manic depressive. I can't remember exactly which it was. They seemed to come up with a new diagnosis every week. Either way, the upshot was that I was prescribed various medications, including lithium.

The memories from that time were mixed.

One vivid memory that sprung to mind was of going into the surgery at the Princess Margaret for a weekly blood test. The walls of the surgery were plastered in posters of pop and rock stars so I had the blood tests done while staring at a picture of Gladys Knight and the Pips.

Each time the doctor assured me that the injection he was about to give me wouldn't hurt. 'It will only feel like a scratch,' he'd say, but it was always more than that. It was kind of ironic, I suppose, but I'd had a phobia about needles for years after that. It was a measure of how deep my drug addiction had been that I'd somehow forgotten this and happily injected myself on a daily basis.

On a happier note, I remembered how, after leaving the hospital, I had wanted to give something back and had begun donating boxes of comic books. I'd managed to get myself some work experience in a comic book shop nearby and had persuaded the boss to let me take boxes of unsold magazines for the kids at the hospital. I'd spent many hours playing air hockey and watching video games in the activity room they had in the children's ward so I knew they'd all appreciate something decent to read.

In the main, however, the memories of that time were pretty grim. They opened my eyes to aspects of my youth that I'd never really examined before.

At one point, for instance, we were working on the book on the day after I'd watched a film by the documentary-maker Louis Theroux about how parents in America were using more and more psychoactive medication to treat their kids for disorders like ADHD, Asperger's and bipolar disorders.

It occurred to me suddenly that this was exactly what had happened to me. And it struck me that being treated like this must have had a huge impact on me when I was young. It made me wonder what had come first. It was a chicken and egg question: had I been given the drugs because I was acting up? Or did I start acting up because of all the visits to doctors who convinced me that there must be something wrong with me? Perhaps most scary of all, what effect did all that medication have on me and my young personality? As a young kid I'd considered myself quite a happy-go-lucky character, but since that time I had been what I suppose you'd call 'troubled'. I'd struggled to fit into society and suffered from depression and mood swings. Was there a link? I had no idea.

What I did know, however, was that I couldn't blame the doctors, my mother or anyone else for the way my life had gone since then. Yes, they had played a role, but the buck stopped with me. No one told me to develop a drug problem. No one forced me to drift on to the streets of London. No one made me take up heroin. They were mistakes that I made of my own free will. I hadn't needed anyone's help to screw up my life. I'd done a perfectly good job of that on my own.

If nothing else, the book was an opportunity for me to make that crystal clear.

For a moment my dad was lost for words. The expression on his face was a mixture of disbelief, happiness, pride – and mild apprehension.

'That's a lot of money, Jamie,' he said after a couple of moments, putting to one side the manila coloured cheque I'd just handed him.

'You'd better be careful with that.'

The reality of what had happened hadn't really sunk in until now. Not just for my dad, but for me either. There had been meetings with publishers, contracts signed, even articles in the newspapers. But it hadn't been until I received this cheque for the advance that it finally struck home.

When it had first flopped through the letter box a couple of days earlier, I had opened the envelope and then simply sat there looking at it. The only cheques I'd seen in the past decade had been from the DHSS. They were for small amounts, £50 here and £100 there, never anything with more than a couple of noughts on it.

Compared to some people, especially in London, it wasn't actually that large a sum of money. For a lot of the commuters walking past me each day on their way to the City of London, I guess it wasn't even a month's salary. But for someone for whom £60 was a very good day's wage, it was an eye-watering amount of cash.

The arrival of the cheque, though, had brought two immediate problems. I was terrified of frittering it away but, even more of a worry, I didn't have a bank account into which I could pay it. I'd had an account years ago but hadn't managed it very well. I'd got used to living on cash and for the last few years had taken all my cheques to a 'cash converters'. Which was why I'd travelled to my father's house in south London.

'I was hoping you could look after it for me,' I'd asked him over the phone. 'I can then ask you for money as and when I need it.'

He'd agreed and I'd now had the cheque endorsed over to his name. (Not a huge change because we shared the exact same initials and surname.)

Rather than meeting as usual at Victoria, he'd invited me over to his neck of the woods. We went for a couple of drinks in his local and chatted for a couple of hours.

'So is this going to be a proper book?' he asked me, the scepticism he'd displayed ever since I'd told him about it resurfacing once more.

'What do you mean?'

'Well, is it a picture book or a children's book? What is it going to be about exactly?' he said.

It was a fair question, I suppose.

I explained that it was the story of how I met Bob, and how we'd helped each other. He looked a little nonplussed.

'So will me and your mother be in it?' he asked.

'You might get a mention,' I said.

'I'd better get on to my lawyers then,' he said, smiling.

'No, don't worry. The only person that comes out badly in all this is me.'

That made him change tack a little.

'And is this going to be a long-term thing?' he continued. 'You writing books.'

'No,' I said, honestly. 'I'm not going to become the next J.K. Rowling dad. There are thousands of books published every year. Only a tiny minority of them become bestsellers. I really don't think a tale about a busker and recovering drug addict and his stray ginger cat is going to be one of them. So, yes this is going to be a short-term thing. It's a nice windfall, and no more.'

'All the more reason to be careful with the money then,' he said, seizing the opportunity to give me some sensible fatherly advice.

He was right, of course. This money would ease the stress on me for a few months, but not much longer. I had debts to clear and my flat was badly in need of some refurbishing. I knew I had to be realistic which meant that I had to keep my job with *The Big Issue* going. We talked about this for a little while, but he then went off into a lecture on the relative merits of various investments and savings schemes. At that point, I did what I had so often done when my parents spoke to me. I tuned out completely.

Chapter 12

The Joy of Bob

Being with Bob has been such an education. I'd not had many mentors in my life and had spurned the few well-meaning people who had tried to guide and advise me. I always knew better than them, or so I imagined.

It is a bizarre thing to admit, but with Bob it has been different. He has taught me as much, if not more, than any human I've come across. Since being in his company I've learned important lessons about everything from responsibility and friendship to selflessness. He has even given me an insight into a subject I thought I'd never really understand – parenthood.

I doubted whether I would ever have children. I wasn't sure whether I'd be up to the job and, truth be told, the opportunity hadn't really presented itself. I'd had a couple of girlfriends over the years, including Belle, to whom I was still really close and thought the world of. But starting a family hadn't ever been on the horizon. As Belle once succinctly put it, I was too busy behaving like a child myself most of the time.

Caring for Bob has, however, given me a glimpse into what it must be like to be a father. In particular, it has made me realise that parenthood is all about anxiety. Whether it is fretting over his health, watching out for him when we are out on the streets, or simply making sure he is warm and well fed, life with Bob often feels like one worry after another.

It actually chimes with something that my father had said to me after I'd been missing in London for a year or so. It had been at the height of my addiction and both he and my mother had been beside themselves with concern about me.

'You have no idea how much a parent worries about his or her child,' he had shouted at me, furious at what he called my selfishness in not being in touch with them.

It hadn't meant much at all to me then. Since being with Bob I have begun to appreciate what hell I must have put my parents through. I wish I could turn back the clock and save them all that grief.

That is the bad news. The good news is that, in amongst the anxiety and worry, 'parenthood' brings with it a lot of laughter too. That is another thing Bob has taught me. For far too long I'd found it hard to find much joy in life. He has taught me how to be happy again. Even the slightest, silliest moments we share together can bring an instant smile to my face.

One Saturday lunchtime, for instance, I answered a knock on the door and found the guy from the flat across the hallway standing there.

'Hi, just thought I'd let you know that your cat is out here.'

'Sorry, erm, no. Must be someone else's. Mine's in here,' I said, turning around to scout around the living room.

'Bob. Where are you?'

There was no sign of him.

'No, I'm pretty sure this is him out here. Ginger isn't he?' the guy said.

I stepped out into the hallway to discover Bob sitting around the corner, perfectly still on top of a cupboard on the landing with his head pressed against the window, looking down on the street below.

'He's been there a while. I noticed him earlier,' the guy said, heading for the lift.

'Oh. Thanks,' I said.

Bob just looked at me as if I was the world's biggest party pooper. The expression on his face seemed to say: 'Come on up here and take a look at this view with me, it's really interesting.'

'Bob, how the heck have you got there?' I said, reaching up to collect him.

Belle was visiting and was in the kitchen rustling up a sandwich.

'Did you let Bob out?' I asked her back inside the flat.

'No,' she said, looking up from the worktop.

'I can't work out how he got out into the hallway and hid himself up on top of the cupboard.'

'Ah, hold on,' Belle said, a light coming on somewhere inside her head. 'I popped downstairs about an hour ago to put some rubbish out. You were in the bathroom. I shut the door behind me but he must have slid out without me noticing and then hidden away somewhere when I came back up. He's so damned clever. I'd love to know what's going on in his mind sometimes.'

I couldn't help laughing out loud. It was a subject I'd speculated on quite a lot over the years. I'd often found myself imagining the thought processes Bob went through. I knew it was a pointless exercise and I was only projecting human behaviour onto an animal. Anthropomorphising I think they call it. But I couldn't resist it.

It wasn't hard, for instance, to work out why he'd been so happy finding his new vantage point out in the hallway today.

There was nothing Bob loved more than watching the world go by. Inside the flat, he would regularly position himself on the kitchen window sill. He could sit there happily all day, monitoring the goings on below, like some kind of security guard.

His head would follow people as they walked towards and then past our flats. If someone turned into the entrance to the building, he'd stretch himself until he had lost sight of them. It might sound crazy, but I found it incredibly entertaining. He took it so seriously that it was almost as if he had a list of people who were allowed to travel this way at certain times and in certain directions. He'd see someone passing and look as if to say 'yes, OK, I know who you are' or 'come on you're running late for the bus to work'. At other times he'd get quite agitated, as if he was thinking: 'Oi, hang on! I don't recognise you' or: 'Hey. You don't have clearance, where do you think you're going. Get back here.'

I could easily while away half an hour just watching Bob watching others. Belle and I used to joke that he was on patrol.

Bob's escape into the hallway today was typical of something else he seemed to love doing as well, playing hide and seek. I'd found him hiding in all sorts of surprising nooks and crannies. He particularly loved anywhere warm.

One evening, I went to have a bath before I went

to bed. As I nudged the bathroom door open, I couldn't help thinking it felt a little odd. Rather than swinging open easily it needed an extra nudge. It felt heavy somehow.

I didn't think much more of it and started running a bath. I was looking in the mirror by the sink when I noticed something moving on the back of the door amongst the towels I kept in a rack. It was Bob.

'How on earth have you got up there?' I said, howling with laughter.

I worked out that he must have climbed on to a shelving unit near the door and then, somehow, jumped from there on to the towels, pulling himself up on to the top of them. It looked pretty uncomfortable as well as precarious but he seemed really happy.

The bathroom was a favourite spot for hide and seek. Another frequent trick of his was to hide inside the clothes horse I often used to dry my washing in the bath tub, especially during winter.

Several times I'd been brushing my teeth or even sitting on the toilet, and suddenly noticed the clothes moving. Bob would then appear, pushing the clothes apart like curtains, his face wearing a sort of *peek-a-boo* expression. He thought it was great entertainment.

Bob's ability to get into trouble was another source of endless entertainment.

He loved watching television and computer screens. He could while away endless hours watching wildlife programmes or horse racing. He would sit there, as if he was mesmerised. So when we walked past the gleaming new Apple store in Covent Garden one afternoon, I thought I'd give him a treat. The place was bursting with shiny new laptops and desktops, none of which I could remotely afford. But the Apple philosophy was that anyone could stroll in and play around with their technology. So we did.

We had spent a few minutes playing with the computers, surfing the internet and watching YouTube videos when Bob spotted a screen that had a kind of aquarium-style display, with exotic and really colourful fish swimming around. I could see why he was attracted to it. It was absolutely stunning.

I took him over to the giant screen and let him gape at it for a few moments. It was funny to watch. He would follow a particular fish as it progressed around the screen and then disappeared. He would then do a sort of double take. He couldn't fathom what was happening and darted behind the giant screen, expecting to find the fish there. But when all he saw was a wall of silver and a tangle of leads, he darted back again and started following another fish.

It carried on like this for minutes until he suddenly started getting frenzied and got wrapped up in a cable. I'd been temporarily distracted and turned around to see his paw wrapped around a white cable. He was pulling on it and was threatening to drag one of the giant consoles with him.

'Oh God, Bob, what are you doing?' I said.

I'd not been the only one to spot this. A couple of Apple 'geniuses' were standing there laughing.

'He's a star, isn't he?' one of them said.

Unfortunately, they were soon joined by another, more senior member of the team.

'If he breaks anything, I'm afraid you'd have to cover the costs,' he said. Given the prices of the products on display in the store, I wasted no time in untangling him and getting the hell out of there.

For Bob, London is an endless source of opportunities to get up to no good. Even the underground has become a place where he can misbehave.

When we first got together he would cling to me closely whenever we travelled underground. He didn't like going down the escalators and lifts and felt intimidated by the crowds and the claustrophobic atmosphere during the rush hour. Over the years, however, he has conquered his fears. He even has his own identity card, given to him by the staff at Angel tube station and behaves just like any other Londoner, going about his or her business. He trots along the tunnels, always walking as near to the wall as possible, probably for security. When we get to the platform, he stands behind the yellow line, unflustered when the train pulls into the station, despite the noise it makes. He waits for it to go past him, then waits patiently for the doors to slide open before padding quietly on board and checking for an empty seat.

Londoners are notorious for not engaging with their fellow commuters, but even the most ice-hearted melt a little when they see him sitting there, studiously taking in the atmosphere. They snap away with their camera phones then head off to work smiling. Living in London can be such an impersonal and soul-destroying existence. The idea that we are somehow lightening people's days makes me smile.

Travelling on the tube has its perils, however.

One evening we'd headed home from central London and got the tube to Seven Sisters, the nearest tube station to my flat. There was a lot of maintenance and repair work being done within the tube at the time and Bob had been fascinated by the various bits of equipment and heavy-duty gear that was visible here and there.

It was as we were coming up the escalator that I noticed Bob's tail was sticky. When I looked at it a little closer, I could see some sort of black, tar-like material on his tail. I then saw that it was also streaked along his body, from the middle of his ribcage back to halfway along his tail.

It was pretty obvious he'd rubbed up against something during his ride on the tube because it wasn't there beforehand. I was at a loss to know what it was exactly. It looked like engine oil or some sort of heavy grease. It definitely looked like it had come from something mechanical. I guessed he must have rubbed up against some of the engineering equipment somehow.

The one thing I did know was that it was potentially harmful. Bob seemed to have worked this out as well. I saw that he'd spotted the mess and had already decided that giving it a lick wasn't a good idea.

My phone was low on credit but I had just about enough to make a call and rang a friend, Rosemary, a vet who had helped us out once before when Bob had been ill. She loved Bob and was always willing to help. When I explained what had happened she told me that whatever it was I needed to get it washed off.

'Motor and engine oil can be highly toxic to cats, especially if it's ingested or inhaled. It can cause really bad inflammation and burning of organs, especially the lungs. It can also cause breathing problems, seizure and even death in really bad cases,' she said, scaring me. 'So you really need to wash it off him. Does Bob let you bathe him?' she said. 'If it doesn't come off, you should take him to the Blue Cross or another vet first thing in the morning,' she said just before I ran out of credit and my phone cut out.

Cats seem to fall into two categories when it comes to bath time: there are those who hate it and those that love it. Luckily, Bob falls well and truly into the second camp. In fact, he is a bit obsessed with his bath.

He loves nothing more than climbing into the tub when I run a bath. He has learned that I always run a warm bath rather than a steaming hot one and hops into the tub so that he can paddle around in it for a few minutes.

It is funny – and, of course, very cute – to watch him walking around afterwards as he lifts and shakes one paw at a time.

He also gets very possessive about the bath plug and steals and hides it. I end up using a makeshift plug only to find the real plug lying on the living room floor where Bob has been playing with it.

Sometimes I have to put a jug with a weight on it over the plug to stop him from stealing and hiding it.

So given all that it was no problem getting him into the bath so that I could get this mystery grease off his tail.

I didn't have to hold him down. I used both

hands to rub his tail and his side using some cat-friendly shower gel. I then hosed him down with the shower head. The expression on his face as the jets of water soaked into his body was hilarious, a mix of a grimace and a grin. Finally I dried him off as best I could with a towel. Again he didn't need much persuasion to be rubbed down. He loved it and was purring throughout.

I managed to get all of the nasty stuff off him. But there was still a faint stain on his tail and body. Over the next few days, however, he was able to lick it and it slowly began to disappear. I popped into the Blue Cross at Islington later that week and got them to give him a quick check up. They told me there was nothing to worry about.

'Easier said than done, there's always something to fret about with this one,' I said to the nurse, realising afterwards that I'd actually begun to sound a little like a parent.

The incident on the tube reminded me of a truth that I always kept in my mind. In the years since we'd found each other, I'd domesticated Bob to a certain degree. When it came down to it though, he remained a stray cat at heart.

I can't be 100 per cent certain, but my gut feeling

is that he must have spent a large part of his young life living off his wits on the streets. He is a Londoner, born and bred, and is never happier than when he is exploring it. I often smile to myself and say *'you can take the cat out of the street, but you can't take the street out of the cat'*.

He has a few favourite haunts. At Angel, he loves visiting Islington Memorial Green, the little park where he is free to rummage around in the bushes, sniffing out whatever caught his interest while he did his business. There are a few overgrown corners where he can discreetly disappear for a few moments of privacy. Not that privacy bothers him too much.

He is also, for instance, very fond of the grounds of St Giles in the Fields churchyard just off Tottenham Court Road. Often, when we walk from our bus stop on Tottenham Court Road towards Neal Street and Covent Garden, he starts moving around on my shoulder letting me know that he wants to make it a port of call.

The graveyard at St Giles is an oasis in the middle of one of the busiest parts of the city, with benches to sit and watch the world go by. For some reason, however, Bob's favourite toilet spot there is actually in full view of the street, by a set of railings on a wall. He is unfazed by the flood of Londoners passing by and quietly goes about his business there.

It was a similar story when we were working on Neal Street where his preferred option was outside an office block on Endell Street. It was overlooked by several floors of conference rooms and offices, so again, wasn't exactly the most private spot in London. But Bob felt comfortable there and always managed to squeeze himself into the shrubbery so that he could get on with things as quickly and efficiently as possible.

Wherever he goes, he is, like all cats, very methodical about it. He digs himself a decent-sized hole, places himself over it while he does the necessary, then starts scrabbling dirt to cover up the evidence afterwards. He is always meticulous in levelling it all off so that no one would know it was there. It always fascinates me to know why cats do this. I read somewhere that it's a territorial thing.

The gardens in Soho Square were another favourite stop-off if we were working in that area. Apart from being one of the most beautiful little parks in central London, it had other attractions for Bob. Dogs were banned, for instance, which meant I could relax a little more if I let Bob off the leash. It was also a place where Bob seemed happy, especially in the summer. Bob was fascinated by birds and Soho Square park was filled with them. He would sit there, wide-eyed, staring at them, making a curious little noise, a sort of *raa, raa, raa*. It sounded really cute, although, in reality of course, it was probably quite sinister. I read somewhere that scientists think cats mimic eating when they see potential prey. In other words, they are practising chomping them to bits in their mouth when they catch them.

That made sense. Bob loves nothing more than chasing mice and rats and other creatures when let loose in parks. On several occasions, he'd wandered over to me with something he'd found – and probably killed – while he was roaming around.

One day, I was reading a comic book in Soho Square when he arrived with something absolutely disgusting dangling from his mouth. It was part of a rat's head.

'Bob, that's going to make you really sick,' I said.

He seemed to know this better than me. I don't think he had any intention of eating it. Instead he took it into a corner and started playing with it, much like he played with his scraggedy mouse at home. Ninety nine times out of a hundred Bob drew admiring glances from passers-by. On that particular occasion, a few people looked at him in utter horror.

I had never been one of those cat owners who saw their pets as little angels, incapable of doing anything nasty. Far from it. I knew all too well that, like all members of his species, Bob was a predator and a highly effective one at that. If we had been living in other parts of the world, I'd have been more concerned. In parts of the USA, Australia and New Zealand, in particular, they have tried to introduce bans on cats being allowed out after dark. They claim domestic cats are doing so much damage that birdlife in particular is being endangered. That wasn't a problem in London. So, as far as I was concerned, Bob was free to do what came naturally to him. As long as he didn't risk hurting or harming himself.

Apart from anything else, it is great entertainment, for him – and for me.

One day, for instance, we were looking after Titch's dog Princess again and I'd decided to take the pair of them to a small park near the flats where I live. It's not the most glamorous green space in London. It's got a rundown basketball court and a tree-lined area. But that was enough for them.

I was sitting on a bench with Bob on the extra-long lead I'd made for him when he suddenly spotted a grey squirrel.

Princess spotted it too and soon the pair of them were bounding towards it. The squirrel, quite sensibly, scampered up the nearest tree, but Bob and Princess weren't deterred.

I watched them as they worked together trying to work out how to flush the squirrel out of the tree. It was like watching a SWAT team trying to winkle a bad guy out of a safe house.

Princess would let out a bark every now and again to try and rattle the squirrel. Every time the squirrel appeared or made a move, the two would adjust their positions. Bob was covering one side, leading back on to the open space towards me, while Princess was covering the squirrel's other potential escape route at the back of the tree.

They carried on with this for twenty minutes before eventually giving up.

I'm sure some people must have thought that I was ever-so-slightly mad. But I sat there grinning and giggling away, engrossed by every captivating minute of it.

Chapter 13

Public Enemy No 1

Another summer was on its way and the midday sun was already blazing as Bob and I settled ourselves in a shady spot outside Angel tube station. I had just got out a bowl and filled it with some water for Bob when I saw two men approaching.

They were both dressed casually, in jeans and jumpers. One was in his late twenties while the other was, I guessed, a decade or so older, probably in his late thirties. Almost in unison, they produced badges from their pockets showing they were police officers, members of the CSU, Community Safety Unit for Islington.

'Hello there, Sir. Can you tell me your name?' the older of them asked me.

'Erm, it's James Bowen, why?'

'Mr Bowen, I'm afraid we have had an allegation of assault made against you. It's a serious matter so we are going to have to ask you to accompany us to the police station to answer a few questions,' the younger guy said.

Plain-clothes policemen were a fairly frequent fixture on the streets and I'd encountered my fair share of them. Fortunately, unlike some of their colleagues, who could be a little aggressive and anti-*Big Issue* vendors, these two were perfectly polite.

When I asked if I could take a minute to pack up my pitch and sort Bob out, they told me to take as much time as I wanted. They then told me that we were going to walk towards their HQ at Tolpuddle Street.

'Shouldn't take us more than a few minutes,' the younger officer said.

I was surprised at how calm I was. In the past I'd have started panicking and would probably have protested, possibly even violently. It was a measure of how much more controlled and together I was these days. Besides, I hadn't done anything. I hadn't assaulted anyone.

The police officers seemed pretty chilled too. As we made our way to the station, they were walking along quite happily in front of me and Bob. Occasionally one would drop back to walk with us. At one point, the younger of the two asked me whether I understood what was happening and whether I knew my rights.

'Yeah, sure,' I said.

I knew I hadn't been charged with anything and that I was just helping them with their enquiries. There was no need to call a lawyer or anything like that, at this stage at least.

Obviously, my mind was churning away, trying to work out who might have made this 'allegation'. I had a few thoughts already.

The most obvious explanation was that this was someone just trying to muck up my day. Sadly, it was pretty common. I'd seen it happen to other vendors and buskers over the years. Someone with a grudge or just an evil streak would make an accusation which the police would be obliged to check out. Sometimes they'd do it simply to get the person away from their pitch and then claim it for themselves. There were a few people around who, I knew, didn't like the fact that I'd made the tube pitch a success and would love to have taken it over. It was nasty, but it was a fact of life, unfortunately.

The other, more sinister, possibility, was that it was someone trying to undermine my book. By now pretty much everyone in *The Big Issue* community knew about it. More newspapers had picked up on the story and several vendors had made comments, positive and negative.

I'd been told by one of the co-ordinators that someone had been putting it around that I shouldn't be allowed to sell the magazine any more. I knew this already because one vendor in central London had made his objections plain and to my face. He had also called me 'a f***ing hippy poser', which was rather charming I thought. Stupidly, I'd imagined that I was doing something positive for the magazine. Instead, it felt at times like I'd turned into every vendor's Public Enemy No 1.

By the time we got to the station both of the police officers were on first name terms with Bob. They seemed really smitten with him, so much so that he was their first priority when we arrived at the station.

'Right let's get Bob settled before we take you into the custody suite,' the older officer said.

We were soon joined by a blonde, uniformed female PC in her late twenties. She immediately focussed on Bob, who was still wrapped around my shoulders, trying to take in the unfamiliar scenery.

'OK, is this Bob?' she said, reaching up to him and giving him a stroke. He seemed to take an instant shine to her and was soon rubbing his face on her hand, purring away as he did so.

'Do you think he'd mind if I picked him up?' she said.

'Sure, if he will come to you then go for it,' I said, sensing that he was already really at ease with her.

As I suspected, he let her scoop him up.

'Why don't you come with me and we can see if

we can sort you out with something nice to eat or drink?' she said.

I watched as they headed behind the main reception desk to an office area with desks and photocopiers and fax machines. Bob was fascinated by all the red lights and buzzing machines and was happy in there. So I left him there as I headed off with the officers.

'Don't worry, he's safe with Gillian,' the younger officer said to me as we went through a set of doors into the custody suite. I felt certain he was telling the truth.

As we headed into an interview room, I suddenly felt butterflies in my stomach. It had been explained to me that I was being questioned about one of the so-called 'trigger offences'. These were offences in which drug users or dealers committed crimes like shoplifting, robbery and assault in order to buy drugs. So as a result of this, I knew that I would probably need to be tested for drugs as well as fingerprinted.

How times had changed? A year or so earlier and I'd have been seriously concerned about this. But now I had no qualms at all as they conducted the so-called Cozart test and swabbed my mouth for traces of heroin or cocaine. I knew I was clean. I told the officers this but they said they had no option.

'It's regulation now I'm afraid,' one of them said.

Once that was over, they sat me down and asked me some questions.

They asked me whether I'd been in a location somewhere in Islington a day earlier. The address didn't sound at all familiar. They then mentioned the name of a woman.

Years earlier, at the depths of my drug addiction, when I'd been arrested a couple of times for shop-lifting I'd learned to simply answer 'no comment' to any questions like this. But I knew this was really irritating for the police, so I tried to be co-operative.

'I'd like to help you, but I honestly don't know what you are talking about,' I said.

They didn't get angry or pushy in their question-ing at all. There was no 'good cop, bad cop' routine. They just nodded at my answers, took down some notes and that was it. After about ten minutes, or less, we were done.

'OK, Mr Bowen, well we need you to stay here for a bit while we look into this further,' the younger officer said.

By now it had turned into a very bright, sunny afternoon outside. I was impatient to be reunited with Bob and to get back to work. But the clock kept ticking and before I knew it the shadows were lengthening. It was really frustrating and I was also worried about Bob. At one stage a duty PC offered me a cup of tea so I asked about him.

'It's OK, he's with Gillian still downstairs,' he said. 'Think she's been out to get him some treats, so he's a pretty happy chappie down there.'

Eventually, the two officers who'd first appro-ached me, came back into the interview room.

'I'm afraid I think we've wasted your time and our time,' they said. 'The person who made this accusation on the phone hasn't been willing to come down to give a formal statement. So there's no corroborating evidence against you and so there will be no charges.'

I was obviously relieved. I felt angry as well, but decided to bottle it up. There was no point in making a formal complaint or threatening legal action, especially as everyone had been so decent. It was best to just get the hell out of there and get back to work.

My main concern, once more was Bob. What had they done with him for all this time?

I had to go down to the reception area to sign out. Bob was there with Gillian, looking as content as when I'd left him. But the moment he saw me his tail started swishing and his ears perked up. He leapt into my arms.

'Gosh, someone's pleased to see you,' Gillian said.

'Has he been a good boy?' I asked her.

'He's been a star. Haven't you, Bob?' she said.

I saw that she had set him up in a corner of her

office. She told me that she'd been out to the shops and bought him some cat milk, a pouch of meaty food and an enormous packet of his favourite treats. No wonder he was so happy, I thought.

We chatted for a moment or two while they got my bag and tabard from wherever it had been put during my interview upstairs. Gillian told me in normal circumstances he'd have been placed with any stray dogs that were being held.

'If you'd been kept in overnight we'd have had to think about putting him there,' she said. 'But luckily that won't be necessary now.'

I'd soon been officially released. The two officers were apologetic again.

'Just someone being spiteful I guess,' I said to them, shaking their hands as I left.

By the time I had left the station it was getting towards sunset. All day I'd been paranoid that someone had stolen my pitch so I headed back to Angel just to check. To my relief, there was no one there.

'You all right, James?' one of the flower sellers asked me.

'Yeah, just someone's idea of a joke. Reporting me for assault.'

'Really? What's wrong with people?' he said, shaking his head in disgust.

It was a good question, one to which I had absolutely no answer unfortunately.

Around a week to ten days later, Bob and I were selling magazines during the rush hour, when an attractive, blonde lady came up to us. Bob seemed to recognise her and arched his head towards her when she knelt down beside him.

'You don't remember me, do you?' she said to me as she made a fuss of him.

So many faces were flashing past us each night outside the tube, it was hard to register everyone. She could obviously see I was struggling.

'Tolpuddle Street station? I was the one who looked after Bob the other week,' she smiled.

'Oh, yes, of course. Sorry,' I said, genuinely mortified. 'It's Gillian, isn't it?'

'Looks like you are both doing well,' she said.

Community police officers had stopped to talk to us over the years, but she didn't seem to be 'on duty'.

She wasn't in uniform for a start.

'On my way home from the end of my shift,' she said, when I mentioned this.

'We didn't really have much of a chance to talk when you were at the station the other day, for obvious reasons,' Gillian said. 'So how did you two get together?'

She smiled and laughed out loud a couple of times as I recounted our early days together.

'Soul mates by the sound of it,' she said.

She could tell that I was busy and that the rush hour was about to begin, so was soon on her way.

'I might pop in and see you again if that's all right,' she said.

'Sure,' I said.

She was true to her word and was soon stopping by to see us regularly, often bringing gifts for Bob. He seemed to have a genuine soft spot for her.

Gillian was generous to me as well. On one occasion she brought me a coffee, a sandwich and a cookie from one of the smart local sandwich bars. We chatted for a little while, both of us skirting around what had happened at the station a few weeks earlier. A part of me was curious to find out who had made this allegation against me, but I knew she couldn't go into too much detail. It would have been too risky for her.

I explained to her what was happening to us with the book and how it seemed to have generated more animosity than anything else.

'Ah don't worry about that. People are always jealous of other's success. It sounds great,' she said. 'Your friends and family must be so proud of you.'

'Yeah, they are,' I said, giving her a sheepish smile and lighting up a cigarette.

Of course, the truth was that I didn't have too many friends. Aside from Belle, there was no one to whom I could turn – in the good times or the bad times. I had Bob and that was about it.

It was, in part, the life that I'd made for myself. I was a product of the environment in which I'd spent the past decade.

When I'd been on drugs I'd withdrawn from the world. My most important relationships back then were with my dealers. But even now that I was clean, I found it hard to establish friendships. There were several reasons. Money, for a start. To make friends you had to go out and socialise, which cost money so I very rarely did that. But on a deeper level, I also found it hard to trust people. During the worst period of my drug dependency, I'd stayed in hostels where you knew that anyone could rob you of all your possessions any moment. Even when you were asleep. So I'd become very wary. It was sad, but I still felt that way to a large extent. The events of the past couple of weeks had underlined that. Someone had made a fictitious assault accusation against me. For all I knew it could have been someone I saw every day of the week. It could have been someone I regarded as a 'friend'.

So as I looked at Bob interacting with Gillian, a part of me wished my life could be as simple and straightforward as his. He had met her in strange circumstances but had immediately sensed he could trust her. He knew in his bones that she was a decent person and so he had embraced her as a friend. I knew it wasn't going to be easy, but I needed to do that more. I needed to take that same leap of faith. To do that, however, I had to change my life. I had to get off the streets.

Chapter 14

Pride and Prejudice

It was the first Saturday of July and the streets of central London were packed for the annual Gay Pride celebrations. The West End was a sea of colour – well mostly pink – as the hot weather had drawn even more revellers than usual. According to the news, a million people had ventured out on to the streets to watch the huge parade of floats, filled with drag queens, dancers and spectacular costumes snake its way from Oxford Circus, down Regent Street to Trafalgar Square.

I'd decided to kill two birds with one stone, and had spent the day watching the floats and fabulous outfits while also selling a few magazines at a pitch on Oxford Street near Oxford Circus tube station.

It was a lucrative day for all *The Big Issue* sellers so, as a 'visitor' from Islington, I had been careful to make sure I stayed within the rules. Some pitches, like my slot outside Angel tube station, are designated to only one authorised vendor but others, like this one, are free to anyone, provided there is no one else working there. I'd also been careful not to 'float', the term used to describe selling whilst walking around the streets. I'd fallen foul of that rule in the past and didn't want to do so again.

During the decade or so that I had been on the streets, Gay Pride had grown from a small, quite political march into one of the city's biggest street parties. Only the Notting Hill Carnival was bigger. This year the crowds were packed four or five deep in places, but everyone was in an incredibly good mood, including Bob.

He'd got used to being in big crowds. There had been a time when he had a slight phobia of people in really scary outfits. He'd run off years earlier after seeing a guy in a weird, over-sized suit outside Ripley's Believe It Or Not in Piccadilly Circus. His years of walking the streets of London and Covent Garden in particular, seemed to have eased his fears, however. He'd seen everything from weird, silver-painted human statues to French fire-eaters to giant dragons during Chinese New Year. Today, there was no shortage of outrageous outfits and people blowing horns and whistles but he took it all in his stride. He sat on my shoulder throughout, soaking the party atmosphere up and loving the attention he was getting from the huge crowds. Quite a few people knew him by name and asked to have their picture taken with the pair of us. One or two even said they were looking forward to reading about us in our book.

'We need to write it first,' I half-joked.

As the main parade drew to an end late in the afternoon, Bob and I headed towards Soho Square where there was a music stage and some other events and turned into Old Compton Street, home to many of London's most popular gay bars. The street was absolutely crammed full of people, many of them members of the procession who were now relaxing over a few drinks. About halfway along the street, I decided to have a cigarette. I didn't have a lighter on me so stopped at a table outside one of the pubs and asked to borrow one. To my surprise, a gay guy wearing nothing but a pair of pink Y-fronts, a pair of angel wings and a halo, produced one. I didn't want to think where he'd been keeping it.

'Here you go, mate. Nice cat by the way,' he said as he lit my cigarette for me.

I was still chatting to the guy when I felt a tap on my shoulder. I turned round to see an outreach worker called Holly. Judging by the way she was dressed in shorts and a t-shirt, I assumed she was off duty, mistakenly as it turned out.

'James. You're floating,' she said.

'No I'm not, Holly. I stopped to ask that guy for a light. Ask him if you like,' I said.

'You were floating, James. I saw you,' she said, adamant. 'I'm going to have to report you.'

I was gobsmacked.

'What? Oh, come on, Holly. You are going to report me for trying to get a light?' I protested, grabbing hold of the bag in which I now had only a couple of magazines left unsold. 'I'm done for the day. I didn't even have my magazines out.'

'Yeah, right,' she said, in a really sarcastic tone before sliding off into the crowd.

I wasn't sure whether to take her threat seriously or not. Every outreach worker was different. Some carried through on their threats, others made them purely to make a point. I decided that she wasn't going to spoil my day and carried on enjoying the party atmosphere.

I took the Sunday off and went back to work on Monday, as normal. By then I'd forgotten completely about Holly. It was on Wednesday that the trouble began.

Arriving in Islington just before midday, I went to see Rita, the co-ordinator on Islington Green to buy new supplies of magazines.

'Sorry, James, I can't sell you any. You are on the "To Be Seen" list,' she said.

'What?!'

'Apparently someone saw you floating in the West End. You know the drill. You've got to go over to Head Office in Vauxhall.'

'Bloody Holly,' I said to myself.

It was infuriating for all sorts of reasons. First and foremost, of course, it was a complete nonsense to say I'd been floating. I'd had this problem before, mainly because so many people approached me and Bob when we were walking around London.

I knew I wasn't supposed to sell magazines when on the move. I could only do so from a fixed pitch. I'd always tried to explain this to people and, whilst some were confused and even offended, they usually moved along without giving me anything. Unfortunately, all it needed was for another *Big Issue* seller or an outreach worker to see me having any kind of exchange with a member of the public and they'd put two and two together to make five.

It was a real bore having to travel over to Vauxhall, but I knew I had to keep my pitch at Angel going. The book was just a passing phase, I knew I couldn't turn my back on what was still my bread and butter.

At *The Big Issue* office, I had to sit around for half an hour before I could see a supervisor. When I eventually got called in, this guy told me that I had been mentioned at the weekly outreach worker meeting where they discuss pitch disputes, misbehaving vendors and other issues.

'I'm afraid you are going to have to serve a one month suspension because an outreach worker saw you table-top floating,' he said.

I tried to defend myself. But it was a waste of breath. With *The Big Issue* you were guilty unless you formally appealed. I'd been through that process before, when I'd been based in Covent Garden. Again, I'd been unfairly accused of floating and it had come down to my word against theirs. My word apparently wasn't worth much and I'd lost.

I knew it was pointless appealing this time so I decided to take it on the chin and accept the suspension. I signed the relevant paperwork, handed in my tabard and ID card and headed home, upset but resigned to the fact that this was the way the cookie crumbled.

'What's that saying? No good deed goes unpunished,' I said to Bob as we sat on the tube heading back home.

I figured that, with the book still to be written, I would spend the month working on that, doing a little busking and return to Angel tube station in a month's time. If only it had been that simple.

At the end of the month, I went back to *The Big Issue* office. I wasn't certain that I'd get my tabard and ID back that day so took my guitar with me, in case I needed to carry on busking. I needn't have worried. I was told I had served my 'sentence' and

got my stuff back. I also bought a supply of magazines to take back to Angel.

'Back to business, Bob,' I said as we caught a bus
and headed back across the Thames.

Arriving back at Angel, I emerged from the
station and saw my pitch was empty. It was still
registered to me, so no one else should technically
have been there although I wouldn't have been
surprised if someone had chanced it. So I set up as
normal and got back to work.

I'd been there for about half an hour when
another vendor arrived. He was a guy I'd seen
around occasionally. He was relatively new to *The
Big Issue* and had a rather scruffy and bad-tempered
old dog.

'What are you doing? This is my pitch' he said.

'No it's not,' I said, looking bemused. 'This has
been my pitch for more than a year now.'

'It might have been your pitch a year ago, but it's
mine now. I'm registered with head office.'

'What? I really don't know what you're on about,
mate. Bob and I are part of the furniture here.
They've even written about us in the newspapers,'
I said, trying to remain reasonable.

He just shrugged his shoulders and blew out his
cheeks.

'What can I say?' he muttered. 'Go and talk to
Rita. She'll fill you in.'

'I will, mate, don't you worry about that,' I said,

marching straight across the High Street towards the co-ordinator's spot on Islington Green.

It was obvious immediately that something was wrong because Rita's face crumpled when she saw me.

'Oh, hi, James,' she said, refusing to make eye contact.

'Look. It wasn't my decision. I told him it was your pitch and that you were on a month's suspension. He stayed away for a fortnight but then he went down to Vauxhall and someone there went over my head. They told him he could have it full time. There was nothing I could do.'

I was stunned. For a moment I was lost for words.

It may sound boastful, but I had turned that pitch into a money-spinner for *The Big Issue*, and myself, obviously. Until I had arrived there, no one had wanted to work there. The conventional wisdom had always been that people were in too much of a hurry to slow down at that spot. They didn't have time to engage with a vendor. But, largely thanks to Bob, of course, I had established myself there. Even the outreach workers had said that the number of people who came to see us was amazing. As were sales of the magazine.

'I can't believe they've done this to me,' I said to Rita, scrambling to work out why this had happened. 'Is it because I've got this book deal and they assume

I don't need to sell any more?' I said. 'Because if it is they've got it all wrong. That's only a flash in the pan. I need to keep working long term.'

But Rita wasn't responding. She just kept shaking her head and saying 'I don't know' or 'I'm sorry'.

In the end I just stormed off, with Bob on my shoulders.

Looking back, I am not proud of what I did next, but I felt so cheated and badly treated that I decided to take matters into my own hands.

I headed back to the tube station and confronted the guy again.

'Look mate, here's £20 for the pitch. How's that?' I said.

He pondered it for a moment then grabbed the note, picked up his magazines and headed off with his dog in tow. I had barely been there ten minutes when he arrived back, this time with Holly in tow.

'James, this isn't your pitch any more,' she said.

'Yes, it is. I just paid the guy £20 to get it back,' I said.

'It doesn't work that way and you know it, James,' she said.

My head was spinning now. I couldn't understand why they were doing this to me. Had I behaved so badly? Was I that unpopular amongst *The Big Issue* fraternity? I must have been. They all seemed to have it in for me.

'So can I have my £20 back?' I said to the guy.

'No. I haven't earned anything yet,' he said.

I could see that he hadn't bought any magazines, so he couldn't have spent the £20. I lost it this time and started busking about twenty feet away from my usual pitch.

'James, what are you doing?' Holly said. I just ignored her and played on.

She slipped away briefly but reappeared with a police officer and another outreach worker, John, in tow.

'I'm afraid I'm going to have to ask you to move on, Sir. Otherwise I will have no option but to caution you,' the PC said.

'James you are also going to have to hand in your tabard and your ID,' Holly said. 'You are going to get another suspension for this.'

I'd only got them back a couple of hours earlier. But I handed them over.

This time I knew *The Big Issue* were going to be even harsher in their punishment, and I'd be given a six month suspension. I decided that enough was enough. I decided that I would end my association with them. I didn't feel great about it. Selling the magazine had done wonders for me. But I just felt a deep sense of injustice.

I wasn't an angel. To be honest, I don't think anyone who sells *The Big Issue* really is. We've all got our faults. We wouldn't be working on the streets if we didn't, would we? I also realised that I had probably over-reacted and lost my temper when I'd discovered my pitch had been given away. I just felt betrayed, especially because Bob and I had become unofficial ambassadors for the magazine. After we'd gone on the first Night Walk, we'd effectively been the public faces of the event and had featured in a lot of the publicity for a second one that had taken place. By this point I'd also been in the *Islington Tribune* a couple of times and the *Camden Journal*. The *Independent* had even published a piece. Each and every one of them mentioned that I was selling *The Big Issue*. It was the kind of feel-good coverage they wanted. We embodied the ethos of the charity: they had helped us to help ourselves. Or at least, so I thought.

I began to wonder whether they saw it differently. Maybe they thought I was getting too big for my boots. I actually dug out my original contract with them to see if I'd perhaps broken any rules by agreeing to write a book. But, perhaps surprisingly, there was nothing. *The Big Issue* sellers obviously didn't generally get contracts with big publishers to write their stories.

It was really confusing. I really didn't know what to think. Once again, I began to wonder whether the high profile Bob and I were winning was a double-edged sword. But I knew what I had to do.

I didn't go to Vauxhall to sign my six month

suspension. As far as I was concerned, I'd sold my last copy of the magazine. I was sick of all the politics and the back-stabbing. It was bringing out the worst in people – but more worryingly, it was bringing out the worst in me. From now on I needed to concentrate on Bob, the book and all the things that brought out the best in me.

Chapter 15

The One That Saves Me

The drama at Angel left me feeling depressed and lost for a little while. Deep down I knew I'd done the right thing, but I still had my moments when I worried that I'd made a bad move. I fretted that I'd made an enemy of *The Big Issue* and that it might come back to bite me somehow.

It took me a week or so to snap out of it. I gave myself a talking-to. I told myself that I couldn't dwell on it forever. I had to move on and, in particular, I had to focus on the positives, especially the book.

It had been delivered to the publishers who seemed pleased with it. A part of me had wondered whether they'd read it and get cold feet. My story wasn't the most romantic or glamorous of tales. The life on the streets I'd described was grim and, at times, deeply unpleasant. For a week or two after Garry and I handed in the manuscript, I half expected a phone call saying 'sorry, we've made a terrible mistake'. But that didn't happen. Instead they told me they were going to publish it in the following spring, in March.

I now had a target to aim for, but in the meantime I had to keep earning money, so I headed back to busking – and to Covent Garden.

I had mixed feelings. On the negative side, after a couple of years selling *The Big Issue*, it felt like a little bit of a backward step. Busking is, in some ways, only one rung up from begging. I thought I'd put those days behind me.

The other problem was that my voice had deteriorated. Shouting out 'Big Issue, Big Issue' hundreds and hundreds of times a day was more demanding on the larynx than singing a tuneful song every now and again. So when I picked up my guitar and started singing again I felt that I was well below par, certainly from the previous time I'd been performing. Playing the guitar for long periods took some getting used to as well. I didn't have callouses on my fingers for a start.

They were the negatives, but there were some positives too. I tried to focus on them.

Most significantly, it was a step into independence. *The Big Issue* had, without question, been a force for good in my life. Its guiding mantra had always been that it offered a helping hand rather than hand-outs. That had certainly been true in my case. It had helped me bring a little stability to my life. Without them I would probably never have been asked to write a book.

Yes, I'd found it hard to abide by the rules of an organisation. Some of it was bad luck, some of it was down to personality clashes, but some of it – I had to hold my hands up – was down to me. I wasn't very good at dealing with authority. I never had been.

So being my own person again, felt good. I felt I'd got my freedom back.

Of course, the other really positive thing was that Bob and I were better known now. Thanks to the various pieces in newspapers and on the internet, we were minor local celebrities.

From the first day busking, it was clear to me that we were now drawing bigger crowds than previously. There would be times when little semi-circles of tourists and shoppers would surround us, snapping away with their cameras and kneeling down to stroke Bob. I was shocked at how many people speaking foreign languages that I didn't even recognise would smile, point and say: 'Aaaah, Bob.'

Bob seemed to relish it. One of the most requested songs I played was 'Wonderwall' by Oasis. It was an easy song to play. I just put a capo on the second fret of my guitar and started strumming away. I'd played it a hundred times, but now, each time I played those familiar chords, the lyrics hit home much harder, in particular that line in the chorus that goes: *'Maybe you're gonna be the one that saves me'*. As I looked down at Bob, I realised it could have been written for him. There was no maybe about it. He had saved me.

Another positive about being in Covent Garden, of course, was that life was never, ever dull there. I soon remembered that the place had a rhythm and life all of its own. The busiest time of the day was the evening rush, around 7pm, when hordes of people headed home from work and an even bigger horde flooded in to visit the bars, restaurants, theatres and opera houses.

Watching the world go by from our position on Neal Street, it was never difficult to spot who was headed where. You could spot the kids who were out for a night's clubbing a mile away. They were all mini-skirts and towering heels, leather jackets and hair gel. The opera lovers were generally the best dressed, often with the men in black tie and the women in grand evening dresses with a generous helping of bling thrown in for good measure. You could hear some of them rattling down the road in the direction of the Piazza and the Royal Opera House. The area was full of characters. As we settled back into the routine, we seemed to attract more than our fair share of them once more.

One afternoon, a couple of weeks into summer, I noticed an unfamiliar face on the pavement a few yards away from us.

It wasn't uncommon for other people to set up in the area, trying to earn a few quid. I didn't have any problem with that, as long as they didn't interfere with our livelihood. The only rivals who really annoyed me were 'chuggers', the freelance charity workers who would swarm around an area from time to time, pestering people.

I wasn't being hypocritical. We all had a living to earn, and I had been a bit pushy myself when I was selling *The Big Issue*. But the chuggers took things too far and their behaviour could be so downright rude and intrusive it was bordering on harassment.

This guy was definitely not one of them, however. He was dark skinned and dressed quite smartly, in a suit. He had an odd-looking basket, which he placed on the floor. I guessed he was some kind of street entertainer, but I had no idea what to expect.

I was intrigued and sat there watching him for a few moments, hoping he might ease the boredom of another day. I wasn't disappointed. He had soon dipped into his basket and produced a yellowish snake which he then proceeded to drape around his neck. I was no expert on snakes, but I'd have described it as an albino python. It was quite thick and about three feet long. He then started playing around with it, asking for donations from passers-by.

'Look Bob, we've got a snake charmer,' I smiled as I watched the impressive-looking creature coiling its way around the guy.

Bob was weighing up the situation carefully, but it was obvious he didn't really understand what was happening. We were a good thirty feet away so he couldn't really see properly, so he settled back into his favourite position in the shade and started his afternoon snooze.

The guy had been there for about forty minutes or so when he came over to say hello. He still had the snake draped on his neck as if it was a rather large piece of jewellery.

'OK, guys, how are you today?' he said, in a strong accent that I guessed was Portuguese or possibly Brazilian.

Bob had been dozing away in the afternoon sun but perked up and took a good look at the curious visitor. I could tell his mind was hard at work, trying to work out what this creature was – and whether it was a welcome presence in his world? It didn't take him long to reach his conclusion.

As Bob tilted his head forward to take a better look, the snake decided to stick out its long, forked tongue and deliver a rather scary hiss. It was like something out of *The Jungle Book*.

Bob completely freaked. He made this really loud, yowling sound and jumped up at me imploring me to stick him on my shoulders. I was pretty sure that if I hadn't had his harness connected to me he would have bolted and run off, as he'd done once over in Angel, when an aggressive dog had lunged at him.

'Sorry, dude, didn't mean to scare your cat,' the guy said, realising what he'd done and sliding the snake off his shoulders. 'I'm going to move away from here and see how I get on further down the road.'

Bob spent the rest of the afternoon on edge. He was so paranoid about meeting another snake that he kept attacking the straps on my rucksack. He'd been sitting on this rucksack for years and had never had a problem. But suddenly anything that reminded him of the yellow python was to be treated with extreme suspicion. He kept grabbing the straps in his teeth and flicking them in the air, as if to test whether they were alive or not.

It took Bob a few days to get over the snake. He was a little nervous whenever anyone came up to us in the street or elsewhere and kept checking out their shoulders as if he was worried there was someone lurking there. It must have been confusing for him. For all these years, he'd been the only creature that rode around the streets, draped across a man's neck. I think it completely threw him to see another creature there, especially such an alien and scary-looking one.

Of course it was all part of being back in the wacky world of Covent Garden.

Not everyone on the streets was so understanding. It remained a competitive and sometimes aggressive place, full of people only looking after No 1.

Bob and I were happily whiling away an afternoon on Neal Street when a young guy pitched up with an amplifier and a microphone. He was dressed in skater boy clothes and was wearing a baseball cap and Nike trainers. I spotted him setting up and waited for an instrument to appear, but there wasn't one. All he had was a microphone.

I ignored him and got back to playing my own music.

I wasn't able to shut him out of my mind for long though. Within minutes I heard an ear-splitting, repetitive noise booming out. The young guy was strutting around with his mic against his lips, 'beat boxing'. I'm a fan of most forms of music but this really wasn't my cup of tea. As far as I was concerned it wasn't remotely musical, it was just noise.

Bob shared my opinion, it was obvious. Maybe because he'd spent so long listening to me play acoustic guitar, he seemed to like that kind of music. He had also got used to slightly heavier rock. He made his opinion of this 'music' plain immediately. I looked down at him and saw him casting his eyes down the street with what I can only describe as complete disdain spread across his face.

There were times when I was led by Bob and this was one of them.

He stood up, tilted his head at me and let me know in no uncertain terms that we should move. I gathered my stuff and moved about 70 yards down the street where I began playing again. I could still hear the din from the young kid down the street, but at least I could hear myself think.

It was a false dawn.

The noise this kid was making was so loud that others must have complained because within half an hour or so a police van arrived. I watched from a distance as a couple of officers got out and approached him. I saw the boy waving his arms around in protest, but it didn't get him anywhere. A couple of minutes after the police's arrival I saw him disconnect his mike and start to pack up.

You could almost hear the sighs of relief that

must have been breathed in the offices, cafés and restaurants.

'Thank goodness that's over, eh Bob?' I said.

My joy was short-lived. The police officers saw Bob and me sitting on the pavement and came over to talk to us.

'You're not licensed to play here, mate,' one of them said.

I could have argued the toss and said we had a right to be there, which we kind of did. But I decided not to push it. Easing myself back into life in Covent Garden was difficult enough without aggravating the police. Choose your battles, James, I told myself, rather wisely, as it turned out.

It was just after midday on Neal Street and the crowds of tourists and shoppers were beginning to thicken. Bob and I had come out a little earlier today, partly because it was the first decent weather in a week but partly because we needed to get away by late afternoon so that I could get back home for a doctor's appointment.

I had developed a really bad chest problem and I'd had a week or so of sleepless nights coughing and wheezing. I had to get something done about it. I was getting really strung out by the lack of sleep.

I'd barely got myself set up and started playing when I saw a lady in a ribbed blue jumper and trousers walking purposefully towards me. I could tell she was not a tourist. As she drew close, I saw that her jumper had epaulettes and badges and had a familiar logo on it. She was from the RSPCA.

In ordinary circumstances, I was a big fan and supporter of the RSPCA. They do a great job in preventing animal cruelty and promoting animal welfare in general and had been a huge help to me in the past. When I'd first found Bob injured in the hallway of my block of flats I'd taken him to a nearby drop-in clinic. As well as giving me a prescription for the medicine Bob would need to heal his wounds, the vet there had passed on lots of sound and sensible advice on how to treat and care for him.

That now seemed like a very distant memory. Today, I got the distinct impression that their presence wasn't going to be good news.

'Hello, James, how are you today?' the lady said, producing a card with her ID on it. It showed that she was an Inspector.

I was a bit thrown by the fact that she knew my name.

'Fine, thanks. What's the problem?'

'I've been asked to come and see you because I'm afraid we have had complaints that you are mistreating your cat, Bob isn't it?' she said.

'What?! Mistreating him? How?'

I was horrified. My head was spinning. Who had complained? And what had they said I was doing to Bob? I felt physically sick for a moment, but knew I had to keep my wits about me in case this got serious.

'I'm sure they are unfounded allegations. I was actually watching you for a little while before I came over and I can see that you treat Bob well,' she said, giving him a little tickle under the chin. 'But I do need to have a chat with you and then examine him to make sure there's nothing wrong if that's OK.'

'Be my guest,' I said, knowing that I didn't really have a choice.

She dropped her rucksack to the floor, got out a notebook and a couple of instruments and kneeled down to start examining Bob.

He didn't always take kindly to people poking and prodding him. He had reacted to a couple of vets over the years and had snarled and scratched at one nurse who had handled him a bit roughly once. So I was a bit concerned about how he'd react to this latest stranger, especially if he picked up on my nervousness. That was all I needed, I thought to myself.

It wasn't the first time people had accused me of mistreating him, of course. I'd heard all sorts of accusations levelled against me. The complaints generally fell into three categories. The first was that I was exploiting and 'using' him for my own benefit. My answer to that argument was always the same. As someone once said, a cat will be your friend, but it will never be your slave. A cat is never, ever going to do something it doesn't want to do. And it is never going to be with someone it doesn't want to be with, no matter what that person does to it. Bob was a very strong character, with a free will of his own. He wouldn't have hung around if he didn't trust and like me. And it was his choice whether he wanted to come out with me each day.

There were still days when he didn't fancy taking to the streets. They were rare, to be honest. He genuinely enjoyed being out and about, meeting people and being fussed over. But when he hid away or refused to follow me out the door I always respected his decision. There would always be those who wouldn't believe that, of course, but it was the truth.

The second common accusation was that I was mistreating him by having him on a lead. If I'd had a pound for every time I'd heard someone say 'oh, you shouldn't have him on a leash, he's a cat not a dog' I'd have been a very rich man. I'd explained the reasoning so many times I was bored at hearing myself say the words. On both occasions he'd run off, at Piccadilly Circus and in Islington, he'd been really relieved and clingy when I'd found him. I'd sworn never to let it happen again. But, again, I could keep saying it until I was blue in the face as far as some people were concerned. For them it was an open and shut case: I was some kind of animal abusing monster.

The third, and most upsetting allegation that had been made against me was that I was drugging Bob. I'd only heard that a couple of times, thankfully. But it cut me to the quick both times. Given what I'd been through in the past ten years and the battle I'd fought to kick my heroin habit, I found that the most hurtful insult of all. I found it really, really offensive.

As I watched the Inspector checking Bob I felt pretty certain that someone had raised one, two or even all three of these issues with the RSPCA. But I knew she wasn't going to tell me, not until she'd completed her examination and written some kind of report, at least.

She took out a microchip reading device to check that he was micro-chipped, which he was, of course. The device showed up my name and address as Bob's legal owner.

'That's a good start,' she smiled. 'You'd be surprised how many cat owners don't chip their pets, even these days.'

She then checked his fur for fleas, took a look at his teeth and checked his breath, I assumed to see if there was anything wrong with his liver or maybe his kidneys. She also checked his eyes to see if they were cloudy. That made me wonder whether someone had tried to accuse me of drugging him. It made my blood boil to think someone would say that to the RSPCA.

I didn't bother busking while all this was going on. Instead I reassured the small scrum of people who had stopped that everything was OK. I just hoped it was.

As I paced around I tried to put all those thoughts to the back of my head. I had to be positive, I told myself. I hadn't done anything wrong.

After a few minutes she'd finished the inspection and started asking me questions.

'Any health problems that you are aware of, James?' she asked me, her pen poised over her notebook.

'No,' I said. I made sure to tell her that I regularly took him to the weekly drop-in Blue Cross clinic in Islington. They had always praised me for the way I looked after him and always gave him a clean bill of health. 'They've not spotted anything so I think he's pretty healthy,' I told her.

'That's good to know, James,' she said. 'So tell me, how did you two get together in the first place?'

I told her the story and she nodded and smiled throughout.

'Sounds like you two were meant to be together,' she laughed.

She seemed pretty happy with everything, in fact she looked up and gave me a smile.

'He's a fine fellow, isn't he? Don't suppose you have a phone number that I can reach you on,' she asked.

My battered old Nokia was still working – just – so I gave her the number.

'OK, well I'm happy for now but I may need to follow up with another visit. Are you here every day?'

'Yeah, pretty much most days at the moment,' I said, already feeling uneasy.

'OK, I will give you a call or drop in to see you soon.'

She then gave Bob a final ruffle and headed off into the crowds.

On the one hand I was pleased that she had left without any major drama. All sorts of scenarios had been going through my head. What if she'd found something that I didn't know about, health wise? What if she'd said she needed to take him away? That was the worst conceivable outcome as far as I was concerned. I would have been sick with worry.

But my relief was tempered by other worries.

I knew the RSPCA had significant powers when it came to pet owners, from being able to confiscate a pet, to starting legal proceedings against anyone deemed to be guilty of abusing an animal. Why was she doing a follow-up visit? What was she going to tell her superiors? What sort of report was she going to write? What if I was prosecuted and, heaven forbid, Bob was taken away from me? I couldn't help all these things going through my head, however little control I had over the situation.

I gave myself a good talking to. I was being paranoid again. That wasn't going to happen. There was no reason for it. I had to put those thoughts to one side.

As I headed home that evening, however, I still had a knot of anxiety in my stomach. I had an awful feeling that this was going to hang over me for a while.

It was about a week later when the RSPCA inspector appeared again. She was a lot friendlier and more relaxed this time. Bob responded well to her as well as she once more knelt down to check him out.

I felt a bit more confident this time so engaged her in conversation.

Again, she made some notes and asked me a couple of questions about what we'd been up to that week and what we had planned in the coming days.

She sat and watched us interacting together and with the passers-by. RSPCA inspectors are obviously trained to read animal behaviours and she could see that he was perfectly content to be there and to be doing his little stunts for his audience.

She then headed off again and said she'd be in touch very soon. As she left, she gave Bob another friendly stroke, shook my hand and smiled.

I carried on for an hour or so, but my heart wasn't in it. I was about to pack up when I saw a familiar face striding over. It was the housing manager of one of the blocks of flats on Neal Street. We'd clashed before, over my busking, which she objected to for some reason. She had a face like thunder. She had obviously been watching from a window and had seen the RSPCA officer shaking my hand and walking off.

'People are trying to sleep upstairs,' she said.

'It's two o'clock in the afternoon,' I said, genuinely baffled.

'Never mind that,' she said as if I was some three-year-old child. 'You shouldn't be busking here. Can't you read the sign?', she said, pointing at a plaque across the road on the side of the building where she worked.

'But I'm not busking there, I'm busking on the other side of the road,' I said. 'And I am entitled to do that if I want. The outreach workers and even the Police have told me as much.'

Again, she wasn't interested in having a debate about it. She just wanted to rant and rave at me.

'I've had enough of you and that bloody cat, I'm going to call the police and have you removed,' she said, marching off. She seemed even angrier than when she'd arrived.

Her argument was actually ridiculous. How on earth could I disturb people from their sleep in the middle of the afternoon? I didn't have an amplifier, so it wasn't as if I was blasting out a huge amount of sound. And besides, this was a busy street with a lot of traffic passing through at all hours of the day and night. If anything was going to wake up her residents, it was the constant din of delivery vans and lorries and police sirens. It was crazy.

Despite all this, however, I knew that she did have the law on her side to an extent. There were restrictions on busking in the area and I had to be very careful. So I kept an eagle eye out for the police for the rest of the afternoon.

Sure enough, about half an hour after I'd had the confrontation with the lady, I saw a Police van drawing into the street a hundred yards or so away from our pitch.

'Don't like the look of that, Bob,' I said, unstrapping my guitar and packing up.

By the time two policemen had walked over, I was ready to leave.

'You have to move on,' they said.

'Yes, I know. I'm off,' I said.

The incident had really riled me. I became

convinced that this lady was the one who had reported me to the RSPCA. Now that tactic seemed to have failed, she had changed tack. She would go to any lengths to drive us away, it seemed.

Back at the flat that evening, the RSPCA inspector rang me on my mobile and said that I had absolutely nothing to worry about.

'He's a special creature, and you're doing a grand job,' the lady said. 'My advice to you is to ignore those who tell you any different.' It was the wisest advice I'd had for a long time. And, unusually for me, I took it.

Chapter 16

Doctor Bob

I was finding it harder and harder to haul myself out of bed in the morning. For the past few weeks I'd actually grown to dread the sight of the late winter sun, leaking light through my bedroom window.

It wasn't that I didn't want to get up. I wasn't sleeping well and was usually awake by first light in any case. My reasons for wanting to hide, motionless under the duvet, were very different. I knew that the moment I got up, I would just start coughing again.

I'd suffered from chest problems for some time, but recently they had begun to get really bad. I reasoned it was because I was always on the streets, working outside. But now, no sooner had I got up in the morning, than my lungs and chest were filling up with phlegm and I was coughing really violently almost constantly. At times it was so bad that I was doubling up in pain and I would begin retching and vomiting. It really wasn't pleasant for me – or anyone else, to be honest. The sounds I was making were pretty horrendous. I was embarrassed to be in public places.

I was getting really worried about it. I'd been smoking since I was a 13-year-old back in Australia and had inhaled a lot more than just plain cigarettes over the years. Also, an ex-girlfriend from way back had died of tuberculosis after smoking a lot of drugs a few years earlier. The memory of her coughing uncontrollably in her final months had remained with me. I'd heard somewhere that TB was actually contagious. Had I contracted it from her? Were my lungs collapsing? Try as I might, I couldn't stop all sorts of crazy thoughts whizzing around in my head.

I had tried to get rid of the coughing by dosing myself with cheap medicines from the supermarket. But it had gotten me nowhere. I'd seen a doctor, but at that stage it could easily have been a seasonal cold and he'd fobbed me off with a suggestion that I should take a few paracetamol, rest and cut down on smoking. That hadn't achieved much at all.

Bob had again sensed I was unwell and started paying me attention. He would wrap himself around me as if taking some kind of measurements. I'd learned the lessons of the past and didn't dismiss him this time.

'Here comes Doctor Bob,' I joked one day.

There was no question in my mind that he was performing some kind of diagnosis. When I was lying on the sofa or on the bed, he would often spread himself out on my chest, purring gently.

I'd read about cats having the power to heal bones with their purring. Apparently there's something about the frequency at which they vibrate that somehow strengthens bones. I wondered whether he was trying to somehow heal my chest. More worryingly, I wondered whether he knew something I didn't?

In a way, that was the scariest thing of all. I knew how intuitive cats are when it comes to sniffing out illness in humans. There's evidence that they can predict epileptic fits, seizures and other illnesses. One cat I read about, from Yorkshire, would give its male owner 'strange looks' before he was about to have a fit. Famously, there was a cat called Oscar who lived in an old people's home in America and would come and sit with residents who were in their final hours. No one was quite sure whether he was picking up on something visual or whether he was able to tune into the smells produced by the bio-chemical changes in a person's body when they die. What was in no doubt, however, was the fact that Oscar's ability to anticipate people's passing was uncanny, so much so that people dreaded seeing him sidling up to them. It was as if the cat was some kind of Angel of Death. I did hope Bob wasn't the same.

After a while I made another appointment, this time with a young doctor that a friend had recommended as being very good. He certainly seemed a little more sympathetic. I told him about the coughing and the vomiting.

'I'd better take a listen to your lungs,' he said. After checking me out with a stethoscope he made me do a peak-flow check, testing the strength of my breathing and chest. I'd had childhood asthma so I knew my chest wasn't the strongest.

He didn't say too much. He just sat there making notes, rather too many of them for my liking.

'OK, Mr Bowen, I'd like you to have a chest X-ray,' he said, eventually.

'Oh, OK,' I said, worried already.

He then printed out a form which he handed to me.

'Take this along to Homerton Hospital and they'll know what to do,' he said.

I knew he was being careful in his language. But there was something about his face that spooked me a little. I didn't like it.

I took the form home and stuck it on the

sideboard in the front room. I then quietly forgot about it. A small part of me couldn't face the hassle. It wasn't that long ago that I'd been hospitalised with DVT. What if I had to be admitted again? What if it was something even worse? I really didn't like hospitals.

On top of this, I'd been to Homerton Hospital before and I knew it was a nightmare. I pictured in my mind one of those long days waiting in a queue and just getting frustrated. I told myself that I couldn't afford to waste a day there not earning money.

Of course, these were all rather limp excuses. The truth was that I was terrified of what an X-ray might find. It was pure, ostrich-like stubbornness. I assumed that if I stuck my head in the sand and forgot all about it, the coughing and vomiting and all the other unpleasantness would simply go away. Of course it didn't. It only got worse.

I reached breaking point one day when I visited the publishers. I had, at last, begun to believe that the book was finally happening. They'd mocked up a cover, with Bob sitting Zen-like on my rucksack. On the back was a picture of me, while inside was a brief note on 'the author'. I still had to pinch myself to believe it was happening. Unfortunately, I'd had a coughing fit in the middle of the meeting. I'd began retching and could feel like I was ready to throw up. So I'd made an excuse about needing the toilet and dashed off there. I'm sure they had their suspicions that I was up to no good and I wouldn't have blamed them if they did. I was a recovering drug addict, after all.

I knew it must have looked pretty bad, and that I couldn't repeat it in March. The publication of the book was looming into view and I'd been told that I might be doing a few media interviews, even an appearance on television. There was also talk of book signings where I'd meet members of the public. It all seemed pretty far-fetched, but to be on the safe side I decided I had to get to the bottom of this and go for the X-ray.

By now I'd lost the form, so I went back to the surgery to see the same doctor.

'You don't seem to have had your X-ray,' he said, scrolling through the records on his computer.

'No, erm, I didn't go. I haven't had time. I'd lose a day if I went there,' I said, slightly embarrassed. 'I've been writing a book.'

'OK,' he said, looking at me disbelievingly then tapping away and then printing out another form.

'This is for an emergency appointment. It's a walk-in service. You won't have to hang around for long.'

'OK,' I said, a little reluctantly.

I knew that, this time, I couldn't really duck out of it.

I went along to Homerton and was led into a

large room by a couple of nurses, one of whom asked me to take off my shirt and stand in a contraption. She then proceeded to place a big metal plate on my chest before retiring behind a screen.

Again, it could have been paranoia on my part but I was disconcerted by the fact that she wrote a lot of notes afterwards.

'How did it look?' I asked her, fishing for a clue.

'Fine, but we will send a full report to your doctor. Should be there in a few days.'

I took some solace from her reassurance, but was still a bundle of nerves for the next 72 hours.

I went along to see the doctor with a real sense of foreboding.

I have a tendency to think the worst so I was braced to hear something terrible. I was slightly taken aback when the doctor looked at the notes attached to his copy of the X-ray images and said: 'Your lungs are completely clear, Mr Bowen.'

'Really?' I said.

'Yes. There's not a single black spot, which is frankly remarkable given that you tell me you've been smoking since you were 13.'

'In fact,' he continued, 'I would go so far as to say that you seem to have super healthy lungs,' he added.

'So why am I coughing my guts up all the time?' I asked, confused.

'I suspect you've got an infection of some kind.

Nothing has shown up in the tests we've done. But I think your lungs are simply trying to expel all the rubbish that they are accumulating there. So let's try and treat the infection,' he said, prescribing me some heavy duty antibiotics.

'That's it? Antibiotics,' I said, relieved but slightly shocked to discover it was that simple.

'Well, let's see if they work,' he said. 'If not we will have to explore things a bit more.'

I was sceptical. It couldn't be that simple, I told myself. But it was. Within days my chest was feeling much better and the coughing was easing off.

My agent, Mary, had been worried about my health. She'd been anxious that the publicity and the signings that would soon be coming up might be too much for me. She had my best interests at heart, I knew that.

'You seem a lot better,' she told me when we met for a chat about the publication of the book which was now just weeks away.

But it was when I got another opinion that I really knew I was in the clear.

I was lying on the bed reading a comic book. Out of nowhere, Bob appeared and jumped up. He slid up to me in the same way he had done over the previous few weeks, placing himself on my chest and purring quietly away. After a moment or two, he put his ear to my chest, doing his feline stethoscope act. He lay there for a moment, listening intently. And then, as quickly as he'd arrived, he'd gone. He just picked himself up and hopped off the bed in the direction of his favourite radiator. I couldn't help smiling.

'Thanks, Doctor Bob,' I said.

Chapter 17

Basic Instincts

They say that March comes in like a lion and goes out like a lamb. The month had barely begun but the weather was already living up to its reputation. There were days when the wind blowing down the alleyways of Soho and the West End made such a raw, rasping noise it could almost have been a lion's roar. Some days I struggled to feel the tips of my fingers as I played my guitar. Fortunately, Bob was a little better insulated than me.

Even now with spring around the corner, he was still sporting his rather luxurious winter coat. His midriff was also still carrying some of the extra weight he'd put on over Christmas. The cold hardly seemed to bother him at all.

Bob and I missed Angel, but if I was honest, we were enjoying life more in Covent Garden.

We'd become a double act and seemed somehow more at home amongst the jugglers and fire-eaters, human statues and other street performers that roamed the Piazza and surrounding streets. It was a competitive place, of course, so, as we settled back into daily life in central London, we polished up our act.

Sometimes I would play my guitar while sitting cross-legged on the pavement with him. He'd always loved that and would drape himself across the body of my guitar, just like he'd done during our early days together, years earlier. We shook hands and he'd stand on his hind legs to collect treats. We also had a new party piece.

It had been born back at the flat one day while he had been playing with Belle. As usual, he was tossing his shabby old scraggedy mouse around. Belle wanted to take it off him so that she could give it a decent wash.

'God knows what germs it's collecting, Bob,' I heard her telling him. 'It needs a good scrubbing.'

He was reluctant to surrender his precious play-thing. He always was. So she offered him a treat. Choosing between the two was a real dilemma and he dithered for a second before going for the treat. He released the mouse from his jaws long enough to receive the little snack – and for Belle to whisk the toy from under his nose.

'Well done, Bob,' she said afterwards.

'Give me five,' she said, putting her hand in the air like an American footballer or basketball player, inviting his team-mates to celebrate a score.

I was sitting there and saw him raise his paw to give her an acknowledegment. 'That was cool,' I laughed. 'Bet you can't get him to do it again.'

'Bet I can,' Belle said, before proceeding to do exactly that.

Since then he'd come to associate it with receiving a treat. On Neal Street it had pulled in all sorts of admirers, including some rather famous ones.

It was around 4pm on a Saturday afternoon and a couple of little girls had stopped to admire Bob. They were about nine or ten years old and were accompanied by a small group of adults, including a couple of big, burly bouncer-like guys in dark glasses. To judge by the way they were anxiously surveying the scene while the girls stroked Bob they must have been security minders.

'Daddy, look at this,' one of the girls said excitedly.

'Oh yeah. That's a cool cat,' a voice said.

I froze to the spot. I recognised the voice immediately.

'It can't be,' I said. But it was.

I turned round and standing behind me was the unmistakeable figure of Sir Paul McCartney.

I wouldn't have expected one of the greatest figures in popular music of all time to engage with a lowly street performer. He was, after all, in a slightly different league to me when it came to knocking out a tune. But he seemed charming.

I had my early edition of the book alongside me on the floor and saw it catch his eye. I also had a wad of flyers advertising the first book signing the publishers had organised. It was now just three days away.

The event was going to mark the beginning – and probably the end – of my career as a published author. I was feeling apprehensive about it already and had been frantically handing the flyers out to anyone who showed an interest, in the hope that I'd at least avoid the embarrassment of sitting in an empty bookshop the following week. I felt sure if I fished around in the bins of Covent Garden I'd find most of them there.

Inside my head a little voice was saying *oh, go on, give him one.*

'Erm, I've written a book about me and Bob,' motioning to my ginger companion sitting at my feet. 'I'm having a signing next week if you want to come along,' I said, handing him the flyer.

To my amazement he took it.

'I'll take a look,' he said.

By now a sizable crowd had begun to form around us and his minders were getting a bit twitchy. People were flashing away with their cameras. For once it wasn't Bob they were snapping.

'We'd better move along kids,' the lady with him said. By now I'd worked out who she was. It was Sir Paul's new wife, Nancy Shevell, who he'd married the previous autumn. She seemed really cool.

'Take care man and keep it going,' Sir Paul said as he hooked his arm into hers and rushed off with his entourage.

I was slightly dizzy afterwards. Starstruck I suppose would have been a more accurate description. I stayed in Neal Street for another hour or so but headed home on Cloud Nine.

There wasn't a snowball's chance in hell of Sir Paul McCartney coming along to the signing. Why would he come? No one else was going to show up, I said to myself. All that really didn't matter now. If it achieved nothing else and sold only five copies, the book had already allowed me to achieve the impossible. I'd chatted to a member of The Beatles.

Bob attracted so much attention these days that small crowds would often gather around us. Late on the afternoon of the Monday after I'd met the McCartneys, a dozen or so Spanish-speaking students were clustered on the pavement, each of them snapping away with their cameras and phones. It was always great to meet people, it was part of the attraction of what I did. But it could be distracting and, given the nature of street life, getting distracted was never a great idea.

As the crowd broke up and headed off in the direction of Covent Garden, I sat down on the pavement to give Bob a couple of treats. With the light already beginning to fade, the chill was really setting in again. Tomorrow was the day of the book signing in Islington. I wanted to get a reasonably early night, although I knew I wouldn't sleep much. I also didn't want to keep Bob out for much longer. As I stroked him, I noticed immediately that his body language was very defensive. His back was arched and his body was stiff. He wasn't much interested in the food either which was always a sign something was wrong. Instead, his eyes were fixed on something in the near distance. Something – or someone – was clearly bothering him.

I looked across the street and saw a rough-looking character who was sitting, staring at us.

Living your life on the streets, you develop an instant radar when it comes to people. I could spot a bad apple instantly. This guy looked rotten to the core. He was a little bit older than me, in his late thirties probably. He was wearing battered jeans and had a denim jacket. He was sitting on the pavement, legs crossed, rolling up a cigarette and sipping on a can of cheap lager. It was obvious what he was looking at – and what his intentions were. He was working out how to relieve me of my money.

In the space of the last few minutes, most of the Spanish students and several others had dropped coins into my guitar case. One rather cool-looking black guy had given me £5. We'd probably collected £20 in the space of half an hour. I knew better than to leave too much money on display to the world and had scooped up most of it, slipping it in my rucksack. He'd obviously registered this.

I wasn't going to confront him, however. As long as he kept his distance, there was no need. I'd been in his shoes myself. I knew how desperate people could get. I sensed he was trouble, but unless he proved that I was going to give him the benefit of the doubt. Let him cast the first stone and all that, I said to myself.

Just to make sure, however, I looked across at him and nodded, as if to say: 'I've spotted you, and I know what you're thinking. So just forget about it.'

Street people speak the same language. We can convey a hundred words with a simple look or expression, so he understood me immediately. He just growled, got himself up and slinked off. He knew he'd been rumbled and didn't like it. He was soon heading off in the direction of Shaftesbury Avenue, probably to prey on someone else.

The instant the guy disappeared around the corner, Bob's body language lightened and he had a renewed interest in the snacks.

'Don't worry, mate,' I said, slipping a little biscuit into his mouth. 'He's gone on his way. We won't see him again.'

The street was particularly busy that day and we'd soon collected more than enough to get Bob and me a few days' worth of shopping in our local shop. When I started packing up, Bob didn't need a second invitation to jump up on to my shoulders. It was getting colder by the minute.

I knew he'd need to do his business before we got the bus home, so we headed for his regular spot outside the posh office block on Endell Street.

To get to this spot we had to walk down one of the narrower and less well lit streets in the area. As we did so, the world suddenly turned quiet. London could be like that at times. One minute it was full to bursting, the next it was deserted. It was part of the city's many contradictions.

I was halfway down the street when I felt Bob moving on my shoulder. At first I thought he was simply dying to go to the toilet.

'Hold on for another second, mate,' I said. 'We're almost there.'

But I soon realised he was repositioning himself and, unusually for him, had turned himself to look backwards rather than forwards.

'What's wrong, Bob?' I said, turning around.

I looked down the street. There was a guy locking up his coffee shop for the evening and that was about it. I thought nothing more of it. The coast seemed clear enough to me.

Bob didn't seem quite so convinced. Something was definitely bothering him.

I'd barely taken a dozen steps when all of a sudden he made the loudest noise I'd ever heard him make. It was like a primal scream, a piercing *wheeeeeow* followed by a really loud hissed *hsssssssss*. At the same time I felt a tug on my rucksack and then an almighty scream, this time from a human.

I swung round to see the bloke who had been staring at us earlier on Neal Street. He was bent over double and was holding his hand. I could see the back of it and saw that there were huge scratches. Blood was gushing from his wounds.

It was obvious what had happened. He had made a lunge for my rucksack. Bob must have dropped himself over my back and lashed out with his claws. He'd dug them deep into this guy's hands, ripping into the skin. He was still in fighting mood too.

Bob was standing on my shoulder, snarling and hissing.

But the guy wasn't finished. He lunged at me with his fists but I managed to dodge him. It was hard to do much with Bob balanced on my shoulder, but I landed a well-directed kick to the guy's leg. I was wearing my really heavy Dr. Martens boots so it had the desired effect and he dropped to his knees for a second.

He was soon back on his feet, though. For a moment we just stood there shouting at each other.

'F***ing cat, look what it's done to my f***ing hand,' he said, waving his bleeding arm at me in the gloom.

'Serves you right, you were going to mug me,' I said.

'I'll f***ing kill it if I see it again,' he said pointing at Bob. There was another brief standoff while the guy looked around the street. He found a small piece of wood which he waved at me a couple of times. Bob was screeching and hissing at him more animatedly than ever. The guy took one step towards us with the piece of wood then thought better of it and just tossed it to one side. After letting fly with another stream of expletives, he turned on his heels and stumbled off into the gloom, still holding his hand.

On the bus back home, Bob sat on my lap. He was purring steadily and had tucked his head under my arm, as he often did when he – or I – felt vulnerable. I guessed we were both feeling that way after our encounter, but I couldn't be sure, of course.

That was the joy and frustration of having a cat. 'Cats are mysterious kind of folk – there is more passing in their minds than we are aware of,' Sir Walter Scott wrote. Bob was more mysterious than most. In many ways, that was part of his magic, what made him such an extraordinary companion. We had been through so much together, yet he still had the ability to startle and surprise me. He'd done it again this evening.

We'd had our fair share of confrontations over the years, but we'd never been attacked like this. And I'd never seen him react and defend me in that way either. I'd not been switched on to the threat this guy posed at all, but Bob had.

How had he sensed the guy was not to be trusted from the minute he set eyes on him? I could read the signs from a human perspective, but how did he know that? And how had he detected his presence when we were walking away from Neal Street? I'd seen no sign of him anywhere. Had Bob caught a glimpse of him hiding in an alleyway? Had he smelled him?

I didn't know. I just had to accept that Bob possessed abilities and instincts that were beyond my understanding – and would probably always remain that way.

That was the frustrating part. He was exhilarating company at times, but he was also an enigma. I would never truly know what went on in his feline brain. Yes, we were best friends. We had an almost telepathic bond. Instinctively, we knew what each other were thinking at times. But that understanding didn't extend to being able to share our deepest thoughts. We couldn't really tell each other what we felt. As silly as it sounded, I often felt sad about that. And I did so now.

Holding him close to me as the bus lurched its way through the London traffic, I had an almost overwhelming urge to know what emotions he'd gone through back there in the side street. Had he been scared? Or had he just fallen back on his basic instincts? Had he just sensed the need to defend himself – and me – and acted? Had he just dealt with it in the moment? And did that mean that he'd already forgotten about it? Or was he thinking the same kind of thoughts as me? I am fed up with this life. *I am sick of having to look over my shoulder all the time. I want to live in a safer, gentler, happier world.*

I suspected I knew the answer. Of course he'd rather not be fighting off scumbags on the streets. Of course, he'd rather be sitting somewhere warm rather than freezing on a pavement. What creature wouldn't?

As my mind ticked over, I dipped into my pocket

and pulled out a scrunched up flyer. It was one of the last that I had. I'd given the rest away. It had a photo of me with Bob on my shoulders and read:

**Come and meet
James Bowen and Bob the cat
James and Bob will be signing copies of
their new book
A STREET CAT NAMED BOB
at Waterstones, Islington Green, London
on Tuesday 13th March 2012 at 6pm**

Bob looked at it and tilted his head ever-so-slightly. It was, again, as if he recognised the image of the pair of us.

I stared at the scrap of paper for what must have been a couple of minutes, lost in my thoughts.

I'd been wrestling with the same old questions for so long now. Truth be told, I was thoroughly sick of them. But tonight had brought them to the fore again. How many more times would I have to put myself and Bob in the firing line? Would I ever break this cycle and get us off the streets?

I flattened the flyer out neatly and folded it away in my pocket.

'I hope this is the answer, Bob,' I said. 'I really do.'

Chapter 18
Waiting for Bob

It was barely 9am but my stomach was already churning away like a cement mixer.

I'd made some toast but couldn't touch it for fear of being physically sick. If I felt like this now, I asked myself, how on earth was I going to feel in nine hours' time?

The publishers had organised the signing, thinking it would be a good opportunity to generate some London publicity, and maybe attract a few people to buy a copy or two at the same time. As well as handing out flyers down in Covent Garden I had even detoured via Angel a couple of times. We still had a few friends there, thankfully.

Waterstones in Islington had been the obvious venue. The store was part of my story in more ways than one. Not only had the staff there helped us when we'd had nowhere to go a year or so earlier, they even featured in one of the more dramatic scenes in the book. One weekday evening, I'd run in the front door, desperate and panic-stricken, when Bob had run off after being scared by an aggressive dog at Angel tube station.

In the days running up to the event I'd started giving interviews to more newspapers but also to radio and television. To help me get used to this, I'd been sent to a specialist media trainer in central London. It was a bit intimidating. I had to sit in a sound-proofed room having myself recorded and then analysed by an expert. But he had been gentle with me and had taught me a few tricks of the trade. During one of the first recordings, for instance, I'd made the classic mistake of fiddling with a pen while talking. When it was played back to me all I could hear was the sound of me tapping the pen against the desk like some manic rock drummer. It was incredibly distracting and annoying.

The trainer prepared me for the sort of questions I could expect. He predicted, quite rightly, that most people would want to know how I'd ended up on the streets, how Bob had helped changed my life and what the future held for us both. He also prepared me to answer questions about whether I was clean of drugs, which I was happy to do. I felt I had nothing to hide.

The pieces the newspapers and bloggers had been writing were almost universally nice. A writer from the *London Evening Standard* had said some lovely things about Bob, writing that he 'has entranced London like no feline since the days of Dick Whittington'. But he also upset me a little by writing about the holes in my jeans and my 'blackened teeth and nails'. He also described me as having the 'pleading manner of someone who is used to being ignored'. I'd been warned to expect that kind of thing; it went with the territory and the bottom line was that I knew I was 'damaged goods' as that same writer called me. It wasn't pleasant though.

The signing had been scheduled two days ahead of the official publication date, March 15th, which also happened to be my 33rd birthday.

I hoped that wasn't going to put a hex on everything. Birthdays hadn't exactly been a cause for celebration in my life, certainly not since my teens.

I had spent my 13th birthday in a children's ward at the Princess Margaret Children's Hospital in Western Australia. It had been a miserable time in my young life and had only accelerated my downward spiral. Not long afterwards I'd started sniffing glue and experimenting with marijuana. It was the start of my long descent into drug addiction.

Fast forward ten years, to my 23rd birthday, and

I'd been on the streets of London. I might have spent it in a hostel, but I could just as easily have been sleeping rough in an alleyway around Charing Cross. At that point my life was at rock bottom and I had absolutely no recollection of it. The days, weeks, months and years had all blended into each other. The chances are that, if I had been aware it was my birthday, I'd have spent the day trying to beg, borrow or – most likely – steal the money I needed to treat myself to an extra wrap of heroin. I'd probably taken the same reckless gamble I'd taken a hundred times before and risked overdosing by taking an 'extra hit'. I could easily have ended up like that guy I'd seen on the landing of my flats.

Ten years further down the road, my life had finally taken a positive turn. That period now seemed like another life and another world. When I looked back I found it hard to believe that I'd lived through that period. But, for good or bad, it would always be a part of me. It was certainly a part of the book. I'd decided not to sugar-coat my story. It was virtually all there, warts and all, which was another one of the reasons I felt so racked with nerves.

In the hours before the signing, I was due to be filmed by a photographer and cameraman from the Reuters international news agency. He wanted to take a series of photos of Bob and I going about our normal, day-to-day life, travelling around on the tube then busking on Neal Street. I was quite glad of the distraction. By the time I'd finished with the photographer, it was early evening.

A damp chill was beginning to descend when we got back to Islington and made the familiar walk from Angel tube station. There was no sign of the guy who had 'acquired' my pitch outside the tube station. A flower seller told me that the guy and his dog had been causing all sorts of trouble and had already been stripped of the pitch by the co-ordinators. There was now no one from *The Big Issue* selling magazines outside Angel.

'What a waste,' I said. 'I'd built that pitch up into a nice earner for someone.' But that wasn't my concern any more. I had other things to worry about.

Bob and I walked through Islington Memorial Park towards Waterstones. We were early so I let Bob do his business and sat on the bench to enjoy a quiet cigarette. Part of me felt like a condemned man, enjoying a final, fleeting moment of pleasure before going to face the firing squad. But another part of me felt a sense of anticipation. I felt like I was on the verge of a fresh start in my life; that, for want of a better phrase, a new chapter in my life was beginning.

I felt queasier than ever. I had so many conflicting thoughts fighting for space in my head. What if no one turned up? What if loads of people turned up and thought the book was rubbish? How would Bob react if there was a crowd? How would people react to me? I wasn't a typical author. I wasn't a polished public personality. I was a guy who was still operating on the fringes of society. Or at least, that's how it felt. I knew people would love Bob, but I was terrified that they'd hate me.

I drew on the last remnant of my cigarette, making it last for as long as possible. The nerves had solidified inside me to such an extent that I felt like someone had punched me really hard in the stomach.

Luckily Bob was being extra cool for both of us. He spent a couple of minutes rooting around in a favourite little spot then sauntered back to me. He just gave me a look as if to say: 'it's all right, mate, it's all good.'

It was uncanny how he was able to calm me.

Arriving at the bookshop about half an hour before the signing was due to start, there were four or five people standing in line outside. *Ah well, someone has turned up at least,* I said to myself, relieved. They all smiled at us and I gave them a sheepish wave. I couldn't quite get my head round the idea that people were giving up an hour of their evening to come and meet us. There were a few more people inside the store as well. They were all stood in a queue to pay and were all holding copies of the book.

Alan, the manager, invited me upstairs to the staff room where I could wait for the signing to start.

'You can have a glass of wine and Bob can have a saucer of milk. You can take it easy for a minute before things get under way,' he said, sensing my nervousness.

I wasn't sure whether to keep a clear head or to have a drink for Dutch courage. I decided on the former. I'd have a glass of wine afterwards.

Belle, Mary, Garry and a bunch of people from the publishers were there to wish me luck. There was also a stack of books for me to sign for general sale in the store. Someone had come up with the rather bright idea of having a paw-shaped stamp so that Bob could also 'sign' each book. I got to work scrawling on the first copies. Belle added the final flourishing touch with the paw stamps. There were at least two dozen books in the pile. Were they sure they'd even sell this many?

The staff from the store seemed positive. At one point one of them arrived beaming.

'It's stretching all the way around the block,' she smiled.

'What is?' I said, stupidly.

'The queue. It's stretching all the way back around the corner. There's probably a hundred people there with more joining all the time.'

I was speechless. I didn't think it was possible to feel any more anxious, but somehow I did. There was an open window next to me. For a moment, I thought about climbing out of it, shinning my way down the drainpipes and making a hasty escape.

As the clock ticked down towards 6pm, Bob climbed up on my shoulder and we headed back down to the main store. On the landing at the bottom of the first flight of stairs, I knelt down and took a sneaky look down on to the shop floor. My heart jumped into my throat. It was heaving with people.

A table stacked with books had been laid out ready for me and Bob. The line of people waiting to file past it was stretching along the bookshelves all the way to the entrance and out into the dark March evening. They were right. There must have been a hundred people and more in it. At the other side of the store, a separate queue of people were lined up, buying copies of the book. There was even a group of photographers and a television cameraman there.

It was surreal, an out-of-body experience. Until now we'd been hidden from view but as we started walking down the final flight of steps, the cameras began flashing and photographers began shouting.

'Bob, Bob, this way, Bob.'

There was even a ripple of applause and a couple of cheers.

My years on the street with Bob had taught me to expect the unexpected. We'd learned to adapt, to roll with the punches, sometimes literally. This time, however, it felt like we were entering totally uncharted territory.

One thing was clear, however. We'd come too far to pass on this chance. If we took it, our time on the street might, just might, start drawing to a close. That new chapter might just open up for us.

'Come on, Bob,' I whispered, stroking the back of his neck before taking a final, deep breath. 'No turning back now.'

Epilogue
Always

That night in March 2012 was probably the most important of my life. Afterwards there were no more doubts. It really was a new beginning for me and Bob. The book signing in Islington was a success way beyond my expectations. Paul McCartney didn't quite make it, but more than 300 other people did. The numbers clamouring to meet us caught everyone by surprise, even the bookshop, who were cleaned out of every one of their 200 or so copies within half an hour.

'So much for my prediction that we'd only sell half a dozen,' I joked with Alan, the store manager, when I eventually got to share a glass of wine with him after three hours of signing and interviews.

No one could work out how we'd drawn such a big crowd. The flyers and the publicity had obviously played their part. We'd set up a Twitter account which had attracted a hundred or so followers, but even then it didn't quite explain the passion with which people had embraced Bob and myself.

It was the first sign that something amazing was about to take place.

When *A Street Cat Named Bob* went on general sale two days later it seemed to strike an immediate chord and became, what *The Times* described as, 'an instantly bestselling memoir'. It entered the best-seller list on the first weekend after publication – and remained in the UK bestseller list for the best part of a year, most of that time at No 1. Each Sunday, I would pick up a newspaper and look at the latest chart, shaking my head slowly. Why was it so popu-lar? What had captured the public's imagination? After a while I gave up trying to work it out. Even more miraculously, the book swiftly found a foreign audience too. At the last count, it was set to be trans-lated into 26 other languages. In Italy it was *A Spasso Con Bob (A Walk with Bob)*. In Portugal it was *Minha História Con Bob (My Story with Bob)*. It seemed to have some universal appeal. Whatever the language, people seemed to love the story, and most of all, of course, they simply adored Bob.

As a result, Bob and I became, to all intents and purposes, minor celebrities, appearing on television and radio programmes to talk about the book and its popularity. It wasn't something for which I was prepared, even after my afternoon of media train-ing. Our first major appearance, on the BBC's

Breakfast programme was typical. I arrived at the studios in West London at the crack of dawn a bundle of nerves. I was paranoid that Bob would be scared of the lights or the strange surroundings. But he'd taken to it all, sitting on the sofa serenely watching himself on the monitors in front of him. He'd naturally been the star of the show, even managing to do a series of high fives for the hosts who seemed to be every bit as bewitched by him as everyone else. It was the same when I made other appearances.

Wherever we went I was asked the same questions. In particular, people would begin to wonder how the success of the book was changing life for the both of us.

The most significant and obvious change was that Bob and I no longer needed to put ourselves in harm's way on the streets. It took a little while for the financial rewards of the book's success to trickle in, so for a few months we had continued to busk on Neal Street. Gradually, however, we were able to ration our appearances. It was such a huge relief to wake up each morning knowing we wouldn't have to face the cold and the rain and that I wouldn't have to experience that sense of uncertainty and quiet desperation that I felt each day I used to set off for Angel or Covent Garden.

A small part of us would always remain there of course. You can take the busker off the street . . . and Bob has always loved the attention he gets from admirers. So we continued to make occasional appearances, the only difference being that we now did so in order to help other people rather than ourselves.

At the beginning of 2013, for instance, we formed a relationship with the animal charity, Blue Cross. We began collecting money for them both online and via public appearances and our occasional days busking. We raised almost £5,000 in the first week. It felt fantastic to be able to give something back. They were so kind to me during my early days with Bob and continued to help us when we popped into their weekly clinics on Islington Green. I remembered how I'd often felt that Bob was my reward for some act of kindness that I'd bestowed on someone earlier in my life. I'd felt like it was karma. By adopting the Blue Cross, I felt like I was now reciprocating their generosity, performing another act of karma. I aim to do the same thing for homeless charities at some point in the future.

Of course people also asked me if the book had made me rich. The answer to that was yes and no. Compared to where I'd been financially, I was, by any stretch of the imagination, comfortable. But I didn't become an overnight millionaire. The important thing was that, for the foreseeable future, at least, I knew I wasn't going to be reduced to scouring the shelves of supermarkets for 10p tins of past-the-sell-by-date baked beans. For years I had to rely on my wits and a few state hand-outs. Now, for the first time in many years, I had a bank account and even an accountant to help me manage my affairs, including my taxes. I hadn't earned enough money to be eligible to pay tax in the past decade. The fact that I now began doing so was important to me.

When you are homeless or selling *The Big Issue* you know you aren't contributing to society – and you know that society resents you for that. A lot of people take great pleasure in telling you so. To your face. 'Get a job, you scrounging git,' had been a common refrain for me for a decade. The result of this is that you become gradually more marginalised by that society. People don't understand that the lack of self-esteem and general hopelessness you feel when you are homeless, busking or even selling *The Big Issue* is partly down to this. You want to be part of society, but that society is, effectively, driving you away. It becomes a vicious circle.

Paying my way was the most tangible sign that I was once more 'a member' of society. And it felt good.

There were so many other positives to the book's success.

It improved my relationship with my parents. Among the throng at Waterstones on that March evening was my father, who I'd persuaded to come partly out of curiosity and partly for moral support.

The bewildered but delighted look on his face when he witnessed the queues will live in my memory for a very, very long time. After all the disappointments, I felt like I'd given him something to be proud about. At last.

He was touched when he was shown the note I'd written thanking him and my mum in the acknowledgements. Apparently he shed a tear when he read the book back at home. He called me up to say well done, and said the same thing again on other occasions. He still told me to get a haircut and a shave, of course, but at least he stopped nagging me to 'get a proper job'.

We didn't talk about our feelings about the past in huge detail. That was not his style. He's not the kind of person to have a big heart to heart. I suspect I knew what he was thinking but I also knew that he couldn't express it. He couldn't formulate the words, but that was fine. Knowing was enough for me.

I also travelled to Australia again to spend time with my mother. She'd read the book and wept as well. She told me she felt guilty about many of the things that had happened but was honest enough to say that, as a teenager, I was a nightmare who would have challenged even the most sainted mother. I accepted that.

We were open and honest with each other and realised that we'd be friends from now onwards.

Another satisfying aspect of the book's success was the impact it seemed to have on people's attitude to *The Big Issue* sellers and the homeless in general. Schools and charities wrote, telling me how the story of Bob and I had helped them to better understand the plight of the homeless.

Bob and I were on Facebook and Twitter. Every day it seemed we got a message from someone explaining how they no longer walked past *The Big Issue* vendors. Many told me they now made a point of always engaging them in conversation. I knew I'd had my difficulties with the magazine, but I felt a huge sense of pride in that. It is a fine institution that deserves everyone's support, especially in these dark economic times.

On a more profound level, our story also seemed to connect with people who were facing difficult times in their lives. Hundreds of them wrote to me or contacted us via social media. Some read our story of survival and drew their own strength from it. Others recognised the power animals possess to heal us humans. Again, I was immensely proud every time I received a message of this kind. I never in a million years expected that I'd touch the life of one person, let alone thousands.

A few people got a little carried away and bestowed some kind of divinity on Bob and me. Bob might have been a saint but I wasn't, that was for sure. You can't spend a decade fighting for your day-to-day existence on the streets of London without being shaped by that environment. You can't live a chunk of your life dependent on heroin without being damaged by that experience. I was a product of my past.

So I knew it would take me a long time to iron out the rougher edges of my personality. And I would never quite shake off my past, not least because people would always pop up to remind me of my lost years. Medically, I still carried the scars of my drug-addicted twenties too. The punishment I inflicted on my body would continue to extract a price. In short, Saint James of Tottenham didn't exist. He never had and he never would. The person who most definitely did exist, however, was someone who had been given his second chance in life and who was determined to seize it. And if I ever lost sight of that, I now had constant reminders of why that second chance was so important.

I recently received a letter from a lady in a small, rural community in Wales whose close friend had just lost her long fight against cancer. The lady had given our book to her friend during her final days. She had been so touched by it that she had, in turn, given a copy to her local Minister. During his oration at the friend's funeral in the small village chapel, the Minister had held up a copy of our book in front of the congregation. He mentioned how much the book had meant to the lady at the end of her life and praised our 'wonderful journey of hope'. Bob and I were, he said, an example of the power of 'faith, hope and love'. Reading this moved me to floods of tears. It was unbelievably humbling. It remained in my head for days.

For far too many years those three precious qualities – faith, hope and love – had been sorely missing in my life. But then a twist of fate delivered me all three. They were each embodied in the mischievous, playful, canny, occasionally cantankerous but always devoted cat who helped me turn my life around.

Bob had helped me restore my faith in myself and the world around me. He had shown me hope when I really couldn't see much of it. Most of all he had given me the unconditional love each of us needs.

During one of my television appearances on the BBC, a presenter asked me a question which threw me at first.

'What will you do when Bob is not around any more?' he asked.

I got a little emotional at the very thought of losing him, but once I'd gathered myself, I answered as honestly as I could. I said I knew that animals didn't live as long as us humans, but that I would cherish every single day that I shared with him. And when the time came for him to leave, he would live on in the books that he inspired.

They may have been the truest words I ever uttered.

The world as it was before I met Bob seemed a harsh, heartless and, yes, a hopeless place. The world I have grown to see through his eyes is a very different one. There was a time when I couldn't distinguish one day from the next. Now I cherish each one. I am happier, healthier and more fulfilled than I have ever been. For now, at least, I have escaped from life on the streets. I can see a clear path ahead of me.

I have no idea where our adventure will lead us next. But I know that, for as long as he is around, Bob will be at the heart of all the good things that come to pass. He is my companion, my best friend, my teacher and my soul mate. And he will remain all of those things. Always.

Acknowledgements

Writing this book has been a collaborative process and I need to thank the team of incredibly talented and supportive people who helped me cross the finishing line. Garry Jenkins was my principle guiding hand, skilfully extracting the stories then shaping the manuscript. At Hodder, I have to thank Rowena Webb and Maddy Price along with Ciara Foley, who edited the script. I would also like to single out the brilliant publicists Emma Knight, Kerry Hood and Emilie Ferguson. A big thanks also to Dan Williams for his superb line drawings. At Aitken Alexander I'm totally indebted to my fantastic agent Mary Pachnos as well as the team of Sally Riley, Nishta Hurry, Liv Stones and Matilda Forbes-Watson. Thanks also to Joaquim Fernandes at Aitken Alexander and Raymond Walters at R Walters & Co for their invaluable guidance and help. Closer to home I'd like to thank my best friends Kitty and Ron, for being at my side through what has been a pretty crazy year or so. It hasn't been easy at times, but they've remained steadfast and loyal and I owe them more than I can say. I'd also like to thank my mother and father for their love and support, not just in the past year but throughout the darker and more difficult earlier years when I was, I know, far from the easiest of sons. I can't let this opportunity pass without thanking the legions of people who have written to me either directly or through social media, passing on their good wishes and sharing their experiences. I've done my best to reply to as many as possible but hope that I can be forgiven for not getting back to each and every one of you. The response has been, at times, overwhelming. Most of all, of course, I'd like to thank the little guy who remains my constant companion. I still don't know whether I found Bob or he found me. What I do know, however, is that without him I'd be utterly lost.

James Bowen, London, May 2013

For the latest news, stories and pictures from James and Bob, follow them on Twitter at www.twitter.com/streetcatbob, or visit their Facebook page at www.facebook.com/streetcatbob.

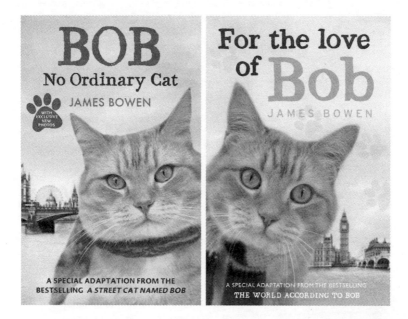

Bob: No Ordinary Cat and *For the Love of Bob* are special adaptations of the story of James and Bob for children aged 11 and above.

Also, don't miss the heartwarming *A Gift from Bob*, as Bob teaches James the true meaning of Christmas.